USING QUALITATIVE METHODS IN PSYCHOLOGY

*The editors dedicate this text to their partners,
without whose support and understanding
this project would not have been possible.*

USING QUALITATIVE METHODS IN PSYCHOLOGY

MARY KOPALA
LISA A. SUZUKI

Editors

SAGE Publications
International Educational and Professional Publisher
Thousand Oaks   London   New Delhi

For information:

SAGE Publications, Inc.
2455 Teller Road
Thousand Oaks, California 91320
E-mail: order@sagepub.com

SAGE Publications Ltd.
6 Bonhill Street
London EC2A 4PU
United Kingdom

SAGE Publications India Pvt. Ltd.
M-32 Market
Greater Kailash I
New Delhi 110 048 India

Printed in the United States of America

Library of Congress Cataloging-in-Publication Data

Main entry under title:
    Using qualitative methods in psychology / Edited by Mary Kopala,
Lisa A. Suzuki.
        p. cm.
    Includes bibliographical references and index.
    ISBN 0-7619-1036-0 (cloth: alk. paper)
    ISBN 0-7619-1037-9 (pbk.: alk. paper)
    1. Psychology—Research—Methodology. I. Suzuki, Lisa A.,
1961– II. Title
    BF76.5 .K68 1998
    150′.72—ddc21

This book is printed on acid-free paper.

99 00 01 02 03 04 05 7 6 5 4 3 2 1

Acquisition Editor:	Peter Labella
Editorial Assistant:	Renée Piernot
Production Editor:	Wendy Westgate
Editorial Assistant:	Stephanie Allen
Typesetter:	Lynn Miyata

Contents

SECTION 1: Foundational Issues in Qualitative Methods

PART I: The Philosophical Foundations of Qualitative Methods in Psychology

Section 2: Applying Qualitative Methods in Psychology

PART V: Qualitative Methods in Action Research and Evaluation

Preface

Early observations of behavior formed the foundation of the field of psychology. Freud and Piaget made major contributions to the discipline by using observational qualitative methods. Their theories continue to be major cornerstones of psychological thinking. Historically, promotion of the scientific method in psychology and the emphasis on experimental methodology was an attempt to give the discipline legitimacy and an identity as a "hard science." Despite the contributions of early observational research, some members of the academic community thought it was important to pattern the field after the hard sciences. This phenomenon had such an impact that the emphasis on quantitative methodology continues even though much psychological research may be irrelevant to actual practice.

Neglect of qualitative methods in psychological research has limited the kinds of questions that can be studied. The field of psychology has broadened to include areas that may not be appropriate for study with traditional methods—for example, questions about the meaning of experiences for specific populations. When researchers select measures to represent the variables under study, the flexibility needed in understanding the experiences of the participants is sacrificed. Consequently, important questions go unanswered.

The field of applied psychology encompasses diverse areas, such as multicultural counseling, diversity, health psychology, family systems theory, feminism, development of new theory, career, and developmental issues. The authors of this text promote the need to return to qualitative methods to study relevant questions in these areas. Most psychology research methods books, however, focus solely on quantitative methods or include a token chapter that introduces the reader to qualitative methodology. The use of qualitative methods is complex, and one does not develop understanding, nor can one become a competent qualitative researcher, by reading one chapter. Consequently, individuals are poorly equipped to answer questions that require a qualitative method.

The editors of this text have served as cochairs of the Special Interest Group on Qualitative Methods in Teaching and Research in the Division of Counseling Psychology for the American Psychological Association. During annual meetings, discussions were held repeatedly regarding the need for a comprehensive text focusing on qualitative methods and their specific application to questions in psychology. This text represents an answer to this call.

This book is divided into five parts. Part I provides a philosophical foundation for the conduct of qualitative research. The authors reflect on issues that can help researchers form a qualitative identity and understanding of their roles in the research process. Part II provides basic information and illustrations that make much of the discussion in Part I concrete. Parts III, IV, and V provide examples of how qualitative methods have been successfully applied to questions appropriate for psychology. In these parts, the authors share their experiences in engaging in the qualitative process.

Acknowledgments

We thank all of the chapter authors for their dedication to this text. Without their expertise and knowledge regarding qualitative research, the field of psychology would not be moving forward to embrace a different methodology. From the inception of this project, their enthusiasm to create a book representing the foundations of qualitative research and its application have been unwavering. Many authors displayed honestly the struggles and challenges in conducting qualitative research and the evolution of various projects from start to finish. In addition, the book highlights changes in research identity as particular researchers moved from a more quantitative orientation to a qualitative focus. For their commitment and desire to communicate the importance of qualitative methods, we are grateful.

We thank Peter Labella at Sage for his support of this project. His confidence in the project enabled us to complete the book in a timely manner.

We also acknowledge the assistance of Ellen Short, a doctoral student in the Counseling Psychology Program at New York University, for her assistance in the preparation of this manuscript. Her honest opinions regarding various chapters provided important input regarding the perceptions of students in training.

About This Text

Part I of this text provides discussions of issues that emanate from the philosophy of science and provides a foundation for the use of qualitative methods in psychology. In Chapter 1, David Rennie discusses the nature of inquiry and the observation of philosophers that "all inquiry is interpretive." Building on thoughts of philosophers of science, he suggests ways that qualitative researchers can be more objective and perhaps satisfy the criticism of positivists.

In Chapter 2, Lisa Hoshmand discusses how knowledge is generated and applied. She asserts that individuals identify problems and are motivated to pursue research questions on the basis of their values and personal agendas. In an effort to develop a qualitative research praxis, she makes an argument for locating research genres in the larger social and cultural context.

Elizabeth Merrick explores issues of "reliability" and "validity" in qualitative research in Chapter 3. She reformulates the definitions of these constructs to make them relevant to qualitative research. Merrick asserts that "reliability and validity depend on the relationship between the researcher and the research process, as well as between the research and the interpretive community." She urges the researcher to be personally reflexive and self-disclosing.

Chapters 4 and 5 focus on the role and identity of the qualitative researcher. Dan Sciarra, in Chapter 4, asserts that the choice of a quantitative or qualitative approach is determined by how one "knows" and that this understanding determines the researcher's relationship to those he or she seeks to understand. The quantitative researcher approaches his or her subject with a belief that truth exists "out there" independent of the researcher. In contrast, the qualitative researcher enters the world of those he or she attempts to understand; the researcher and the participant contract meaning together. This philosophical difference determines one's approach to doing research and one's role as a researcher.

In Chapter 5, the last chapter of this section, drawing on their expertise in multicultural counseling, Joseph Ponterotto and Ingrid Grieger suggest an alternative to Sciarra's position and suggest that researchers can maintain both a qualitative and a quantitative identity simultaneously. Like individuals who are bicultural, they maintain that researchers can "incorporate multiple ways of understanding reality and of solving problems."

Part II of this text discusses practical foundations for the conduct of qualitative research. This begins with Chapter 6, in which Cori Cieurzo and Merle Keitel focus on ethical issues relevant to qualitative research in the field of psychology. They discuss ethical dilemmas that may emerge when psychologists conduct qualitative research. These authors discuss the impact of values and personal agendas that motivate researchers to study particular communities and to interpret others' realities, yet they stress that this must be done ethically.

Patricia Libutti, in Chapter 7, briefly examines the history of the use of computer technology in the conduct of qualitative research and identifies ways that individuals have studied computer cultures. She expands the discussion of ethics by examining the unique research situations presented by computer technology—specifically, several components of the Internet (e.g., Web sites, chat rooms). She reminds the qualitative researcher that these are cultures that can be examined anonymously by researchers and identifies the ethical dilemmas that can arise when using this as a source of qualitative data.

In Chapter 8, Sally Stabb relates her own experiences and "personal view on teaching qualitative research in psychology." In addition, she shares feedback that she has received from students regarding her course and includes a syllabus. Stabb's chapter provides information regarding the importance of incorporating qualitative methods in research training.

Constance Fischer, in Chapter 9, concludes this part of the text by sharing her insight about publishing qualitative research. She explains that many mainstream editors are uninformed about qualitative methods and suggests that how the information is presented is crucial to the editor and to fellow researchers. Using her own experiences as a qualitative researcher, she illustrates a way to present information that informs the reader about the researcher's process as well as the findings of the study.

The chapters in Part III of this text illustrate qualitative research with a focus on examining communities within a particular cultural and/or developmental context. In Chapter 10, Lisa Suzuki, Maria Prendes-Lintel, Lauren Wertlieb, and Amena Stallings describe the process of conducting collaborative qualitative research with diverse racial/ethnic populations. Their retrospective qualitative study of Cuban refugees illustrates the importance of understanding one's own motivations and interests in particular communities (especially if one is an outsider), entering and establishing relationships with community members, integrating multiple sources of information, and identifying representative themes.

Nancy Salkin Asher and Kenneth Chavinson Asher discuss similar issues in conducting a qualitative study of lesbian women and body image in Chapter 11. They identify the importance of the qualitative method in examining an area in which research has not been conducted. Benefits of the qualitative process are highlighted in exploring the complexities of the construct of body image, which may include identity, esteem, sexuality, cultural mores, and health issues.

In Chapter 12, Niobe Way and Kerstin Pahl examine the process of conducting a large-scale qualitative study of friendships among urban, ethnically diverse adolescent boys from low-income families. The diversity of relational themes that could only be discovered through a qualitative method are highlighted. In addition, the authors identify particular issues that arose in condensing interview material into relevant themes for interpretation.

Part IV of this text includes chapters that focus on issues relevant to conducting research in a therapeutic context. The studies used to illustrate the points in each chapter reflect not only the importance of qualitative methods but also the study of relationships within the psychotherapeutic domain. In Chapter 13, Joy Tanji addresses how researchers and practitioners can move toward a more integrated understanding of the family therapy process through use of qualitative methods. In her study, she incorporated therapists, a reflecting team, and families engaged in Milan systemic therapy. Issues of understanding qualitative epistemology, debriefing, enhancing entry and immersion skills, triangulation of data, peer examination, and member checks with participants of multiple stakeholder groups are noted.

Virginia O'Brien and Mary Kopala examine the use of a qualitative method in exploring clinical supervisory relationships in Chapter 14. They discuss the evolution of their qualitative project, which includes dilemmas that arose in examining a relationship in which the participants were not co-equal (supervision occurs between a junior and a senior member of the helping profession). In addition, the authors discuss issues of power in the research process, given that they were also in positions of authority. Addressing dilemmas and resulting modifications in procedure are highlighted as part of the overall process of conducting qualitative research.

In Chapter 15, Michelle Maher discusses her role as a feminist researcher in the context of a qualitative project designed to understand lesbians' supportive and unsupportive experiences of therapy. Aspects of the qualities of feminist research are provided and then integrated into the study of therapy. Issues of relationship between the researcher and the participant are noted. In addition, the importance of moving toward social change is described.

Part V of this text contains chapters that illustrate the diversity of methods that can be incorporated in qualitative research. Unlike the preceding chapters in this section, which use primarily an individual interview, authors in this part selected methods that incorporate other formats. In Chapter 16, John O'Neill, Barbara Small, and John Strachan describe the use of focus groups within a participatory action research environment. Specifically, their study addresses issues surrounding employment for persons with HIV/AIDS. The authors discuss the organizational principles of action research and illustrate the integration of new information (changes in HIV/AIDS realities) as the study progresses. Focus group methodology is also discussed in the context of the study.

In Chapter 17, Leo Goldman highlights the use of qualitative research methods in program evaluation. Various kinds of evaluations are identified with regard to the author's experiences in evaluating counseling programs in educational settings. A project involving a review of the guidance and counseling activities of an inner-city high school is used to illustrate the various components of evaluation research using qualitative methods.

SECTION 1

Foundational Issues in Qualitative Methods

CHAPTER 1

Qualitative Research

A Matter of Hermeneutics and the Sociology of Knowledge

David L. Rennie

Within the last decade, qualitative research methods have been exploding onto the scene in several disciplines, particularly education, nursing, and social work. Its uptake is less strong in psychology, however; although it seems reasonably popular in the United Kingdom, it is less so in other countries. In the United States, only a handful of university departments of psychology can be said to feature qualitative research—similar to the situation in Canada and in Western Europe (especially the "Germanic" countries)—whereas most departments either pay little attention to it or ignore it altogether. Correspondingly, other institutions exerting power over the development of knowledge in psychology, such as granting agencies and professional journals, have come to consider qualitative research projects and manuscripts but generally not to the point of treating them as on par with positivistic efforts. Meanwhile, psychologists engaged in qualitative research generally are passionate about it because it seems to be a way of addressing the more interesting subject matter of their discipline.

In a way, the entrenchment of positivism in psychology is an attempt to continue the grand modernist project that began around the time of Descartes and got consolidated by Kant—the project that displaced a reliance on faith with a reliance on reason as the source of knowledge. In the 20th century, this approach to questing certainty through the application of reason has come under attack by postmodernists, pragmatists, and philosophical hermeneuts (see below). This challenge holds that nothing is certain, that all knowledge production is relative to frames of reference. The difficulty is that the postmodern and related arguments lean heavily toward skepticism, and skepticism does not sit well in the corridors of power. Indeed, governments, granting agencies, and hence institutions of learning are going in the opposite direction, toward an emphasis on accountability (e.g., the value being placed on "empirically validated" psychotherapy [see the October 1996 issue of *American Psychologist* on outcome assessment in psychotherapy]).

The symptoms of this conflict can be seen clearly in the various rationales given for qualitative research. Some qualitative researchers ally themselves with societal sentiment and attempt to work out a kind of positivism (e.g., Miles & Huberman, 1984), whereas others pick up relativism with gusto by attaching importance of democratic dialogue and, going with it, by appealing to consensus as the criterion of goodness in qualitative research (e.g., Guba & Lincoln, 1989; Packer & Addison, 1989). Is this state of affairs satisfactory? Some reviews of work on this topic, by myself and students, have indicated that some hold the answer to be yes. Those with this opinion seem to be holding out for a general shake-up in social science.

I am not so sure. I am inclined to think that the need for certainty is still so strong in society that it will continue to reinforce positivism. So, what can be done? To collapse under the strain and submit to positivism would be to undo the instinct for more meaningful knowledge about human affairs that girds qualitative research. To go the other way and march valiantly under the banner of relativism not only would be futile, but I'm not sure it would even be correct. Relativism is appealing because it presents a strong argument that is internally consistent. But then, the same can be said for objectivism. Rather than adopt one or the other, the challenge is to take both into account and somehow reconcile them (for contemporary efforts by philosophers in this regard see, e.g., Margolis, 1986; Putnam, 1990).

Kvale (1996) has recognized the twin perils of objectivism and relativism and how difficult it is to chart a methical course between them. The route he appears to favor is a kind of methical pluralism wherein the inquirer may draw on either positivistic or relativistic approaches, depending on the perceived requirements of the particular study (Rennie, 1998a). There is much sense in this strategy, but I find it unsatisfying because it does not grasp the nettle. Philosophers have observed that although, of course, all inquiry is interpretive, inquiry in the human sciences involves a double hermeneutic (Giddens, 1976; see also Taylor, 1971): Both the inquirer and the "entity" being inquired into are self-interpreting. If it may be granted that qualitative research is an instantiation of human science (Fischer, 1977; Giorgi, 1970; Rennie,

1995a), then the claim that qualitative research ineluctably is hermeneutical is on firm ground. The question is, Can hermeneutics be methodical? I believe it can, and is, in the form of qualitative research. My argument is as follows, beginning with a brief history of hermeneutics.[1, 2]

BRIEF HISTORY OF HERMENEUTICS

Hermeneutics refers to the practice of interpreting the meaning of text. It is an ancient tradition, having its origins in the exegesis of religious and judicial texts (Palmer, 1969). It has close connections with rhetoric because hermeneutics has no hard and fast laws or rules; instead, it is a matter of understanding, and the strength of the understanding is indicated through argument. Hermeneutics came into prominence during the Reformation, in keeping with the interest, characteristic of that period in history, in interpreting the meaning of religious texts (Teigas, 1995). More recently, in the 19th century, Friedrich Schleier-macher combined faith and idealism, maintaining that it is possible to divine the "spirit" of a given text that may exceed its author's understanding of it. Later, Wilhelm Dilthey came to believe that it is possible to approach the hermeneutical study of history empirically and objectively, but not positivistically, on the grounds that positivism precludes the study of meaning. Supporting his claim to objectivity, he worked out a concept of objective mind, universal human values, and an empathic approach to understanding another person's experience that involves the application of induction, analysis, construction, and comparison (Rickman, 1961, 1976).

Twenty years his junior, Edmund Husserl both was influenced by and influenced Dilthey (for introductions to Husserl see, e.g., Smith & Smith, 1995; Spiegelberg, 1960). Husserl, too, was skeptical about positivism but for a different reason: He believed that, through phenomenology, which he thought could be made scientific, it is possible to be objective in a way that transcends the kind of objectivity yielded by positivism. After all, positivism is "merely" empirical or, as Husserl sometimes put it, merely psychological, in that it is based on perceptions gained through the senses and, correspondingly, is limited by the senses. Moreover, he recognized that perception is influenced by expectations, hypotheses, anticipations, assumptions, and frames of reference. Perception in terms of sensory input and such psychological influences is what he referred to as the "natural attitude." The trick in phenomenology is to get beyond the natural attitude so that reality may be perceived objectively. The way to do this is to become aware of such influences on perception and to put them aside, or to "bracket" them (Husserl came upon the metaphor of "bracketing" when thinking that the activity involved is like putting in parentheses the natural way of seeing the phenomenon). Correspondingly, the phenomenologist should consider the phenomenon of interest from all angles—to think about its variations imaginatively—and be alert to the commonality cutting across all variations. Alertness to this commonality allows for the *description* (objective) of the *essence* of the phenomenon and, again, the essence is not limited by what can be known about the phenomenon empirically. Thus, Husserl is generally considered a subjective idealist who aspired to objectivity.

Dilthey was attracted to Husserl's notion of phenomenological bracketing because he saw it as a way of enhancing objectivity in methodical hermeneutics, although I can find no clear evidence (in the English translations of Dilthey's works) that he actually attempted to institute the procedure. In any case, both Dilthey's and Husserl's claims to objectivity came under powerful attack by Heidegger (1927/1962) and Gadamer (1960/1992), both of whom, in advancing what has come to be known as *philosophical hermeneutics,* make a compelling argument that it is impossible to escape the subjectivizing influences of language, culture, ideology, expectations, or assumptions. Thus, Heidegger and Gadamer support the postmodern and pragmatic position on relativism. Meanwhile, in turning Immanuel Kant upside down by making the nature of being (ontology) primordial over the application of reason in involvement in the world, Heidegger makes the human individual *a part of* reality, rather than an ego dualistically separated from the world, thereby reconciling relativism and realism (or objectivism). Heidegger's realism is more practical than rational, however, and so it is difficult to find a way through him (and thus Gadamer) back to reason, knowledge production (epistemology), and, hence, method. The challenge is thus to recognize Heidegger's strong argument regarding relativism while extending his realism in a way that makes room for method.

QUALITATIVE RESEARCH AS
METHODICAL HERMENEUTICS

When we look at the various genres of qualitative research, we can see how each has recognized the importance of relativism while each has failed to reconcile it with objectivism. For example, although empirical phenomenologists (e.g., Giorgi, 1985) are alert to perspectivism, they have tended to maintain that they are *describing* phenomena; they have seemed reluctant to support Paul Ricoeur's criticism that Husserl's phenomenology is interpretive, not descriptive (Thompson, 1981). The originators of grounded theory, Glaser and Strauss (1967), have, in their various works, in effect combined strands of pragmatism, positivism, phenomenology, and hermeneutics without making any attempt to explain coherently how they tie together (Rennie, 1998b). Meanwhile, although coming at it from a different route (through French deconstructionism, postmodernism, and social constructionism [Gergen, 1985]), narrative analysts (e.g., Polkinghorne, 1995) and discourse analysts (e.g., Potter & Wetherell, 1987) are inclined to share with the hermeneutics of Packer and Addison (1989) a tendency to lean too far toward relativism.

The shoal that threatens to block the passage between objectivism and relativism is the double hermeneutic: When qualitative researchers acquire texts in response to "live" inquiries such as interviews, the text itself is reflexive. The interviewee has been self-interpreting when providing the text, and this self-interpretation has much to do with the interviewer and the interview situation. Meanwhile, of course, the interviewer is either wittingly or unwittingly injecting his or her horizon of understanding into the interview. The result is a relativized co-construction of the interviewee's experience. On top of that, of course, the qualitative researcher proceeds to interpret this already relativized text. It is difficult to argue convincingly that a foundational, "true," or "bottom line" representation of the participant's experience can be expected to come out of such activities. Meanwhile, apart from these kinds of subjectivizing influences, both participants are communicating within a given language and cultural frame, which further add to the relativism. It is these kinds of relativizing influences, taken collectively, that Heidegger and Gadamer are aware of and have leveled against Dilthey's claim that hermeneutics can be objective and methodical.

I do not think we have to be so quick in coming to that conclusion. I believe it is possible coherently to bring objectivity back into the picture provided we steer more clear of Kant than Dilthey was inclined to do, and instead revise methodical hermeneutics in the light of certain features of both ancient and contemporary philosophy. I am speaking of a relativized version of Husserl's bracketing, a feature of Charles Sanders Peirce's pragmatic theory of inference, and rhetoric. Each of the three elements making up this revised methodical hermeneutics is addressed in turn.

Bracketing

Heidegger and Gadamer and followers of them go too far when concluding that there is little point in even attempting to bracket. The fact of the matter is that it is possible to bracket at least some influences on the understanding of a phenomenon under investigation. Moreover, once the false subject-object dichotomy is dispensed with as part of the release from positivism, it is also possible to feel less inhibited about declaring one's biases. At a minimum, this way of doing inquiry does not build it *around* a hypothesis or hypotheses made in advance of the inquiry, as is characteristic of the hypothetico-deductive mode of inquiry so often favored by positivists. Qualitative research is about the development of understandings, and *consequent to,* not prior to, the analysis of text.

Although it cannot be total by any means, the declaration of biases that clearly were operating during the achievement of understanding amounts to an attempt to explicitate the subjective. In taking this step, qualitative researchers who bracket *let the reader in on* their subjectivity and in this sense objectify it (more on this below, on rhetoric). Meanwhile, of course, the focus of the inquiry in qualitative research is typically an entity external to the researcher—such as someone else's experience. In this sense, the inquirer is interested in an external "object" of attention. Thus, an object outside the inquirer is attended to, but it is recognized that this objectification invariably is influenced by subjective factors. In turn, in recognition of that influence, the attempt is made to explicate the subjectivity, thereby objectifying it, at least to some extent. For both reasons, then, the qualitative researcher achieves a certain degree of objectivity. Correspondingly, bracketing in qualitative research helps reconcile objectivism and relativism.

Peirce's Theory of Inference

Bracketing in the way described is not sufficient to warrant a claim by qualitative researchers that their understandings are not merely hypothetical but instead have been, by virtue of the procedures used in arriving at them, validated in their own right. When qualitative researchers take at face value the conventional view that the scientific method involves the inductive development of general understandings from particulars that are then tested deductively, they can easily feel defenseless. To compensate, one approach is to claim that qualitative research feeds into conventional science by producing good ideas; good ideas have "grab value," and because qualitative inquiry is a royal road to good ideas, *that* is the justification for the approach. (This is the rationale used by Glaser and Strauss, e.g., especially in their early works, and is adhered to by Glaser today.) Another approach is to use language to soften the hard edge of positivistic canons. Thus, in this approach, "credibility" is substituted for "validity," "consistency" for "reliability," "triangulation" for "test," and so on.

Meanwhile, although they may have difficulty explaining it, qualitative researchers generally feel deeply that their understandings are grounded in their "data" (or better, texts) while not being able to justify the claim logically, at least not to the satisfaction of positivists. I have come to believe that Peirce's theory of inference offers an appropriate justification for this belief. Peirce (1965) spent much of his brilliant career trying to sort out how modern logic applies to modern natural science. Peirce reasoned that inference has not two but three modes: induction, deduction, and abduction. Of these, of course, abduction is the new element. *Abduction* is a hypothesis or idea that could explain a scientific finding. The most interesting and significant aspect to Peirce's logic is that *deduction* is circular. There is nothing more in the conclusion of a deduction that is not already contained in its premises. New knowledge comes about, not through the relationship between deduction and induction, but instead from the interplay between abduction and induction. For Peirce, abductions are tested through induction.

Once I became acquainted with these notions, I saw what seems to be a direct implication for the practice of the grounded theory method, and possibly for many, if not most, other approaches to qualitative research as well. First, the understanding—of a given portion of text of a text as a whole that is represented as a category, structure of experience, or narrative theme—is an *abduction*.

Second, the abduction is validated internally by *induction* by virtue of the fact that the qualitative researcher insists on a number of instances, in one form or another, supporting the abduction before concluding that it speaks to the text as a whole. Thus, abduction and induction depend on each other symbiotically (Rennie, 1998b). Third, reminiscent of the hermeneutical circle (the influence of the parts of a text on the understanding on the whole of it, and vice versa), abductions may be formed first and are then made subject to induction. Or, induction may be carried out first, whereupon abductions are interpreted commonalities among the individual items compared inductively in this approach and checks are made to ensure support for the abduction. Fourth, this interplay between abduction and induction may be applied to single texts or to multiple texts; when the latter approach is engaged, hermeneutics is taken beyond its focus on the individual, claimed by Dilthey, to a focus on collectivities. Correspondingly, then, to use the language of Jerome Bruner (1986), qualitative research may be about paradigmatic knowing (general knowing in terms of commonalities, regularities, structures, or in natural science, laws), as well as narrative knowing (knowing about an individual). Last and most important, the symbiosis of abduction and induction means that qualitative research is *internally validating,* and not merely ancillary to real science, as positivists would have it.

Another feature of Peirce's philosophy of science provides a link between qualitative research and science as well. In developing and promoting pragmatism, Peirce effectively became allied with relativism when recognizing the subjectively idealistic involvement in the pursuit of truth. Correspondingly, he maintained that it is impossible to achieve absolute knowledge. Instead, people increasingly approximate truth, and at any given moment truth is a matter of consensus. Thus, Peirce may be thought of as an early postmodernist. Going with this recognition of the role of relativism and of consensus, Peirce held that rhetoric constitutes one form of logic (thus undoing a division between them that had been put in place by Aristotle and endorsed ever since). This contribution by Peirce—which, again, was made in the interest of *natural science*—has important implications for qualitative research because the warranting of claims to understanding, made logically on the grounds of the symbiosis of abduction and induction, cannot stand on its own but rather is supported by a less conclusive but nevertheless fitting form of argument. The warranting at bottom is a matter of rhetoric (Rennie, 1995a, 1995b).

Rhetoric

Historically, the connection between hermeneutics and rhetoric has always been close. Aristotle made a distinction between *epistēmē* (or epistemology) and *phronesis* (having to do with politics, law, and practical affairs generally). *Epistēmē* involves reason and logic; *phronesis* involves practical judgment and argument. In fact, Aristotle counseled that, in *phronesis*, it is important to appeal to what people understand, rather than to their logic. The kinship between *phronesis* and rhetoric, on the one hand, and what we have come to describe as human science, on the other, is readily apparent. In human affairs, laws like those in the biological and other natural sciences do not apply unless one wishes to take the extreme, reductive position that ultimately even human affairs are resolvable to physics. What are the components of this rhetoric? I see three, in the main.

First, it is important to convey to the audience that the qualitative inquiry was thorough and systematic. I find it significant that, when students defend their theses or dissertations based on a qualitative method, examiners very seldom challenge the students on this ground. Instead, the examiners are typically overwhelmed by how much work went into the analyses and are inclined to take the returns from the method at face value. The same principle applies to journal manuscripts. Although the writer is limited by the space allotted to the specification of method, it is important to be as detailed as possible: The detail carries weight.

Second, it is important to tie understandings to the text giving rise to them. In the language of grounded theory analysis, which is highly generalizable on this score, the understandings should be *grounded.* Otherwise, the reader has difficulty combating the fear that the claims to understanding arose unduly from the qualitative researcher's subjectivity. At the same time, it is important not to overburden a write-up (of any sort) with illustrations because this tactic bogs down the reader. It now becomes difficult to see the forest for the trees. To a considerable extent, conceptualizations, whether presented in the form of categories, structures, or themes, when grounded, will make sense to a reader sharing the same culture as the researcher.

Last, it is important to be reflexive. This requirement (and freedom) more than any other distinguishes qualitative research from positivism. In positivism, it is expected that the researcher has separated him- or herself from the phenomenon under inquiry; the phenomenon is the object, and the researcher is the subject. Thus, any declaration of subjectivity violates this norm. For this reason, in write-ups by positivists, personal considerations do not appear. It is as if such authors are either unaware of the importance of the objectivism-relativism duality or pretend it does not exist. Qualitative research does not make this mistake. As indicated throughout this chapter, it recognizes the duality directly and attempts to work with it. Procedurally, this work resolves to giving full rein to reflexivity. Thus, as seen, when generating text through "live" inquiry such as interviews, qualitative researchers bring the participant into the inquiry as a co-researcher while recognizing as fully as possible the contextualizing influence of the inquiry itself. Also, as seen, qualitative researchers pay attention to and explicate the subjective influences on their attempts to understand the phenomenon under inquiry. In making this report, they help objectify their subjectivity. This objectification gives the write-up strength and increases its rhetorical impact.[3]

CONCLUSION

As indicated, I developed the foregoing understanding of the rationale for qualitative research through the avenue of working with grounded theory. I am convinced that it explains well the practice of this particular genre (Rennie, 1998b). The extent to which it applies to other approaches to qualitative research and, indeed, whether all qualitative researchers would even be willing to unite under a common rationale, are open questions. Several considerations are involved: (a) whether all qualitative researchers would agree that, at bottom, qualitative research is hermeneutical; (b) whether it involves a symbiosis of abduction and induction; and (c) whether claims to understanding are made rhetorically in the ways described.

As I survey several genres in the light of my current understanding of them—which is sketchy in many respects—I think contemporary empirical phenomenologists would find much in common with my formulation. They advocate bracketing; in effect, they make a claim to paradigmatic knowing; and, in keeping with the last point, it seems to me, they engage the symbiosis of abduction and induction. Whether they would accede to the additional assertions that their approach is hermeneutical and that claims to understanding amount to rhetoric are open questions. It is possible that these points would not sit well with their placement of a high value on objectivity. In contrast, narrative and discourse analysts may be inclined to resist the role of reflexivity, both in bracketing and in self-disclosure, on the grounds that it is a lapse back into modernism in that it implies the activity of an autonomous ego. As in all the genres of qualitative research, the actual research practices, more than dogmatic statements on position, would tell the tale. As for the hermeneutics of Packer and Addison, it seems unlikely that they would complain about my attempt to generalize hermeneutics, although they might take issue with my attempt to resurrect Dilthey in a new guise.

Thus, a lot of inquiry and thought are necessary to sort out the generalizability of the formulation. In the interim, one feature of it more than any other should be enticing. This is the notion that the symbiosis of abduction and induction is internally validating. This feature allows the term *validation* to be used coherently within the field of qualitative research, thereby reducing the barrier between qualitative research and positivism. Most important, the symbiosis supports qualitative research as an approach to science that stands on its own. This, more than any other feature of the formulation, has positive implications for the endorsement of qualitative research by the gatekeepers controlling the constitution of knowledge.

NOTES

1. The argument is developed more fully in a paper entitled *Methodical Hermeneutics: A Promising Logic of Justification for Qualitative Research?* available on request from David Rennie, Department of Psychology, York University, Toronto, Ontario, M3J 1P3.

2. Restoring Dilthey in this way thus is a different line on hermeneutics, compared with the one taken by Packer and Addison (Packer, 1985; Packer & Addison, 1989), who attempt to apply the philosophical hermeneutics of Heidegger and Gadamer. Packer and Addison tend to be vague on actual procedures, which is consistent with their appeal to philosophical hermeneutics because Heidegger and Gadamer maintain that philosophical hermeneutics is beyond method.

3. Elliott, Fischer, and Rennie (in press) propose guidelines for the publishability of qualitative research that includes these points about rhetoric.

REFERENCES

Bruner, J. (1986). *Actual minds, possible worlds.* Cambridge, MA: Harvard University Press.

Elliott, R., Fischer, C. T., & Rennie, D. L. (in press). Evolving guidelines for the publication of qualitative research studies in psychology and related fields. *British Journal of Clinical Psychology.*

Fischer, C. T. (1977). Historical relations of psychology as an object-science and as a subject-science: Toward psychology as a human science. *Journal of the History of the Behavioral Sciences, 13,* 369-378.

Gadamer, H-G. (1992). *Truth and method* (2nd ed.) (J. Weinsheimer & D. G. Marshall, Trans. and Rev.). New York: Crossroad. (Original work published 1960)

Gergen, K. (1985). The social constructionist movement in psychology. *American Psychologist, 40,* 266-275.

Giddens, A. (1976). *New rules of sociological method.* London: Hutchinson.

Giorgi, A. (1970). *Psychology as a human science: A phenomenologically based approach.* New York: Harper & Row.

Giorgi, A. (Ed.). (1985). *Phenomenology and psychological research.* Pittsburgh, PA: Duquesne University Press.

Glaser, B. G., & Strauss, A. (1967). *The discovery of grounded theory: Strategies for qualitative research.* Chicago: Aldine.

Guba, E., & Lincoln, Y. (1989). *Fourth-generation evaluation.* Newbury Park, CA: Sage.

Heidegger, M. (1962). *Being and time* (J. Macquarrie & E. Robinson, Trans.). San Francisco: Harper & Row. (Original work published 1927)

Kvale, S. (1996). *InterViews: An introduction to qualitative research interviewing.* Thousand Oaks, CA: Sage.

Margolis, J. (1986). *The persistence of reality 1: Pragmatism without foundations: Reconciling realism and relativism.* Oxford, UK: Basil Blackwell.

Miles, M., & Huberman, M. (1984). Drawing valid meaning from qualitative data: Toward a shared craft. *Educational Researcher, 13,* 20-30.

Packer, M. J. (1985). Hermeneutic inquiry in the study of human conduct. *American Psychologist, 40,* 1081-1093.

Packer. M. J., & Addison, R. B. (1989). Evaluating and interpretive account. In M. J. Packer & R. B. Addison (Eds.), *Entering the circle: Hermeneutic investigation in psychology.* Albany: State University of New York Press.

Palmer, R. E. (1969). *Hermeneutics: Interpretation theory in Schleiermacher, Dilthey, Heidegger, and Gadamer.* Evanston, IL: Northwestern University Press.

Peirce, C. S. (1965). *Collected papers of Charles Sanders Peirce.* Cambridge, MA: Belknap.

Polkinghorne, D. E. (1995). Narrative configuration in narrative analysis. *Qualitative Studies in Education, 8,* 5-23.

Potter, J., & Wetherell, M. (1987). *Discourse in social psychology: Beyond attitudes and behavior.* Newbury Park, CA: Sage.

Putnam, H. (1990). *Realism with a human face* (J. Conant, Ed.). Cambridge, UK: Cambridge University Press.

Rennie, D. L. (1995a). On the rhetorics of social science: Let's not conflate natural science and human science. *The Humanistic Psychologist, 23,* 321-332.

Rennie, D. L. (1995b). Plausible constructionism as the rigor of qualitative research. *Methods: A Journal for Human Science,* annual edition, 42-58.

Rennie, D. L. (1998a). Forging a way between objectivism and relativism: Review of "InterViews: An introduction to qualitative research interviewing," by S. Kvale (1996), and of "Psychological research: Innovative methods and strategies," by J. Haworth (1996) (Ed.). *Theory & Psychology, 8,* 515-516.

Rennie, D. L. (1998b). Grounded theory methodology: The pressing need for a coherent logic of justification. *Theory & Psychology, 8,* 101-119.

Rickman, H. P. (Ed. and Trans.). (1961). *Meaning in history: W. Dilthey's thoughts on history and society.* London: George Allen & Unwin.

Rickman, H. P. (Ed., and Trans.). (1976). *W. Dilthey: Selected writings.* Cambridge, UK: Cambridge University Press.

Smith, B., & Smith, D. W. (Eds.). (1995). *The Cambridge companion to Husserl.* Cambridge, UK: Cambridge University Press.

Spiegelberg, H. (1960). *The phenomenological movement: A historical introduction* (Vols. 1 & 2). The Hague, The Netherlands: Martinus Nijhoff.

Taylor, C. (1971). Interpretation and the sciences of man. *Review of Metaphysics, 25,* 3-51.

Teigas, D. (1995). *Knowledge and hermeneutic understanding: A study of the Habermas-Gadamer debate.* London: Associated Universities Press.

Thompson, J. B. (Ed. and Trans.). (1981). *Paul Ricoeur: Hermeneutics and the human sciences.* Cambridge, UK: Cambridge University Press.

CHAPTER 2

Locating the Qualitative Research Genre

Lisa Tsoi Hoshmand

Much has been written and debated on the nature of qualitative research and the philosophical assumptions that undergird the qualitative tradition. Rennie has focused on the logic of justification in qualitative research, characterizing this research genre as "methodical hermeneutics" (Rennie, 1996; also chap. 1, this volume). He has helped clarify the philosophical differences among grounded theory, empirical phenomenology, narrative inquiry, and discourse analysis. Although some counseling researchers (e.g., Hill, Thompson, & Williams, 1997; "Qualitative Research," 1994) have begun to move the research community toward a greater appreciation for qualitative research, methodological and philosophical issues remain (Polkinghorne, 1994; "Reaction Papers," 1997). Philosophical and procedural differences among qualitative approaches have made it difficult for qualitative researchers to forge a unified proposal and to establish the place of qualitative inquiry in psychology in particular and in the social sciences in general.

In this chapter, I further articulate the nature of qualitative research as a praxis by viewing it in terms of the values, purposes, and collective agency of the communities of research practitioners who exercise particular kinds of intentionality in implementing particular kinds of research agendas. I argue that knowledge-generating activities should be placed not only in an intellectual context governed by cognitive values but also in a broad normative context that includes other social judgments (Hoshmand, 1997). The value of a given form of inquiry is to be gauged by its contribution to knowledge, as well as by its sociopolitical role and cultural relevance. The qualitative research genre can be located in the communities and practices with which it is associated and be evaluated by the shared purposes and values that inform such practices and their future agendas. Pragmatist and cultural perspectives of psychology and other human sciences, as I explain, suggest that we connect qualitative inquiry with the action research mode and the hermeneutical tradition. They support a normative conception of qualitative research praxis in which researchers assume a proactive role in collaborative problem solving and critical inquiry in the human realm. Within this broadened context, I believe, we should locate the qualitative research genre.

PRAGMATIST AND CULTURAL VIEWS OF KNOWLEDGE

How we view existing forms of research practices is a function of our conceptions of knowledge and the role of the disciplines and professions that engage in knowledge production and application. The philosophy of science has in recent years undergone significant changes with the postmodern rejection of universal foundations of knowledge. To avoid the problems of extreme relativism, a pragmatist view has been proposed (Bernstein, 1983; Harre & Krausz, 1996; Margolis, 1991) whereby contingent normative standards and judgments based on communal agreements and the experience of practice can be used to evaluate research and knowledge claims. This pragmatist view is supported by communitarian views of knowledge communities (Habermas, 1984) and the work of sociologists of science that clearly illustrates the social nature of knowledge (Mulkay, 1979). It is consistent with the critical realist and social constructionist orientations in granting the empirical reality and lived significance of those human experiences and actions that are socially appropriated (Hoshmand, 1996; Hoshmand & Martin, 1995).

The pragmatist view of knowledge considers problem solving and the experience of practice as central to knowledge making. Researchers' heuristic reasoning and judgments in problem solving during inquiry are expected to evolve with experience. Improvement of the research enterprise depends on our reflexivity and ability to learn from the experience of prior research practice. In emphasizing knowledge making as a way of acting on reality problems, the pragmatist orientation also implies that the purposes and intentions of researchers in problem finding and problem solving are important. This brings us into a broader normative context that includes the values and knowledge interests of researchers.

The philosopher Jürgen Habermas (1971) differentiated knowledge interests into the technical, the hermeneutical, and the critical. Scientific disciplines such as psychology have emphasized technical application as a goal. Being a social science, however, psychology may also contribute to hermeneutical and emancipatory goals. To the extent that qualitative research reflects the goals of illuminating human experience and enhancing our understanding of culturally constructed meanings in self-interpretation and various forms of intersubjectivity, it may serve these types of knowledge interests. When researchers use qualitative methods to study underresearched problems (e.g., certain experiences of victimization) and to give voice to populations that have not been well understood (e.g., minorities), one may regard their research as examples of purposeful value-based inquiry. Perhaps because of the self-definition of psychology as a science-based discipline and profession, however, the social intentions and values of psychology researchers tend to be given less attention than their scientific and knowledge-generating purposes.

This prevailing communal practice is long overdue as far as having its assumptions questioned. Philosophers of knowledge, including philosophers of science, have acknowledged that all knowledge is value-laden and that science is far from neutral. Naturalistic study of research as a praxis indicates that researchers are motivated by more than epistemic considerations (Hoshmand & Martin, 1996). To disregard the intentions and personal agendas of researchers only gives an incomplete picture of the knowledge enterprise. It promotes a disembodied view of research and isolates research practice and knowledge making from its human context. The implications for professional socialization and the preparation of researchers are such that continuing to ignore the values and interests that can be served by our inquiry would be irresponsible.

I have argued elsewhere that psychology is, to a large degree, a cultural science (Hoshmand, 1996). The cultural view of science places epistemic judgments and other social judgments in communal processes. In this view, scientific/professional discourse is continuous with ordinary discourse, both being culturally derived, a point particularly relevant to psychology as our theoretical language is close to everyday language. Researchers are accountable to the scientific/professional community, as well as to the larger community. In other words, our research practices should be sensitive to the fact that the public has a stake in our research enterprise. The knowledge interests we serve may be open to communal discussion and involve the negotiation of different stakeholder interests. This is recognized by qualitative researchers in program evaluation, for example, which calls for collaborating with the client system and responding to the relevant constituencies.

Both the pragmatist and the cultural view of knowledge emphasize practice and the purposes and values that inform the activities of researchers. These views locate knowledge making and decisions about knowledge claims and scientific contributions in communities of discourse that are embedded in the larger social and cultural context. They direct our attention to qualitative researchers as a community and to qualitative research as a subculture of practice. It follows that discussions about the normative criteria for evaluating qualitative research are ongoing both within the qualitative research community and in its external negotiations with the larger research and scholarly community. These discussions have not been easy, partly because of philosophical and procedural differences among subgroups of qualitative researchers and partly because the restricted attention to epistemic considerations prevents the qualitative research community from forging a strong proposal based on broader normative commitments (Hoshmand, 1997). For research practice to be defined by such shared commitments, prevailing views of what constitutes good scholarship may need to be revised (Lieberman, 1992). For example, collaborative relationships with the community, and other structures and processes developed by a researcher for problem solving, should be valued as part of the generativity of practicing research.

Two traditions with which qualitative researchers may identify their practice are *action research* and *critical hermeneutical inquiry*. These two growing traditions of inquiry are clearly defined by their philosophical, epistemic, and moral commitments. Because this volume includes examples of substantive research, I suggest that the reader refer to those chapters to determine the extent to which qualitative research is consistent with the two traditions described below. Of course, additional examples of qualitative research may be found in other sources.

QUALITATIVE RESEARCH AS A
FORM OF ACTION RESEARCH

The history of action research may be traced to the influence of Kurt Lewin, and its philosophical base is found in pragmatism (Hoshmand & O'Byrne, 1996). It has become identified respectively with action science and participatory action research (Argyris & Schon, 1989; Whyte, 1991), with the former being practiced by those interested in theory development and theory testing, and the latter being practiced by those who emphasize the egalitarian and emancipatory values of action research. Thus, one may think of action research as serving theoretical as well as emancipatory interests. Characteristics of action research, as described in detail previously (Hoshmand & O'Byrne, 1996), include characteristics similar to those of qualitative research in general (Hoshmand, 1989). A respectful, egalitarian attitude is adopted toward the human subject. Research involves collaboration with the participants whose native perceptions and meanings are valued in a consultative, co-constructing process.

Action research is consistent with a pragmatist orientation to knowledge in that knowledge is conceived to be resulting from one's attempt to act on problems. Thus, problem finding is just as important as problem solving. Descriptive and discovery research conducted with the help of qualitative methods of inquiry fall within the realm of action research as far as facilitating problem identification and illumination. In conducting action research, the researchers continuously learn about the requirements of addressing problems realistically. This usually results in the use of multiple methods because action researchers, like pragmatist philosophers, favor methodological pluralism. The choice of method is determined by the nature of the problem and the task at hand. If the qualitative research community were to support an action research mode, it would not be by preference of qualitative methods, but by commitment to a pragmatist approach to knowledge and an interest in applying appropriate means to conduct research that is relevant to solving human problems.

Action research is also sensitive to context and the diversity of stakeholder interests. In program evaluation, the negotiation of stakeholder interests is part of the role of the researcher (Scriven, 1986; Shadish, Cook, & Leviton, 1991). Whereas qualitative research methods are increasingly used in program evaluation to generate information on the evaluation context and to enhance the ecological validity of evaluation data (Patton, 1978, 1990), the political role of the researcher is less examined. Those who study organizations and complex systems have realized the importance of researcher reflexivity. This emphasis is consistent with the use of self as an instrument in qualitative research (Berg & Smith, 1988) and with the view of knowledge as a social, reflexive process (Morgan 1983; Steier, 1991). To the extent that the qualitative research community can exercise sufficient reflexivity in accounting for the researcher's role and be sensitive to the sociopolitical and cultural implications of research, qualitative inquiry may be more aligned with action research.

The problem-solving emphasis of action research can become more of a focus of qualitative research than has been the case. The research community at large has a tendency to regard qualitative research as exploratory or only contributing to problem description and exploration. Qualitative research is not considered a means of problem solving under the theory-testing tradition. Yet researchers can derive generalized theoretical structures from phenomenologi cal descriptions. Grounded theory research often involves theoretical sampling and theory testing. Those who promote "action science" would also point out that what is learned from qualitative inquiry (e.g., the nature of the interpretive systems in an organization) can be used to formulate interventions (e.g., process consultation for the organization members). The problem-solving aims of qualitative research would help define qualitative research practice as a form of action research. Its pragmatic validity, as far as human subjects finding the interpretive data to be useful in their own lives, and ecological validity, in terms of truthfulness to context, will be further indicators of its action research potential. Some of the same considerations apply to qualitative hermeneutical research as well.

HERMENEUTICS AND THE CRITICAL ROLE OF QUALITATIVE RESEARCHERS

Whereas philosophical hermeneutics is a cultural, ontological discipline that examines the fundamental conditions of living underlying our efforts to make sense of human existence (Gadamer, 1976), qualitative hermeneutical research focuses on people's self-interpretation within the webs of meaning generated by our cultural processes of intersubjectivity. The central metaphor is the interpretation of text, including texts of identity. Most qualitative researchers see their task as the analysis of narrative data for themes and patterns of meaning. The term *hermeneutics* has become loosely associated with qualitative research, apart from its historical and philosophical roots. There are certain reasons for maintaining this usage. Hermeneutics involves the kind of researcher reflexivity that is intended in qualitative research. A part-to-whole logic of interpretation and argumentation is often followed. The phenomenological attitude involved in practicing qualitative research is consistent with a hermeneutical mode of understanding.

In contrast, there is much more to the hermeneutical tradition than what has been credited to qualitative research in general. Hermeneutics involves deconstruction and critical examination of the underlying assumptions in any form of cultural text. In grounding social interpretation and judgments in cultural existence, the hermeneutical tradition considers human beings to be governed by particular histories as understood within particular cultural assumptions that can be critically evaluated (Gadamer, 1975, 1987). The cultural, hermeneutical approach encourages empirical inquiry into cultural pragmatics. In other words, not only are narrative texts of self-interpretation important, but the texts of living or historical enactment of texts of identity by individuals and groups can be subjected to hermeneutical analysis. This is where qualitative research may have been lacking in its primary focus on narrated texts and its relative neglect of enacted texts of living. In making this judgment, I do not mean that it is impossible for qualitative research to encompass hermeneutical inquiry into all forms of texts. Ethnographic research, for example, can capture communal texts of living. A qualitative researcher can presumably proceed from narrative ethnographic understanding to more critical inquiry into the conditions of living concerned (see, e.g., Edgerton, 1992).

According to Ricoeur (1980), the concrete utility and existential function of a given text is what matters in life. Textual analysis can be extended from narrated texts to enacted texts of human action in social context. It is significant that the cultural, hermeneutical approach is informed by pragmatist ideas. Hermeneutical inquiry means using a "vocabulary of practice rather than of theory, of action rather than contemplation" (Rorty, 1982, p. 162). And very important, "the pragmatist knows no better way to explain his convictions than to remind his interlocutor of the position they both are in, the contingent starting points they both share" (Rorty, 1982, pp. 173-174). This last statement is good advice for those conducting qualitative hermeneutical research. In comprehending another person's story or action, no one has final authority. Social interpretation and critique imply an irreducible plurality, which is consistent with the perspective in the interpretive social sciences that culture is always multivocal (Rabinow & Sullivan, 1987).

Although some researchers who use qualitative inquiry have identified their work as being of a critical hermeneutical nature (Fox & Prilleltensky, 1997), the critical role of qualitative research is just beginning to be considered by the community of researchers. Knowing how to conduct narrative research does not fully prepare one to assume the critical hermeneutical role. The latter calls for more attention to the sociopolitical aspects of knowledge and the deconstruction of cultural texts. It involves an intentional effort in uncovering cultural and political assumptions, with the aim of empowering the less vocal and those who have been subjugated by the existing social structure and dominant discourse. To participate fully in the hermeneutical process, qualitative researchers would have to be immersed in their understanding of culture and become astute cultural observers. Cultural study requires the types of intensive local observations at which qualitative researchers are supposed to be skilled. Also required would be reflexive understanding of psychology as a cultural science and a willingness to deconstruct our own theoretical narratives. Feminist scholars, for example, have used hermeneutical qualitative research methods for such purpose. By further studying cultural pragmatics such as the realistic societal consequences of certain texts of identity (Hoshmand & Ho, 1995), qualitative researchers can increase their contributions to understanding and improving social living.

Hermeneutics is concerned with human ontology, and qualitative research is looked on by many as a means of improving on the quality of our ontological statements about human beings. Some fear that psychology's loss of romanticism under the dominance of reductionism and objectivism may compromise our humanity. Others challenge human science advocates to rise to the occasion in ensuring that the image of the human would not suffer from routinized, mechanistic assessments such as associated with the evaluation of psychological well-being under managed care. Qualitative research methods can complement measurement-oriented approaches in providing more holistic information about the mental health needs of people, their coping resources, and the types of intervention that are helpful in facilitating problem solving. When combined with the goals of action research, qualitative hermeneutical research can be an important force in maintaining the quality of human life in the face of increasing technological advances and depersonalization.

LOCATING THE QUALITATIVE RESEARCH GENRE IN A NORMATIVE CONTEXT

What are the implications of locating the qualitative research genre in this broadened normative context and of aligning it with the action research and critical hermeneutical traditions?

Those who have held a view of scientific neutrality and objectivity may be uneasy with the notion of locating qualitative research in a value context. Especially in an age of relativism and intellectual autonomy, one finds considerable skepticism toward any unified purpose and reluctance in being identified with any collective effort. Yet qualitative research is not a disembodied technology or merely a craft. As a praxis, it is carried out by persons with particular social purposes in particular cultural and political environments. Even if the norms of practice were not uniformly clear, certain norms and values have emerged from the work of qualitative researchers and the ensuing discourse. A growing sense of community exists among those who practice this form of research, a collectivity that may become more pronounced as qualitative researchers openly share their social purposes and moral commitments. For us to begin to evaluate the qualitative research enterprise as an organized praxis, there is an assumption of collective agency in fostering epistemic and other goals that may be constitutive of social goods. I base this scenario on my own inquiry into professional identity and the transcendental goals of professionals' work (Hoshmand, 1998). It seems clear that intellectual efforts are sustained by communities of practice, as well as by intrinsic, moral commitments.

If qualitative researchers are to become a community, more needs to be done to facilitate our internal discourse. Conversations about criteria and norms for evaluating our own research praxis can be informed by the knowledge of experience in conducting qualitative research. Communal agreements require openness and an investment in the process of discussion. External dialogue with the larger research and scholarly community will be essential, not only within our own profession but also with the other social sciences. Gergen (1994) suggested forming an alliance among the semiotic sciences, a move that would facilitate the organization of knowledge from a sociological standpoint. Again, such an alliance presumes similarities in knowledge goals, interests, and approaches to inquiry. Any community-building effort would involve the development of a common language of understanding to enable metadiscourse and the complex negotiation of horizons.

Implications will accrue for education, training, and the definition of scholarship. Action research and critical hermeneutical inquiry should be specifically included in the qualitative research curriculum. Epistemic development and the learning of research competencies are no longer to be decontextualized or removed from the value context of inquiry. It would seem that students will need role modeling of the types of intentionality and personal commitment associated with these forms of research practice. They can also learn about community by being in a collaborative learning environment or research team where they can be socialized with the values that are consistent with the ideals and norms of such practice. Granted that institutional environments tend to shape academic values, the reward structure within the academic culture should be supportive of collaborative, prosocial problem-solving efforts. The definition of scholarship would need to emphasize the social significance of research beyond methodological rigor or argumentative eloquence. Critical inquiry that challenges prevailing norms and power structures should be taken seriously, rather than be marginalized or censored.

It remains for qualitative researchers to set the future agenda. Given the nature of the mode of inquiry used with qualitative research, it can be empowering of human subjects and affirming egalitarian and collaborative values. More can be accomplished, however, with intentional problem finding and problem solving that would serve hermeneutical and emancipatory interests.

Use of an action research paradigm, with equal attention to narrative texts and texts of living, may help articulate the place of qualitative research praxis as part of a knowledge enterprise that is sensitive to the cultural pragmatics in understanding and addressing human problems. As we apply reflexivity to our own work and maintain a critical community in evaluating the evolution of our research praxis, we may be able to accomplish these goals.

REFERENCES

Argyris, C., & Schon, D. (1989). Participatory action research and action science. *American Behavioral Scientist, 32,* 612-623.

Berg, D. N., & Smith, K. K. (1988). *The self in social inquiry.* Newbury Park, CA: Sage.

Bernstein, R. J. (1983). *Beyond objectivism and relativism: Science, hermeneutics, and praxis.* Philadelphia: University of Pennsylvania Press.

Edgerton, R. (1992). *Sick societies.* New York: Free Press.

Fox, D., & Prilleltensky, I. (Eds.). (1997). *Critical psychology.* Thousand Oaks, CA: Sage.

Gadamer, H. (1975). *Truth and method* (G. Barden & J. Cumming, Trans.). New York: Seabury.

Gadamer, H. G. (1976). *Philosophical hermeneutics* (D. E. Linge, Ed. and Trans.). New York: Pantheon.

Gadamer, H. G. (1987). The problem of historical consciousness. In P. Rabinow & W. M. Sullivan (Eds.), *Interpretive social science* (pp. 83-140). Berkeley: University of California Press.

Gergen, K. J. (1994). *Toward transformation in social knowledge* (2nd ed.). Thousand Oaks, CA: Sage.

Habermas, J. (1971). *Knowledge and human interests.* Boston: Beacon.

Habermas, J. (1984). *Theory of communicative action: Vol. 1. Reason and rationality in society* (E. McCarthy, Trans.). Boston: Beacon.

Harre, R., & Krausz, M. (1996). *Varieties of relativism.* Oxford, UK: Basil Blackwell.

Hill, C. E., Thompson, B. J., & Williams, E. N. (1997). A guide to conducting consensual qualitative research. *Counseling Psychologist, 25,* 517-572.

Hoshmand, L. T. (1989). Alternate research paradigms: A review and teaching proposal. *Counseling Psychologist, 17,* 3-79.

Hoshmand, L. T. (1996). Cultural psychology as metatheory. *Journal of Theoretical and Philosophical Psychology, 16,* 30-48.

Hoshmand, L. T. (1997). The normative context of research practice. *Counseling Psychologist, 25,* 599-605.

Hoshmand, L. T. (1998). *Knowledge, creativity, and moral vision: Narrative study of professional identity and commitment in a postmodern age.* Thousand Oaks, CA: Sage.

Hoshmand, L. T., & Ho, D. Y. F. (1995). Moral dimensions of selfhood: Chinese traditions and cultural change. *World Psychology, 1,* 47-69.

Hoshmand, L. T., & Martin, J. (Eds.). (1995). *Research as praxis: Lessons from programmatic research in therapeutic psychology.* New York: Teachers College Press.

Hoshmand, L. T., & Martin, J. (1996). Epistemology is more than method: Reply to
    Yanchar and Christensen. *Journal of Theoretical and Philosophical Psychology, 16,*
    103-110.
Hoshmand, L. T., & O'Byrne, K. (1996). Reconsidering action research as a guiding
    metaphor for professional psychology. *Journal of Community Psychology, 24,* 1-16.
Lieberman, A. (1992). The meaning of scholarly activity and the building of community.
    Educational Researcher, 1, 5-12.
Margolis, J. (1991). *The truth about relativism.* Oxford, UK: Basil Blackwell.
Morgan, G. (Ed.). (1983). *Beyond method.* Beverly Hills, CA: Sage.
Mulkay, M. (1979). *Science and the sociology of knowledge.* Sydney, Australia: Allen
    and Unwin.
Patton, M. Q. (1978). *Utilization-focused evaluation.* Beverly Hills, CA: Sage.
Patton, M. Q. (1990). *Qualitative evaluation and research methods* (2nd ed.). Newbury
    Park, CA: Sage.
Polkinghorne, D. E. (1994). Reaction to special section on qualitative research in
    counseling process and outcome. *Journal of Counseling Psychology, 41,* 510-512.
Qualitative research in counseling process and outcome [Special section]. (1994).
    Journal of Counseling Psychology, 41, 427-512.
Rabinow, P., & Sullivan, W. M. (Eds.). (1987). *Interpretive social science.* Berkeley:
    University of California Press.
Reaction papers to Hill, Thompson, and Williams. (1997). *Counseling Psychologist, 25.*
Rennie, D. L. (1996, August). *Reconciling realism and relativism: The root of qualitative
    research as methodical hermeneutics.* Paper presented at the International Confer-
    ence on Qualitative Research in Psychotherapy, Düsseldorf, Germany.
Ricoeur, P. (1980). Existence and hermeneutics (K. McLaughlin, Trans.). In J. Bleicher
    (Ed.), *Contemporary hermeneutics: Hermeneutics as method, philosophy, and cri-
    tique* (p. 107). London: Routledge & Kegan Paul.
Rorty, R. (1982). *Consequences of pragmatism.* Minneapolis: University of Minnesota
    Press.
Scriven, M. (1986). New frontiers of evaluation. *Evaluation Practice, 7,* 7-44.
Shadish, W. R., Jr., Cook, T. D., & Leviton, L. C. (1991). *Foundations of program
    evaluation.* Newbury Park, CA: Sage.
Steier, F. (1991). *Research and reflexivity.* Newbury Park, CA: Sage.
Whyte, W. F. (Ed.). (1991). *Participatory action research.* Newbury Park, CA: Sage.

CHAPTER 3

An Exploration of Quality in Qualitative Research
Are "Reliability" and "Validity" Relevant?

Elizabeth Merrick

For some, considerations of qualitative research prompt thoughts of relativism and loosely established truths. A charge is often made that there is no way to establish the validity or truth value of scientific claims or observations in qualitative work (Jessor, 1996). Indeed, what most qualitative researchers consider strengths—a reliance on the human instrument and an acknowledgment that many truths exist   others may see as major threats or weaknesses. With such relativism, it becomes essential to acknowledge the human element involved and to consider, as part of the method, the strengths and limitations of the personal instrument. The latter is a major contribution of qualitative methods: not only to acknowledge the researcher's influence/involvement in making meaning but also to attempt to delineate steps or checks that bound, or at least make visible, this influence. The question remains, How shall we judge the quality of the research process and product?

My approach to the issues involved is informed by my experience as a qualitative researcher and as a consumer of qualitative research. Essentially, I am concerned with fairly practical questions: How do I conduct "good" qualitative research? How do I communicate my findings to others? and How do I evaluate others' work? I take up these questions first through an exploration of reliability and validity. Then I address three areas considered essential to evaluations of quality. I have chosen the first two—trustworthiness and reflexivity—because of the consensus about these as hallmarks of quality work, and the third—representation—because it seems to be a crucial, next issue in the field.

It is important to note at the start that whether the terms *reliability* and *validity* belong in considerations of qualitative research is debatable. (For examples of divergent views, see Becker [1996], Lather [1993], and Wolcott, [1990].) After all, these criteria have traditionally been used to assess the quality of quantitative research. Traditionally, *reliability* is described as the extent to which a research endeavor and findings can be replicated; *validity* refers to the extent to which findings can be considered true (Stiles, 1993).

As these terms have been defined and used in discussions of quantitative work, they are not truly appropriate for discussing qualitative research. Nevertheless, I choose to begin my consideration of quality in qualitative research with an exploration of these terms partly because most psychologists are familiar with, and have been trained to evaluate, research using these criteria. In addition, my choice is rooted in the belief that "reliability" and "validity" have been appropriated by quantitative researchers for too long. My hope, in a vein similar to Lather (1993), is that qualitative researchers may reclaim and redefine the terms needed to discuss qualitative work. Believing that the research we conduct is both reliable and valid, I discuss it as such. Thoughtful use of these terms—not as a defense or an appeal to the positivist paradigm— creates space to consider what is important in qualitative research endeavors.

Acknowledging the many divergent opinions about evaluation criteria for qualitative research, I rely heavily on Denzin and Lincoln (1994) to summarize four positions:

1. The *positivist position* argues that one set of criteria should be applied to all scientific research. These criteria involve assessing internal validity, external validity, reliability, and objectivity.

2. The *postpositivist position* asserts that a set of criteria unique to qualitative research should be developed. Although researchers disagree considerably about what these criteria should be, they do agree that these should be different from those of quantitative research. In the constructivist view, internal and external validity, reliability, and objectivity translate into trustworthiness and authenticity.

3. The *postmodernist position* states that no criteria exist for judging the products of qualitative research. "The very idea of assessing qualitative research is antithetical to the nature of this research and the world it attempts to study" (p. 480).

4. The *poststructuralist position* asserts that an entirely new set of criteria, divorced from positivist and postpositivist traditions, needs to be constructed. This set would flow from the qualitative project itself and might include subjectivity, emotionality, feeling, and other antifoundational factors (pp. 479-480).

In the summary of issues that follows, my treatment can be located within the postpositivist position. The task, then, is to consider and develop criteria for assessing "quality" in qualitative research, redefining reliability and validity in the process. To introduce several central issues and as a way of grounding this discussion with attention to concerns of traditional evaluation, I present a summary of Lincoln and Guba's (1985) delineation of "parallel criteria." This perspective, from naturalistic inquiry, may be situated within the postpositivist/ constructivist position described above. Lincoln and Guba's ideas on evaluation criteria have subsequently changed (see Lincoln, 1995, for a summary of the evolution of her thought); however, these original criteria may be considered foundational. Toward a goal of "trustworthiness," Lincoln and Guba developed four criteria that paralleled those of quantitative methods. These parallel criteria are presented and briefly discussed.

The concept of *internal validity* was paralleled by *credibility*. Lincoln and Guba (1985) proposed several techniques to increase the likelihood that credible findings and interpretations will be produced. These include (a) *prolonged engagement*—investing sufficient time for persistent observation; (b) *triangulation*—checking the accuracy of specific items of data by using different sources; (c) *peer debriefing*—engaging with others about what one is finding and about the research process; (d) *negative case analysis*—a process of revising hypotheses in the light of what is found; and (e) *referential adequacy*— setting aside data to be archived and then compared with findings following analysis. Finally, they recommended (f) *member checking*—the process of informally and formally checking constructions with stakeholders.

The concept of *external validity* was parallel to *transferability*. Although the traditional concept of *external validity* is not relevant, Lincoln and Guba (1985) conceived of transferability as the researcher's responsibility to provide "the thick description necessary to enable someone interested in making a transfer to reach a conclusion about whether transfer can be contemplated as a possibility" (p. 316).

In addition, Lincoln and Guba (1985) paralleled *reliability* to *dependability*. The latter was to be achieved by using an "inquiry audit," which they described as metaphorically analogous to a fiscal audit in which process and product of the inquiry are examined.

Finally, Lincoln and Guba (1985) identified the concept of *objectivity* as parallel to that of *confirmability*. Confirmability refers to the "accuracy of the product" (p. 318). It is "the extent to which the auditor examines the product— the data, findings, interpretations, and recommendations—and attests that it is supported by data and is internally coherent so that the 'bottom line' may be accepted" (p. 318).

The idea of parallel criteria may now seem somewhat defensive and limited, given its reliance on quantitative terms. In general, more recent considerations have moved away from establishing the method's merits and defending its means ("our methods are as good as yours"). Greater acknowledgment of the merits of qualitative methods for all types of research seems to have resulted in less defensive and more creative positions (as well as greater conflict within qualitative circles). Lincoln and Guba's (1985) original ideas are useful, however, for engaging ideas related to reliability and validity and for elucidating several broad concerns, which are generally accepted as the hallmarks of good qualitative work.

An examination of the concepts of *reliability* and *validity* raises important questions and provides insight into how qualitative researchers view the world and their work. These issues are essential to evaluations of quality. In traditional, positivist views, "reliability, or the stability of methods and findings, is an indicator of validity, or the accuracy and truthfulness of the findings" (Altheide & Johnson, 1994, p. 487). In qualitative research, however, the definition of reliability as replication is rejected. Given postpositivist acknowledgments that there is no one "truth" and that all knowledge is constructed, the aim (and even the possibility) of replication is thrown out. Qualitative researchers generally agree that a study cannot be repeated even by the same investigator, given the unique, highly changeable, and personal nature of the research endeavor (Banister, Burman, Parker, Taylor, & Tindall, 1994).

Having rejected reliability as consistency and replication, a larger question of reliability remains. My argument for a consideration of qualitative research as "reliable" relies on a more common, general understanding of reliability. This understanding incorporates a definition of *rely* as meaning "to depend upon confidently." When asking questions about my own and others' research, I address reliability in the sense of asking, Can I depend upon this (the research process, as well as the findings)? In doing so, I focus on issues related to the following: What types of methods were used in collecting the data? With whom? Under what arrangements? What types of methods were used in analyzing the data? and Who conducted this research (what did they bring to the task)? (This assumes, of course, that the material presented allows one to make such judgments.) This has to do, in part, with the trustworthiness of observations or data (Stiles, 1993). The many ways in which qualitative researchers address this concern are discussed in the "Trustworthiness" section.

An examination of definitions of validity in qualitative research also provides useful insights into issues at the heart of the qualitative research endeavor. These rest upon, and are informed by, philosophical considerations that differ from those underlying quantitative research methods. These include qualitative researchers' emphasis on "the socially constructed nature of reality, the intimate relationship between the researcher and what is studied, and the situational constraints that shape inquiry" (Denzin & Lincoln, 1994, p. 4).

In qualitative research, validity is not about establishing the "truth" of "facts" that exist "out there." Although perspectives on validity among qualitative researchers diverge widely (see Altheide & Johnson, 1994), in general the focus has shifted from the "truth of statements" to "understanding by participants and readers" (Mishler, 1990; Stiles, 1993).

For many qualitative researchers, validity is dependent on the audiences or "interpretive communities" and the goals of the research (Altheide & Johnson, 1994). Such a perspective is based on a belief that "[a]ll knowledge and claims to knowledge are reflexive of the process, assumptions, location, history, and context of knowing and the knower" (Altheide & Johnson, 1994, p. 488).

Validity in the qualitative context is integral. As Banister et al. (1994) summarized: "[Validity] has to do with the adequacy of the researcher to understand and represent people's meanings" (p. 143). Validity becomes "a quality of the knower, in relation to her/his data and is enhanced by alternative vantage points and forms of knowing" (Marshall, 1986, p. 197).

This points to the importance of, and the difficulties inherent in, interpretation. If there is no single interpretative truth, how is "interpretive authority" (Hoshmand, 1997) to be established? Questions about whether this "authority" can or should be established are involved in what has been termed a "crisis of legitimation" within qualitative research (Denzin & Lincoln, 1994). Validity within qualitative research can be viewed from different positions, including culture, ideology, language, and relevance (Altheide & Johnson, 1994). Clearly, the issues involved are complex, and perspectives within qualitative circles are evolving. Despite these difficulties, qualitative researchers' emphasis on understanding remains a guidepost for considerations of validity.

One way of addressing validity concerns in qualitative research is to use consensus to achieve interpretive conclusions and enhance quality of judgment. An example is the model of consensual qualitative research forwarded by Hill, Thompson, and Williams (1997). Reliance on consensus or agreement, however, also raises other challenges in terms of validity (e.g., how to consider minority vs. majority views; see Hoshmand, 1997).

An alternative to considering validity only in terms of consensus is the perspective presented by Stiles (1993). Stiles distinguished between those types of validity that depend on (a) the fit or agreement of new observations or interpretations with one's understanding and (b) the change or growth in one's understanding produced by new observations or interpretations. Stiles also differentiated three classes of people whose understandings might be affected by the research: readers, participants, and the investigators themselves.

Stiles (1993) defined the three types of validity that depend on fit or agreement as (a) *coherence*—quality of interpretation determined by readers; (b) *testimonial validity*—accuracy of interpretation as determined by participants; and (c) *consensus/stability/replication*—interpretations as discussed with other investigators, often through peer debriefing. The types of validity that depend on change or growth are (a) *uncovering and self-evidence*—evaluations of fruitfulness and "fit" by readers; (b) *catalytic validity*—the degree to which the research process "reorients, focuses, and energizes participants" (p. 611); and (c) *reflexive validity*—evaluation of how theory or an investigator's way of thinking is changed by the data.

Stiles's (1993) attention to various audiences, as well as to the processes and goals of the research, points to the kind of validity I believe is important in qualitative research. My considerations regarding validity in qualitative research are based on assessing the extent to which the research is "soundly founded on fact or evidence" (the common understanding of validity) and how it meets concerns such as those indicated by Stiles.

In assessing others' qualitative work, my questions include, How were the data analyzed? How did the researcher determine when to stop collecting data? and By what processes were interpretations made? I also ask, Do these interpretations make sense? Were these checked out with participants? With other researchers? and Did changes occur in the researcher's understanding or theory on the basis of what was found? As a researcher, I work to incorporate these issues into the research process.

Reliability and validity, then, are not properties of the research tool as they are in quantitative research. Rather, reliability and validity depend on the relationship between the researcher and the research process, as well as between the researcher and the interpretive community. The researcher's engagement with issues of reliability and validity begins at the conception of the research project and runs through to the dissemination of findings. The weight of providing "evidence" of reliability and validity rests on the researcher; such evidence must be presented for assessment by those seeking to understand the research.

Attempts by qualitative researchers to increase the reliability and validity of the research process and findings are addressed next as they relate to issues of trustworthiness, reflexivity, and representation. All three are interconnected and are primary to evaluations of quality.

TRUSTWORTHINESS

Many qualitative researchers have forwarded trustworthiness as a primary criterion for evaluation of quality. Trustworthiness encompasses elements of "good practice" that are present throughout the research process (Banister et al., 1994; Lincoln & Guba, 1985; Stiles, 1993). Several of these were described in the previous section addressing the parallel criterion of credibility. Elements of trustworthiness, from a review by Stiles (1993), include (a) disclosure of the researcher's orientation, (b) intensive and prolonged engagement with the material, (c) persistent observation, (d) triangulation, and (e) discussion of findings and process with others. As Stiles summarized, it also involves the iterative cycling between observation and interpretation or between dialogue with text. It entails "grounding" the interpretations by using individual examples in the data to support abstractions or higher-level theorizing.

Trustworthiness also encompasses efforts to reduce—or at the very least to make explicit—sources of bias by the researcher. A qualitative approach to the problem of bias is to "increase the investigators'—and readers'—exposure to the phenomenon" (Stiles, 1993, p. 614) by using intensive interviews and by providing "thick descriptions" (p. 614) of the data. In addition, Stiles (1993) identified triangulation, responsible searching for negative instances, and repeatedly seeking consensus through peer debriefing as elements of good practice.

The commitment to revealing, rather than avoiding, the researcher's involvement is consistent with the shift from the truth of statement to understanding by participants and readers. This prompts the need for disclosure and explication of the researcher's orientation. As Stiles (1993) noted, "Having [the researcher's] orientation in mind, whether or not we share it, helps us put their interpretations in perspective" (p. 602). In addition, qualitative researchers may provide an explication of social and cultural contexts and the internal processes during the investigation as they constitute a part of the meaning of the study's observations and interpretations (Stiles, 1993).

Although these elements are generally conceived as accepted steps toward trustworthiness, I agree with Steinmetz (1991) that "trustworthiness is more than a set of procedures . . . it is a personal belief system that shapes the procedures in process" (p. 93). Consistent with this is an awareness that issues of trustworthiness are with us even before we enter the field from the time we conceptualize an object of study. Trustworthiness, then, has to do with how one approaches, collects, analyzes, interprets, and reports data. A primary emphasis is placed on making the steps and influences conscious to the researcher and visible to readers. Implicit in the aim of trustworthiness is a goal of awareness of self-as-researcher engaging in the research process. Qualitative research has an inherent concern with reflexivity.

REFLEXIVITY

Acknowledgment that the researcher is central in the construction of knowledge leads qualitative researchers to emphasize the reflexive aspects of the research process. As Altheide and Johnson (1994) noted, "One meaning of reflexivity is that the scientific observer is part and parcel of the setting, context and culture he or she is trying to understand and represent" (p. 486). Reflexivity is the attempt to deal with this; Wilkinson (1988) defined it as "disciplined self-reflection" (p. 493). Banister et al. (1994) further described it as "an attempt to make explicit the process by which the material and analysis are produced" (p. 149).

Commitment to reflexivity suggests that the research topic, design, and process, together with the personal experience of doing the research, are reflected on and critically evaluated throughout. Wilkinson (1988) identified three types of reflexivity: personal, functional, and disciplinary. Banister et al. (1994) summarized Wilkinson's work in a way that directly expresses the relevant issues for our concerns. Wilkinson's *personal reflexivity* is "about acknowledging who you are, your individuality as a researcher and how your personal interests and values influence the process of research from initial idea to outcome" (Banister et al., 1994, p. 150). *Functional reflexivity* entails "continuous critical examination of the practice/process of research to reveal its assumptions, values, and biases" (p. 151). *Disciplinary reflexivity* involves reflecting on larger issues that include "research methodology and questioning psychology itself" (p. 172).

Assumptions that all findings are constructions incorporating one's personal view of reality and that these are open to change and reconstruction entail the need for qualitative researchers to make explicit the process through which their understandings were formed. Given that the reader evaluates trustworthiness through what is presented, a premium is placed on the researcher's ability to communicate in a compelling way what and how he found what he did, as well as the meaning he makes of it. This endeavor, by extending considerations of reflexivity to the writing process, also presents significant challenges.

REPRESENTATION

A pressing issue in the evaluation of qualitative research stems from an acknowledgment of "expanding conceptions of the nature of knowledge and the relationship between what one knows and how it is represented" (Eisner, 1997, p. 4). Qualitative researchers such as Fine (1994) have emphasized that "Self and Other are knottily entangled. This relationship, as lived between researchers and informants, is typically obscured in social science texts, protecting privilege, securing distance, and laminating the contradictions" (p. 72).

Our efforts to produce research that is reliable, valid, trustworthy, and reflexive are inextricably connected with issues of representation. Representation is not just about "writing up" the findings after concluding the study; rather, it is integral to the research process, and some suggest it may constitute the findings (Denzin & Lincoln, 1994). As previously addressed, the inclusion of narrative and personal material about the researcher and the research process provides a way for readers to evaluate the research. Some qualitative researchers (e.g., Fine, 1992; Lather, 1991) argue that the ways we present our data have as much to do with who we are and say as much about us as they do about our participants and our findings.

One key assumption of qualitative research has been "that qualitative researchers can directly capture lived experience" (Denzin & Lincoln, 1994, p. 11). However, this view has recently been rejected in recent arguments that such experience "is created in the social text written by the researcher" (Denzin & Lincoln, 1994, p. 11). Resultant conflicts have led to what has been called a "crisis of representation" within qualitative research (Denzin & Lincoln, 1994).

Given the difficulties inherent in representation, some researchers have retreated from analysis and withdrawn from interpretation in their writing (Fine & Weis, 1996). Simply presenting the participants' voices, however, is not a satisfying option because researchers—in particular, psychologists—presumably bring something to the endeavor. In this matter, I would extend Altheide and Johnson's (1994) task for ethnographers to psychologists: "[T]he key issue is not to capture the informant's voice, but to elucidate the experience that is implicated by the subjects in the context of their activities as they perform them, and as they are understood by the [researcher]" (p. 491). The task for psychology, then, is to engage with how researchers package what they say about those they study (Fine, 1992; Lather, 1991).

Various ways of dealing with "problems of representation" have been forwarded. One possibility, proposed by Kvale (1996), is that of a narrative approach to interview analysis. Kvale assumes that an interviewee's statements are not collected but are "coauthored" in the sense that "[the interviewer's] questions lead to the aspects of a topic the subject will address, and his or her active listening and following up on the answers codetermines the course of the conversation" (p. 281). Kvale's narrative approach entails "going back to the original story told by the interviewee and anticipating the final story to be reported to an audience" (p. 282).

Another possibility, presented by L. Richardson (1995), is to create "writing stories." As Richardson summarized: "Rather than hiding the struggle, concealing the very human labor that creates the text, writing stories would reveal emotional, social, physical, and political bases of the labor" (p. 191).

As qualitative research continues to evolve, different forms of presenting qualitative work will need to be developed. The means of assessing quality that have been suggested here are not easily incorporated within the traditional formats for "scholarly" research. An immediate problem is that nontraditional forms of writing are not accepted by mainstream psychology journals.

The role of the researcher in the task of representation will also continue to change. More collaborative projects in which work is explicitly coauthored by researchers and participants may emerge (e.g., Lather's [1995] research with women with HIV/AIDS). Such attempts, however, must acknowledge that these efforts neither eliminate the researcher's position of power nor obviate the fact that researchers have set up a relationship for their purposes.

In these matters, I believe that psychology has much to offer in determining the direction that qualitative research takes from this point. In particular, feminist psychology may provide crucial insights. Feminist scholars' attention to issues of power in relationships and the dynamics that result from inequity are especially promising (e.g., Acker, Barry, & Esseveld's [1991] treatment of problems related to "objectivity" and "truth" in feminist research). Feminist psychology, in addition, has shown commitment to dealing with underaddressed populations and with the complexities of representation. Relevant examples include Wilkinson's (1996) and others' (including D. Richardson, 1996; Russell, 1996) explorations of difficulties inherent in what are termed "representing the 'Other.'"

New directions for qualitative research may incorporate radically different criteria for evaluation. One recent example is Lincoln's (1995) proposal that included such elements as (a) *positionality*—displaying honesty about stance; (b) *concern about voice*—attending to who speaks, for whom, to whom, for what purposes; (c) *reciprocity*—studying the relations researchers make; (d) *sacredness*—honoring ecological concerns; and (e) *sharing the prerequisites of privilege*—participants' receipt of benefits from the research. Although it remains to be seen whether qualitative researchers will embrace such new criteria, considerations for "validity" are clearly evolving to engage some of the complex issues indicated.

Our current concerns involve issues of empirical accountability that entail the need to offer grounds on which to accept a researcher's description and analysis, as well as finding ways to establish the trustworthiness of data within the inquiry. Lather's (1993) attempt to "reframe" validity is relevant here. Instead of stressing a concern with "epistemological guarantees," Lather views validity as "multiple, partial, endlessly deferred" (p. 675). She identified the need for "seeing what frames our seeing—spaces of constructed visibility and incitements to see which constitute power/knowledge" (p. 675).

As this treatment points out, answers (and the difficulties inherent in them) to questions about what constitutes quality in qualitative research are complex. My redefined "reliability" and "validity," then, are relevant and necessary but are not sufficient criteria for evaluating quality. At the center are issues about what research is, what it is for, and who ought to have access to it (Lincoln, 1995). These concerns have ramifications beyond those related to qualitative research methods and speak to issues at the heart of psychology.

CONCLUSION

A review of the literature in this area suggests an ongoing conversation about issues of quality in qualitative research. Until relatively recently, scholars of qualitative research worked toward establishing the method's merits and defending its means. Greater acknowledgment of the benefits of qualitative methods, however, has led to less defensive and more creative positions (as well as to increased conflict within qualitative circles). Although qualitative researchers exhibit wide variation in their definitions of, and positions on, criteria for assessing quality, they do exhibit consensus about concerns encompassed by trustworthiness and reflexivity. In addition, recent attention has been given to the importance of representation in qualitative work. In summary, qualitative research may appropriately be called "reliable" and "valid"; however, these terms, even redefined, are insufficient to cover the multitude of complex issues involved in discussing evaluations of quality. The fact that conversations about these issues are ongoing suggests exciting directions for the future.

REFERENCES

Acker, J., Barry, K., & Esseveld, J. (1991). Objectivity and truth: Problems in doing feminist research. In M. F. Fonow & J. A. Cook (Eds.), *Beyond methodology: Feminist scholarship as lived research* (pp. 133-153). Bloomington: Indiana University Press.

Altheide, D. L., & Johnson, J. M. (1994). Criteria for assessing interpretive validity in qualitative research. In N. K. Denzin & Y. S. Lincoln (Eds.), *Handbook of qualitative research* (pp. 485-499). Thousand Oaks, CA: Sage.

Banister, P., Burman, E., Parker, I., Taylor, M., & Tindall, C. (1994). *Qualitative methods in psychology.* Bristol, PA: Open University.

Becker, H. S. (1996). The epistemology of qualitative research. In R. Jessor, A. Colby, & R. A. Shweder (Eds.), *Ethnography and human development* (pp. 53-71). Chicago: University of Chicago Press.

Denzin, N. K., & Lincoln, Y. (1994). Part V: The art of interpretation, evaluation, and presentation. In *Handbook of qualitative research* (pp. 479-483). Thousand Oaks, CA: Sage.

Eisner, E. W. (1997). The promise and perils of alternative forms of data representation. *Educational Researcher, 26*(6), 4-10.

Fine, M. (1992). *Disruptive voices: The possibilities of feminist research.* Ann Arbor: University of Michigan Press.

Fine, M. (1994). Working the hyphens: Reinventing self and other in qualitative research. In N. K. Denzin & Y. S. Lincoln (Eds.), *Handbook of qualitative research* (pp. 70-82). Thousand Oaks, CA: Sage.

Fine, M., & Weis, L. (1996). Writing the "wrongs" of fieldwork: Confronting our own research/writing dilemmas in urban ethnographies. *Qualitative Inquiry, 2*(3), 251-274.

Hill, C. E., Thompson, B. J., & Williams, E. N. (1997). A guide to conducting consensual qualitative research. *Counseling Psychologist, 25*(4), 517-572.

Hoshmand, L. T. (1997). The normative context of research practice. *Counseling Psychologist, 25*(4), 599-605.

Jessor, R. (1996). Ethnographic methods in perspective. In R. Jessor, A. Colby, & R. A. Shweder (Eds.), *Ethnography and human development* (pp. 3-14). Chicago: University of Chicago Press.

Kvale, S. (1996). The 1,000-page question. *Qualitative Inquiry, 2*(3), 275-284.

Lather, P. (1991). *Getting smart: Feminist research and pedagogy with/in the postmodern.* New York: Routledge.

Lather, P. (1993). Fertile obsession: Validity after poststructuralism. *Sociological Quarterly, 34*(4), 673-693.

Lather, P. (1995, April). *Creating a multilayered text: Women, AIDS, and angels.* Paper presented at the annual meeting of the American Educational Research Association, San Francisco.

Lincoln, Y. S. (1995). Emerging criteria in qualitative and interpretative research. *Qualitative Inquiry, 1*(3), 275-289.

Lincoln, Y. S., & Guba, E. (1985). *Naturalistic inquiry.* Beverly Hills, CA: Sage.

Marshall, J. (1986). Exploring the experiences of women managers: Toward rigor in qualitative methods. In S. Wilkinson (Ed.), *Feminist social psychology: Developing theory and practice.* Philadelphia: Open University.

Mishler, E. (1990). Validation in inquiry-guided research: The role of exemplars in narrative studies. *Harvard Educational Review, 60*(4), 415-442.

Richardson, D. (1996). Representing other feminists. *Feminism & Psychology, 6*(2), 192-196.

Richardson, L. (1995). Writing stories: Coauthoring "The Sea Monster," a writing-story. *Qualitative Inquiry, 1,* 189-203.

Russell, D. E. H. (1996). Between a rock and a hard place: The politics of white feminists conducting research on black women in South Africa. *Feminism & Psychology,* 6(2),176-180.

Steinmetz, A. (1991). Doing. In M. Ely (with M. Anzul, T. Friedman, D. Gardner, & A. M. Steinmetz), *Doing qualitative research: Circles within circles* (pp. 41-105) London: Falmer.

Stiles, W. B. (1993). Quality control in qualitative research. *Clinical Psychology Review, 13,* 593-618.

Wilkinson, S. (1988). The role of reflexivity in feminist psychology. *Women's Studies International Forum, 11*(5), 493-502.

Wilkinson, S. (Ed.). (1996). Editor's introduction. *Feminism & Psychology, 6*(2), 167-8.

Wolcott, H. F. (1990). On seeking—and rejecting—validity in qualitative research. In E. W. Eisner & A. Peshkin (Eds.), *Qualitative inquiry in education: The continuing debate* (pp. 121-153). New York: Teachers College Press.

CHAPTER 4

The Role of the Qualitative Researcher

Daniel Sciarra

Often the choice between quantitative and qualitative method is decided by technical or pragmatic reasons. One method is chosen over the other because it will generate the kind of information the investigator is looking for (Hathaway, 1995), an approach commonly known as *situational*. Little, if any, thought is given to the philosophical assumptions differentiating qualitative and quantitative methodology, such as the nature of reality (ontology) and the acquisition of knowledge (epistemology; Hathaway, 1995). This chapter examines the role of the qualitative researcher first by linkage to epistemology. I believe that the assumption of a philosophical stance on how one knows (and therefore investigates) reality determines the researchers' role and positionality before their participants.

The choice between quantitative and qualitative research is more than simple appropriateness for the task at hand. It is more about philosophy of knowledge and how one understands the real. In other words, epistemological rather than technical criteria will determine the role of the qualitative investigator (Bryman, 1984) and the consequential development of a research paradigm. For example, students faced with the daunting challenge of writing dissertations sometimes opt for a qualitative design, on the one hand, because of their dislike of statistics. On the other hand, the option of quantitative research is sometimes made because of the institution's refusal to recognize qualitative research as "scientific." Neither choice is a philosophically informed one. The choice of one methodology over the other implies an understanding of oneself and one's role regarding research participants. The purpose of this chapter is to examine the role of the qualitative researcher by uncovering the philosophical differences between qualitative and quantitative investigation. I hope that such an endeavor will help both students and seasoned researchers make more informed choices about the kind of research they undertake in applied psychology.

QUALITATIVE VERSUS QUANTITATIVE RESEARCH

Qualitative research is often distinguished from quantitative by referring to the former as exploratory done with a smaller sample of participants about a relatively unknown subject and, in this sense, is viewed as a precursor to quantitative research. Another way of stating the difference is that qualitative research is about hypothesis generation and quantitative research about hypothesis testing (Brause, 1991). In this view, the goal of qualitative research is to provide leads, hunches, and hypotheses that, in turn, may or may not be supported by the quantitative researcher employing more rigorous (and therefore more "scientific") methods with a much larger sample. This attempt to reconcile the roles of the quantitative and qualitative researcher emanates from the neopositivist tradition (Schwandt, 1994). Within this framework, however, "qualitative research merely provides fodder for quantitative researchers and so occupies a lower rung on the epistemological ladder" (Bryman, 1984, p. 84). Furthermore, the implication is that qualitative research and quantitative research are not fundamentally opposed and even complimentary, as the former is in need of verification by the latter. If qualitative research is in need of verification, it can hardly be accepted as a valid pursuit of truth in its own right. This view of methodological complementarity between quantitative and qualitative research blurs the very significantly different answers to fundamental questions underlying the investigative paradigm. According to Guba and Lincoln (1994), these fundamental questions are three: (a) the ontological question—what is the form and nature of reality; (b) the epistemological question—what is the relationship between the knower and the known; and (c) the methodological question—how does the researcher go about finding out what can be known? If qualitative research is in some sense preparatory to quantitative research, the implication is that they are sewn from the same philosophical cloth. If we trace historically the philosophical influences—namely, positivism and idealism—behind quantitative and qualitative investigation, then maintaining that the two roles are similar and complementary becomes more difficult.

Positivism

The role of the quantitative researcher is embedded in a 19th-century argument over whether social science research should be conducted in the same ways as research in the physical sciences. In favor of this was a group of philosophers (Compte, Mill, and Durkheim, to name a few) known as "positivists," who put forth the argument that social relationships are to be regarded as "facts," "things" to be investigated in an objectlike manner. The social scientist, like the physicist, is the observer of an independently existing reality (Smith,

1983b), of something that can be known outside oneself. The relationship of social scientists to their subjects is the relationship of the knower (the researcher) to the known (the subject of the research, who is really an object to be known). Within this paradigm, the neutrality of the researchers is emphasized as they must confine themselves to examining *what is*—what is objective (Smith, 1983a)—and dislodging themselves from all bias, emotion, values, or anything *subjective* that would compromise the objectivity of the research.

This position is consistent with the philosophy of realism, which holds that something can be known independent of the knower, that its "reality" has little, if anything, to do with the knower's process of coming to know that reality. As science, the primary aim of social science research is the discovery of laws regarding human behavior and interaction. These laws are viewed as similar to physical laws "in that they would state the necessary and invariant relationships that existed between and among social objects" (Smith, 1983b, p. 7). In short, positivism became associated with the empirical-analytical paradigm of social science research.

Idealism

Alongside 19th-century positivism arose a countermovement that, despite variations, can be classified under the philosophical term *idealism*. The two most prominent names behind this movement were Wilhelm Dilthey and Max Weber.

Dilthey (1924/1954, 1894/1977) challenged the positivists' assertion that human subjects can be investigated and known in the same ways as inanimate objects. Because the object of study in the social sciences is the product of thought or mind, it cannot be separated from the thought and mind of the investigator. The relationship between the social science researcher and that which is being investigated is not one of subject-object, but subject-subject. Although something or someone may be independent of our minds, it only has a meaning and, therefore, an existence (because, in this paradigm, meaning is reality) through the illumination of our own minds or thoughts. Thus, the knowing of someone else cannot be separated from the process of knowing oneself, a process sometimes referred to as *heuristic inquiry*.

Heuristic inquiry lives in the moment (Patton, 1990). The researcher and the participant are both the subject and the object of investigation, "interactively linked with the values of the investigator inevitably influencing the inquiry" (Guba & Lincoln, 1994, p. 110). Thus, any investigation into the social sciences is an investigation of two subjects (the investigator and that which is being investigated), a relationship of intersubjectivity involving the values, emotions, perceptions, and cultural context of both parties.

Dilthey (1924/1954, 1894/1977) took further issue with the positivists in objecting to the goal of social science research as the discovery of laws. Contrary to the actions of inanimate objects, the action of human beings is more complex and less uniform, changing over time and setting. Dilthey introduced the notion of culture as group-determined behavior making the investigation for uniform causality in the social sciences a fruitless endeavor. Social science research ought not be explanatory, but *descriptive*. It should strive to describe as accurately as possible the actions of another and attempt to understand those actions through interaction. Dilthey's notion of understanding is a special one referred to as *verstehen,* interpretive understanding. "Interpretive understanding, in contrast to Durkheim's approach, does not see the world as a collection of objects, but as a question of what is meaningful in human life" (Smith, 1983a, p. 40). The *verstehen* tradition in rooted in phenomenology (Husserl, 1911/1965), which emphasizes description and interpretation of experience as the basis of inquiry. To investigate truly the actions of another, one must, to the greatest degree possible, get inside the mind of the other through a re-creation of the other's experience, which becomes internalized in the observer (the researcher). One can see how close Dilthey's notion of *verstehen* comes to the notion of empathy in the therapeutic relationship. Through *verstehen,* necessarily interactive, one comes to understand the behavior of another and in so doing achieves a greater understanding of one's own behavior.

Dilthey (1924/1954, 1894/1977) went further in his meta-investigation of social science research, incorporating the concept of *hermeneutics.* For Dilthey, the understanding of another must access the *meaning* associated with a particular action, and meaning must be understood within a context. This knowledge of the context or background for the proper interpretation of another is what Dilthey meant by hermeneutics. The notion of hermeneutics gave rise to the interpretivist paradigm in social science research (Schwandt, 1994). The social science researcher must interpret (understand) the other within context, within the group or culture in which the other functions. Consistent with the subject-subject position of social science research, the investigator, in coming to know the context (culture) through which the other is deriving meaning, is also coming to know and possibly question the context(s) of her or his own behavior. Weber (1922/1949) elaborated on Dilthey's notion of *verstehen* by saying that the understanding of another involves two levels: the "what" of an action and the "why" of an action, understood as the difference between descriptive and explanatory understanding. *Explanatory understanding* involves accessing the meaning an individual gives to her or his actions, and this meaning must be understood within context.

In present-day social science research, the paradigm of constructivism seems to be preferred over interpretivism, although many writers acknowledge that constructivist, interpretivist, and hermeneutical paradigms are similar (Guba & Lincoln, 1989; Schwandt, 1994). They share in common the notion that (a) reality is basically a construction of the individual mind, (b) these constructions are the result of the meanings individuals give (construct) for their experiences, (c) human beings act toward things on the basis of these meanings (Woods, 1992), and (d) the constructions of the investigator cannot be (and should not be) separated from those of the investigated (Schwandt, 1994). In social constructionism, the focus is more on the mutually agreed-upon meanings of a particular group and their role in shaping individual constructions (Berger & Luckmann, 1966; Gergen & Gergen, 1991; Guba & Lincoln, 1989; Schwandt, 1994).

THE RELATIONSHIP BETWEEN THE INVESTIGATOR AND THE INVESTIGATED

Given the philosophical distinctions between positivism and idealism, the application of such distinctions would result in different research methodologies. Causality and prediction would lead to a more quantitative approach for the discovery of laws, whereas description and interpretation would lead to a more qualitative one for the discovery of meaning. Furthermore, how investigators understand their role and relationship to the investigated would be fundamentally different.

The realist position, which holds that something can be known independent of the processes of our own minds and social context, results in an empirically oriented investigation centered around a subject-object relationship. Smith (1983a) refers to this perspective as the *quantitative-realist (Q-R) perspective.*

The idealist position, in contrast, which holds that reality is shaped to some degree (and different philosophical schools will disagree as to the degree) by our minds and social context and cannot be known independently, results in a more participatory oriented investigation centered around two subjects. This is sometimes referred to as the *interpretive-idealist (I-I) position* (Smith, 1983a). Therefore, if reality is in some degree mind-dependent, it is impossible to conceive of the investigative process as not influencing the investigated, a belief in direct contrast to the empirical approach.

This distinction creates a very different view of research instrumentation. For the empiricist, research instruments are conceived as separate from the researcher and the object to be measured; therefore, they are considered accurate measures of the object. In contrast, the I-I research paradigm regards instrumentation as an extension of the knower (Smith, 1983a) that serves to understand the meaning of an action or how participants construct their reality. Because truth is mind-dependent and based on contextual agreement, the qualitative researcher regards as true the agreed-upon meanings by individuals within a given society. In contrast, the empiricist, who understands reality as existing independent of the knower, understands truth as that which corresponds accurately to what is "out there" (Smith, 1983a). Contradictions for the I-I perspective pose no problems because multiple meanings, versions, and interpretations can arise out of multiple contexts of the same experience. Whereas for the Q-R perspective, contradictions are not allowed to exist, and the researcher must "scientifically" opt for one as more "true" than the other after careful examination of the data.

This choice of something being more true than something else on the basis of the data has led to the conviction that the Q-R perspective is more objective, whereas the I-I perspective, with its emphasis on the mind of the knower as constructor of reality, has earned the criticism of being subjective in its investigations. For the postmodernists, if reality is constructed rather than objectively "out there," then the only possible investigations are the constructions (meanings, interpretations) of the participants. If qualitative research is criticized as "subjective," it can only come from someone assuming a contrary epistemological position—namely, that of realism. In contrast, if one assumes that reality is constructed at least in part by the mind of the knower and given meaning within a context, the research must be subjective—that is, an investigation into how others construct their reality, getting inside the mind of another, assuming the other's perspective; these and similar phrases are used in the literature to describe the role of the qualitative researcher. "What is seen as a limitation from the Q-R point of view is considered the essence of social inquiry from the I-I perspective" (Smith, 1983a, p. 47).

If objectivity is found in the idealist perspective, it is to be located in the mutually agreed-upon meanings that exist in a group of individuals or the historical/social context of an individual. From this is derived the holistic approach of the qualitative researcher who attempts to understand the individual (a part) in a particular context(s) (the whole) or culture. Quantz (1992) rightly points out that the holistic approach must go beyond the participant's local group to the consideration of larger social forces, that one's culture is the working out of a struggle often between nondominant and dominant discourses. This meaning-in-context(s) approach, previously referred to as hermeneutics, is the essence of interpretive understanding (*verstehen*) and determines fundamentally the role of the qualitative researcher.

DIFFERENCES IN ROLE

The previous sections have articulated the philosophical differences underlying quantitative and qualitative methodology with a view to their implications in the definition of the researcher's role. This section elaborates further and articulates in a more applied fashion the role of the qualitative investigator and its contrast with the role of the quantitative investigator.

Onlooker Versus Actor

Hathaway (1995) describes the difference in role between the quantitative and qualitative researcher as that between onlooker and actor. The quantitative researcher is on the outside looking in, a detached observer using specialized survey or assessment instruments to collect and then analyze the data with the hope of abstracting something objectively true (usually in terms of causality or correlation) about the investigated. In contrast, the qualitative researcher is

more like an actor in a situation with other actors (the research p
Qualitative researchers allow themselves to be taken up into the
participant, becoming a part of that world either through participant
participant observation and extensive interviewing. Qualitative researchers are
on the inside, immersing themselves in the social contexts and minds of the
participants as an interacting student willing to learn about the experiences and
the meanings given to those experiences within the participants' local context
or culture. The role behind interpretive understanding emerges from the researcher's own prior knowledge, interests, values, emotions, and cultural affiliations, which are also subject for scrutiny and examination in the interaction
with participants. Qualitative researchers allow themselves to be affected and
challenged by the cultural meanings that participants give to their experience
that may be different from the researchers' own meanings.

Expert Versus Learner

In any relationship, issues of power and control emerge almost automatically,
and the research relationship is no exception. *Controlled studies* refers to
empirical-quantitative research and implies the researchers' role as one who
controls the experimental setting as a manipulator of variables with the goal of
supporting or not supporting a hypothetical truth about a reality understood as
external to themselves. Quantitative researchers control the research process as
scientists in the role of expert. In contrast, qualitative researchers know of no
such control nor enjoy the psychological luxury of expertness. Social research
becomes an interactive rather than a controlling process (Hamelton, 1994).
Entering a setting as student and learner, qualitative researchers must relinquish control (Kleinman & Copp, 1993); only in this fashion can they truly
enter the world of another. The qualitative researcher enters the participants's
world, "not as a person who knows everything, but as a person who has come
to learn; not as a person who wants to be like them, but as a person who wants
to know what it is like to be them" (Bogdan & Biklen, 1992, p. 79). Even the
researcher with some well-defined working ideas and a semistructured interview format will often experience a sense of directionlessness, of not knowing
where the participant's world is leading. The temptation to regain control is
constant and often framed within the need to give more focus to the research.
The anxiety generated by immersing oneself in an environment that may differ
radically from the researcher's own cultural background can also lead to
retaking some control. Qualitative researchers run the risk of dealing with such
anxiety either by blurring the distinction between researcher and participant
("going native") or by accentuating the distinction and thus sacrificing the
insider's perspective.

At times, however, assuming the role of expert can help the qualitative
researcher gain entrance to a setting and gain access to the data more easily,
thus serving a practical interest. For example, when I was conducting a

qualitative study of teenage pregnancy and motherhood, I used my position as a counselor in the local intermediate school as a way of gaining access to the participants (Sciarra, 1998). Once such access is gained, however, the investigator must relinquish, at least psychologically, the role of expert, allowing him- or herself to engage in a collaborative pursuit of the participants' meaning-making world, substituting a practical interest for an emancipatory interest (Habermas, 1968/1971; Quantz, 1992). This emancipatory interest resides in a democratic form of communication, in a mutual exchange of meaning-making worlds without the imposition of the researcher's dominant discourse.

Detachment Versus Involvement

We have been emphasizing that qualitative research demands an openness on the part of the investigator that allows her or him to enter deeply into the world of another. This kind of closeness generates some critical questions regarding the role of the qualitative researcher, such as closeness, identification, and emotional involvement with the participants. Unlike the quantitative investigator, who would understand such issues as hampering the objectivity of the research, the qualitative researcher must constantly negotiate issues of closeness and intimacy because they are necessary consequences of the serious qualitative endeavor.

Earlier, mention was made of how the researcher's own subjectivity is a critical component in qualitative research. This subjectivity is not only cognitive (e.g., the investigator's beliefs, attitudes, cultural biases) but also affective (the investigator's emotions). The role of this second pole of the subjective experience is now examined.

Emotional Involvement. Not only are emotions allowed in qualitative research, they are crucial. Because entering the meaning-making world of another requires empathy, it is inconceivable how the qualitative researcher would accomplish her goal by distancing herself from emotions (Kleinman & Copp, 1993). Rogers (1959) described empathy as feeling "as if one were the other person" (p. 210). The etymology of the word *empathy* suggests a feeling in, a state of being inside another person, or adopting another's internal frame of reference (Truaff & Carkhuff, as cited in Duan & Hill, 1996). These definitions connote a sense of intimacy and closeness with another person from which is derived the power and centrality of empathy in the qualitative investigation. Theorists argue whether empathy is primarily affective in nature, "responding with the same emotion to another person's emotion" (Gladstein, 1983, p. 468, as cited in Duan & Hill, 1996) or primarily cognitive, "intellectually taking the role or perspective of another person" (Gladstein, 1983, p. 468, as cited in Duan & Hill, 1996). For the counselor, this distinction may be useful; for the qualitative investigator, it is superfluous. Qualitative researchers use both cognition and emotion to enter and identify with the world of their participants.

All emotional reactions, positive or negative, intense or mild, can be
for the investigator. Unlike quantitative researchers who push em
in the name of objectivity, qualitative researchers rely on such emou
further their understanding of the participants' world of meaning and how it
may differ from their own.

Underrapport Versus Overrapport

Not unlike good counseling, crucial to the role of qualitative researchers is
the analysis of their emotions. Valid questions demanding answers are, for
example, What is this strong emotional reaction I'm experiencing telling me
about the world of the participants? About my own world? About the difference
between their world and my world? Stronger emotions are more likely to be
imbued with greater significance but at the same time create a challenge for the
investigator. Strong positive emotions may lead to overrapport with the participants, whereas strong negative emotions may lead to to underrapport. Recent
literature seems to indicate a curvilinear relationship between validity and
rapport (Harkess & Warren, 1993).

Although this chapter is not about validity and qualitative research (for a
thorough treatment of issues of validity in qualitative research, refer to Merrick,
chap. 3, this volume), the curvilinear relationship does raise the issue of proper
boundaries in the qualitative-investigative relationship. Overrapport (or emotional overinvolvement) can compromise the role of the investigators. Dunn
(1991), who studied battered women, and Roth (1989), who studied women
who experienced amniocentesis, talk about experiencing in themselves the
same symptoms and behaviors of their participants. How does one assess such
closeness? Should these authors be congratulated for having achieved the
highest degree of empathy or be criticized for becoming overinvolved with the
participants of their studies? These are not easy questions to answer. I believe
that emotional involvement in qualitative research is not only unavoidable but
a necessary consequence of establishing a good relationship with participants.
However, does becoming involved to the extent of a quasi-symbiotic relationship as evidenced in the above examples compromise the role of the qualitative
investigator?

The answer to this question is yes if investigators do not provide "analytical
space" for themselves. The investigator ought to take a systematic step back
from the data (and this includes the researcher's emotions and emotional
involvement) to analyze and understand what such involvement is revealing
about the participants' and the investigator's worlds of meaning. Much like
good counselors who use their emotional reactions to the client as a means
for greater understanding of both themselves and the client, so too qualitative researchers engage is a dynamic relationship with participants to generate and collect data about the participants' world. The role of qualitative
researchers is to assume an *empathic* stance in the interaction with their

participants and a neutral stance in the analysis of the data (Patton, 1990). The real question, according to Kleinman and Copp (1993), is not whether the researcher's emotions affected the validity of the study, but rather *how* such emotions played a part in the study. Implicit is the assumption that emotions indeed will play a role in qualitative research.

CONCLUSION

Numerous avenues may be taken to approach an understanding of the role of the qualitative researcher. This chapter examined this role by tracing its philosophical underpinnings in the idealist/interpretivist/constructivist tradition and took the position that ontological (the nature of reality) and epistemological (the process of knowing reality) questions fundamentally determine the relationship between researcher and participant. In doing so, contrasts were drawn with the role of the quantitative researcher. If one takes seriously the question of ontology and epistemology, it becomes difficult to reconcile these two investigative approaches. The question remains, however: Can a researcher employ both quantitative and qualitative methods and still maintain a coherent and honest research identity?

In the meantime, the reader is invited to reflect on the following quote:

> The empirical social world consists of ongoing group life and one has to get close to this life to know what is going on in it. The metaphor that I like is that of lifting the veils that obscure or hide what is going on. The task of scientific study is to lift the veils that cover the area of group life that one proposes to study. The veils are lifted by getting close to the area and by digging deep in it through careful study. Schemes of methodology that do not encourage or allow this betray the cardinal principle of respecting the nature of one's empirical world. (Blumer, 1978, as quoted in Patton, 1990, p. 67)

The role of the qualitative researcher can be viewed through Blumer's metaphor of the lifter of veils. Furthermore, because their own constructions of reality are evoked and challenged in the qualitative endeavor, qualitative researchers, by lifting the veil on others, are also lifting the veil on themselves. This chapter explained the challenge facing qualitative researchers in maintaining the proper boundary between themselves and their participants. Much of the role of the qualitative researcher can be reduced to having to negotiate this boundary continuously.

REFERENCES

Berger, P., & Luckmann, T. (1966). *The social construct of reality*. New York: Anchor.
Bogdan, R. C., & Biklen, S. (1992). *Qualitative research for education*. Boston: Allyn & Bacon.

Brause, R. S. (1991). Hypothesis-generating studies in your classroom. In R. L. & J. S. Mayher (Eds.), *Search and research* (pp. 181-206). London: Falmer.

Bryman, A. (1984). The debate about quantitative and qualitative research: A quest. of method of epistemology? *British Journal of Sociology, 35,* 75-92.

Dilthey, W. (1954). *The essence of philosophy* (S. A. Emery & W. T. Emery, Trans.). Chapel Hill: University of North Carolina Press. (Original work published 1924)

Dilthey, W. (1977). *Descriptive psychology and historical understanding* (R. M. Zaner & K. L. Heiges, Trans.). The Hague, The Netherlands: Martinus Nijhoff. (Original work published 1894)

Duan, C., & Hill, C. E. (1996). The current state of empathy research. *Journal of Counseling Psychology, 43,* 261-274.

Dunn, L. (1991). Research alert! Qualitative research may be hazardous to your health! *Qualitative Health Research, 1,* 388-392.

Gergen, K. J., & Gergen, M. M. (1991). Toward reflexive methodologies. In F. Steier (Ed.), *Research and reflexivity* (pp. 76-95). Newbury Park, CA: Sage.

Guba, E. G., & Lincoln, Y. S. (1989). *Fourth-generation evaluation.* Newbury Park, CA: Sage.

Guba, E. G., & Lincoln, Y. S. (1994). Competing paradigms in qualitative research. In N. K. Denzin & Y. S. Lincoln (Eds.), *Handbook of qualitative research* (pp. 105-117). Thousand Oaks, CA: Sage.

Habermas, J. (1971). *Knowledge and human interests* (J. J. Shapiro, Trans.). Boston: Beacon. (Original work published 1968)

Hamelton, D. (1994). Traditions, preferences, and postures in applied qualitative research. In N. K. Denzin & Y. S. Lincoln (Eds.), *Handbook of qualitative research* (pp. 60-69). Thousand Oaks, CA: Sage.

Harkess, S., & Warren, C. (1993). The social relations of intensive interviewing. *Sociological Methods and Research, 21,* 317-339.

Hathaway, R. S. (1995). Assumptions underlying quantitative and qualitative research: Implications for institutional research. *Research in Higher Education, 36,* 535-562.

Husserl, E. (1965). *Phenomenology and the crisis of philosophy* (Q. Lauer, Trans.) New York: Harper & Row. (Original work published 1911)

Kleinman, S., & Copp, M. A. (1993). *Emotions and fieldwork.* Newbury Park, CA: Sage.

Patton, M. Q. (1990). *Qualitative evaluation and research methods.* Newbury Park, CA: Sage.

Quantz, R. A. (1992). On critical ethnography. In M. D. LeCompte, W. D. Millnoy, & J. Preissle (Eds.), *The handbook of qualitative research* (pp. 447-505). San Diego, CA: Academic Press.

Rogers, C. R. (1959). A theory of therapy, personality, and interpersonal relationships as developed in the client-centered framework. In S. Koch (Ed.), *Psychology: A study of a science. Study 1. Conceptual and systematic: Vol 3. Formulations of the person and the social context* (pp. 184-256). New York: McGraw-Hill.

Roth, P. A. (1989). Ethnography without tears. *Current Anthropology, 30,* 555-561.

Schwandt, T. A. (1994). Contructivist, interpretivist approaches to human inquiry. In N. K. Denzin & Y. S. Lincoln (Eds.), *Handbook of qualitative research* (pp. 118-137). Thousand Oaks, CA: Sage.

Sciarra, D. T. (1998). Teenage motherhood among low-income, urban Hispanics: Familial and cultural considerations of mother-daughter dyads. *Qualitative Health Research, 8,* 751-763.

Smith, J. K. (1983a). Quantitative versus interpretive: The problem of conducting social inquiry. In E. R. House (Ed.), *Philosophy of evaluation* (pp. 27-51). San Francisco: Jossey-Bass.

Smith, J. K. (1983b). Quantitative versus qualitative research: An attempt to clarify the issue. *Educational Researcher, 12,* 6-13.

Weber, M. (1949). *Methodology of social sciences* (E. Shiles & H. Finch, Trans.). New York: Free Press. Original work published 1922

Woods, P. (1992). Symbolic interactionism: Theory and method. In M. D. LeCompte, W. D. Millnoy, & J. Preissle (Eds.), *The handbook of qualitative research* (pp. 337-404). San Diego, CA: Academic Press.

CHAPTER 5

Merging Qualitative and Quantitative Perspectives in a Research Identity

Joseph G. Ponterotto
Ingrid Grieger

In Chapter 4, Daniel Sciarra highlighted the apparent conflict between qualitative and quantitative methods on the basis of their rootedness in radically different philosophical positions. Sciarra believes that the schism between methodologies is irreconcilable because of the variant nature of the positivist and constructivist stances. Our position in this chapter is that although qualitative and quantitative perspectives do represent distinct "languages" and "cultures," so to speak, becoming "bilingual" and "bicultural" in research identity is both possible and desirable. Forging a merged qualitative/quantitative research identity as a scholar is a difficult, long-term, and challenging process, but one that we think is well worth the effort.

In this chapter, we share our perspective on the challenges and rewards of developing a merged research identity and offer a road map for developing multimethod research competence. The chapter is organized along five sections. First, we present definitions of key terms used throughout our discussion. Second, we examine the often-discussed gap or tension between proponents of quantitative and qualitative paradigms, respectively; this tension is likened to a cross-cultural difference in which proponents of one research "worldview" have trouble understanding and valuing the "worldview" of the other. Third, we proceed with a discussion of an advocated symbiosis between qualitative and quantitative methods in a merged research identity. Fourth, we outline steps to developing a merged research identity. Finally, we discuss combining qualitative and quantitative methods in the same study.

KEY DEFINITIONS

If you are new or fairly new to qualitative research approaches in applied psychology, as we suspect many readers may be, you will likely be over-whelmed with the cornucopia of terms used in the topical area. For example, do you know the distinctions among ethnography, ethnomethodology, herme-neutics, grounded theory, and symbolic interactionism? Perhaps not, and if it is any consolation, sometimes we are not sure we do either!

One reason for the semantic confusion in qualitative methods is that they involve many schools of thought, integrate many disciplines, and tap many philosophical roots. Different authors classify various "types" of qualitative methods in diverse ways. Sometimes the types overlap markedly, and various terms may be used interchangeably; at other times, noted distinctions between methods are considered (by some authors) significant. Authoritative sources that will help you disentangle the wide variety of types or approaches to qualitative inquiry are Denzin and Lincoln's (1994) *Handbook of Qualitative Research* and Patton's (1990) *Qualitative Evaluation and Research Methods*. We also recommend, of course, revisiting the Rennie (chap. 1, this volume) and Hoshmand (chap. 2, this volume) discussions that opened this text.

Rather than add to the semantic ambiguity found in qualitative literature by using terms loosely, we pause at this juncture and define six terms central to our discussion. In this way, the reader will be clear about our interpretation and usage of these terms throughout the chapter.

Quantitative Methods

Quantitative methods focus on the strict quantification of observations (data) and on the empirical control of variables. This form of research most often incorporates large-scale sampling procedures and the use of statistical tests to study group averages and variances.

Qualitative Methods

Qualitative methods incorporate "any kind of research that produces findings not arrived at by means of statistical procedures or other means of quantifica-tion" (Strauss & Corbin, 1990, p. 17). Or as Taylor and Bogdan (1984) note, "[Q]ualitative methodology refers in the broadest sense to research that pro-duces descriptive data: People's own written or spoken words and observable behavior" (p. 5). Table 5.1 presents some key differentiating characteristics of quantitative and qualitative approaches when considered at extreme contrasts. The dichotomized characteristics presented in Table 5.1 stem from the writings of many scholars in the area and from our own interpretation and digestion of the variant paradigms.

TABLE 5.1 Differentiating Characteristics of Quantitative and Qualitative Approaches

Quantitative	*Qualitative*
Natural Science Perspective (*Naturwissenschaften*)	Human Science Perspective (*Geisteswissenschaften*)
Positivism	Phenomenology, Idealism, and Constructivism
One true reality, measurable	Multiple realities, socially constructed, and context dependent
Comte, Durkheim, Mill	Husserl, Deutscher, Weber, Dilthey
Deductive	Inductive
Theory driven	Theory generating
Hypothesis testing	Hypothesis generating
Predicting	*Verstehen* (Understanding)
Quantification	Description
Understanding laws and causes	Seeking meaning
Outcome oriented, answering questions	Discovery oriented, asking questions
Objective and detached researcher	Involved and interactive researcher
Experimental designs and standardized instruments	In-depth interviews, participant observation, and "researcher as instrument"
Third-person written reports	First-person written reports
Internal validity, external validity, reliability, and objectivity	Credibility, transferability, dependability, and confirmability
Multitrait—multimethod	Triangulation
Methods and procedures are predetermined and followed rigorously throughout study	Methods and procedures are fluid and evolving

SOURCE: From *Handbook of Racial/Ethnic Minority Counseling Research* (2nd ed.), by J. G. Ponterotto and J. M. Casas, in preparation, Springfield, IL: Charles C Thomas. Adapted with permission of J. G. Ponterotto.

Culture and Research Culture

Linton (1945) defines *culture* as "the configuration of learned behavior whose components and elements are shared and transmitted by the members of a particular society" (p. 32). One's *research culture* (e.g., as existing in one's academic training environment) will shape one's worldview about the importance, process, and methods of research.

Worldview and Research Worldview

Worldview can be defined as the "lens" through which people interpret their world; one's worldview is culturally based, stemming from the socialization process (Ibrahim, Ohnishi, & Wilson, 1994). By extension, one's *research worldview* is the lens with which one sees, approaches, and manages the research process. One's research worldview shapes the specific paradigm from which one will conceptualize, conduct, and interpret research.

Paradigm

Simply stated, a *paradigm* can be perceived as a "set of interrelated assumptions about the social world which provides a philosophical and conceptual framework for the organized study of that world" (Filstead, 1979, p. 34). The paradigm selected helps guide professionals in the discipline, helps direct theory and model development in the field, and promotes the use of particular tools of investigation that include methodology, instruments, and forms of data collection (Filstead, 1979; Kuhn, 1970).

Research Identity

An individual's overall personal identity is composed of multiple and reciprocal identities—for example, racial identity, gender identity, religious identity, political ideology, and career identity. A sense of identity in these various interacting areas helps someone feel anchored and connected. A positive sense of identity is related to self-esteem and one's overall self-concept (Ponterotto & Pedersen, 1993). For an academic scholar, a crucial sense of identity revolves around one's *research identity*. This identity defines how one perceives oneself as a researcher, with strong implications for which topics and methods will be important to the researcher. Naturally, one's research identity both influences, and is influenced by, the paradigm from which one operates.

Having defined key terms to be used throughout this chapter, we now turn to a discussion of the often-talked-about schism between quantitative and qualitative methods.

BRIEF CONCEPTUALIZATION OF THE QUALITATIVE-QUANTITATIVE DISTINCTION: A CROSS-CULTURAL PARALLEL

We have come to view the quantitative-qualitative distinction as being akin to a cross-cultural difference. To illustrate this point, we offer the analogy of considering the concept of *marriage* from a cross-cultural perspective. In the United States, a culture that generally values individualism, autonomy, and *self*-actualization, choosing a spouse is most often an individual decision arrived at after a period of dating and other interactive experiences. Marriage is an individual choice sometimes made without much regard for extended family wishes and traditions. By contrast, in other countries, marriage is often arranged by parents, grandparents, and other extended family members. At times, in these cases, the betrothed marry after only one or two meetings.

To many Americans, the concept of an *arranged marriage* is ludicrous. On the one hand, the typical American may think, How can you marry someone you barely know? How dare your parents, grandparents, uncles and aunts, and so on decide whom *you* should marry? On the other hand, those who practice arranged marriages—for example, some cultural groups in India or Pakistan—perceive the American practice of marriage as outrageous. They might ask, How dare you marry someone whom your family elders have not chosen for you? How can you disregard family, religion, and centuries of cultural tradition?

This oversimplified cross-cultural example parallels our view of the qualitative-quantitative distinction. Consider the following two scenarios. A quantitative-oriented researcher may review a qualitatively focused dissertation proposal and remark, "What do you mean, you are only interviewing about eight mental health patients?" "Do you mean to tell us that your interview questions can actually change from one subject to the next?" "Can't some already validated Likert-type scale tap into those questions?" and finally, "Can't you randomly select subjects from randomly selected mental health clinics in randomly selected states?"

In contrast, yet with the same fervor, a qualitative-oriented scholar may review a quantitative-oriented dissertation proposal and remark, "You plan to survey randomly 1,000 mental health patients nationwide by using this 50-item Satisfaction With Therapy Scale, whereupon you will examine the mean score and standard deviation of the collective sample?" OK, but will you really know how any one patient was affected by therapy?" "Will you be able to understand how a subject's personal and family life was affected?" "Will you be able to determine the most crucial incidents in therapy that led to a satisfying experience?" "Will that mean score give you a true sense of the hard work and emotional pain involved in therapeutic growth?" and finally, "Will reading your study make me a better therapist?"

The qualitative-quantitative debate just illustrated parallels the earlier contrast between arranged and independent marriages. Within each case, different worldviews, identities, and procedural paradigms are in operation. In both scenarios, the respective worldviews, particularly at their extreme ends, seem irreconcilable. The reader can now more fully understand Sciarra's position (chap 4, this volume), which maintained that the differing worldviews underlying qualitative and quantitative methods render them mutually exclusive and incompatible. Accordingly, Sciarra questions whether a scholar can develop a coherent and "healthy" research identity while attempting to integrate the two perspectives.

A SYMBIOSIS OF PARADIGMS

In this section, we provide a response to Sciarra's position by highlighting the value and feasibility of developing a merged research identity. Our perspective is that quantitative and qualitative methods can be viewed as complementary, rather than as competing camps. This position is not new; many writers before us have advocated the use of convergent methods (e.g., Brewer & Hunter, 1989; Denzin, 1978; Jick, 1983). Keeping with our cross-cultural perspective, we use the multicultural context to present our position.

Our own research specialties are in the area of multicultural counseling. Literature in this area suggests that it behooves individuals who live in a multicultural society to become bicultural and bilingual (see eight chapters of Part II in Ponterotto, Casas, Suzuki, & Alexander, 1995). Individuals who immigrate to the United States and both maintain their cultural traditions (and language) of origin and acculturate to some degree to the "American" world-view (and English language) learn two modes of managing and coping in society. They develop bicultural strengths that incorporate multiple ways of understanding reality and of solving problems. Similarly, European Americans who are monocultural and monolingual also benefit from embracing more of a multicultural worldview that can be gained through the *intensive* study of another culture and language.

Our position in this chapter is that psychology researchers will be more effective and more enlightened if they develop a bicultural research worldview— coming to a clear understanding of, and developing true competence in, both quantitative and qualitative philosophies and methods. The challenge inherent in our position is echoed well by Trend (1979), who notes,

> [F]ew researchers are equally comfortable with both types of data, and the procedures for using the two together are not well developed. The tendency is to relegate one type of analysis or the other to a secondary role, according to the nature of the research and the predilections of the investigator. (p. 83)

One goal in this chapter is to guide the quantitative-focused psychologist in developing a bicultural research perspective. As you have learned from reading Chapters 1 through 4 of this text, quantitative and qualitative approaches generally answer different questions in different ways. As a summary for the reader, we include Table 5.2, which presents a flowchart outlining common steps to both approaches.

In our experience, most psychologists approach research questions from a positivist, quantitative paradigm (see column 1 of Table 5.2). In essence, they have only one mode of problem solving, one lens through which to interpret the research inquiry. We believe that this single lens is limiting. Most issues or "problems" in psychology are complex and necessitate multiple perspectives to understand more fully the phenomena under study.

TABLE 5.2   Comparative Conceptual Flow of Quantitative and Qualitative
Methodologies

Sequential Steps	Quantitative Research	Qualitative Research
Step 1	Generate psychological theory	Identify general problem or topic of interest
Step 2	Generate specific hypotheses from theory	Develop exploratory research questions
Step 3	Plan and set specific procedures, methods, and instruments	Collect and interpret initial data
Step 4	Collect data	Develop tentative hypotheses
Step 5	Analyze and interpret data	Collect and interpret additional data (look for negative cases, constant comparative method)
Step 6	Determine whether initial hypotheses are supported or refuted	Refine tentative hypotheses
Step 7		Collect and interpret additional data
Step 8		Develop more specific hypotheses
Step 9		Generate theory

SOURCE: From *Handbook of Racial/Ethnic Minority Counseling Research* (2nd ed.), by J. G. Ponterotto and J. M. Casas, in preparation, Springfield, IL: Charles C Thomas. Adapted with permission of J. G. Ponterotto.
NOTE: The suggested qualitative steps follow more of a grounded theory approach.

Having a bicultural research identity and its related competencies allows the researcher more flexibility and options in both gaining a perspective on a research question and planning its investigation. The choice of research paradigm is dependent on the specific nature of the research problem and on the current state of knowledge in the field. For example, an important concern in applied psychology is the underrepresentation of ethnic minority students on the doctoral level (Atkinson, Brown, & Casas, 1996). Many studies on the topic have relied on surveys and questionnaires completed by faculty and minority students in doctoral programs across the country. This research has yielded important nomothetic (large-group focused; normative) information on leading stressors and challenges in recruiting and retaining underrepresented students. Despite the proliferation of these surveys during the last decade, however, the status of minority student enrollment in, and graduation from, doctoral programs in psychology has remained relatively unchanged (Atkinson et al., 1996).

A fruitful paradigm for research on this topic at this point is more idiographic (individual and small-group focused; descriptive) research on the characteristics of successful doctoral training programs with regard to minority student recruitment, retention, and success. Building on the extensive quantitative survey data as a context, some recent qualitative research has examined the characteristics of "successful" training programs (and faculty) vis-à-vis minority student success (Atkinson et al., 1996; Patterson-Stewart, Ritchie, & Sanders, 1997), attributes of training programs that are most salient to prospective minority applicants (Ponterotto, Burkard, et al., 1995), and personal qualities and early childhood experiences of highly successful graduate students (LePage-Lees, 1997). By using qualitative interviews, think-aloud procedures, and a case study methodology, collectively these studies have shed new light on our understanding of the minority student experience in psychology training.

Ultimately, the combination of nomothetic (quantitative) and idiographic (qualitative) research on the topic of ethnic parity in applied psychology led to a clearer appreciation of both student and training program characteristics that are significant in promoting student success. The researcher who can "wear two hats," so to speak, shifting in sequenced and integrative fashion between small-group descriptive and large-group normative approaches, will be more effective and better able to capture the true complexity of the phenomenon under study.

COMBINING QUALITATIVE AND QUANTITATIVE METHODS IN THE SAME INVESTIGATION

Generally, we caution against combining paradigms in a single study for the simple reason that it is often just "too much." At times, graduate students approach us with enthusiastic and energetic visions about a "comprehensive, all-inclusive" study that rests on method triangulation. More often than not, our reaction is, Well that's OK if you want to conduct two doctoral dissertation studies instead of one!

Unfortunately, many doctoral students in psychology have not had basic (never mind adequate) training in qualitative approaches. Their understanding of qualitative philosophy and methods is limited, and they underestimate the work and rigor involved in this form of research. For some of these students, the notion of "method triangulation" or a "multimethod" study simply involves following up a quantitative study with some interviews or field observations to support or flesh out statistical findings or both. Jick (1983), whose pioneering research we highlight shortly, is among the staunch critics of the "qualitative add-on" (our phrase) approach to research.

Although we are cautious in recommending multimethod studies, we do believe that there is a time and a place for combining diverse methods in the same study. Naturally, the philosophy behind the multimethod approach, or method triangulation, is that the systematic synthesis of different methods will compensate for inherent weaknesses of the individual methods (Brewer & Hunter, 1989). It would be instructive to review two studies that demonstrate the potential complementarity of qualitative and quantitative methods. First, we review an older, classic study in organizational psychology (Jick, 1983); then, we review a recent study in counseling psychology (Blustein, Phillips, Jobin-Davis, Finkelberg, & Rourke, 1997).

Jick (1983) studied the effects of a merger on employees during a 14-month period. Informed by early interviews, his investigative focus was on employee anxiety during the company's state of flux. He was interested in employee stress around the topic of job security. In reviewing the literature on employee stress and anxiety in the workplace, Jick noted several ways to measure stress manifestations: (a) Ask the person directly or indirectly (e.g., projective assessments), (b) ask individuals who interact with the employee, (c) observe the person's behavior, and (d) measure physiological symptoms.

Given the expected high demand characteristics of employees in this situation, Jick thought it prudent to incorporate a multimethod approach to the research question. As a result, the methods used by Jick included quantitative surveys and stress measures of randomly selected employees; probing, semistructured interviews (with projective assessments integrated) with a subsample of workers; interviews with supervisors and coworkers of the selected sample to inquire about perceived anxiety levels; telephone interviews with employees who voluntarily left the company; and unobtrusive, nonparticipant observation, as well as archival materials. In a creative methodological twist, Jick solicited the cooperation of the company archivist, who monitored employee usage of the in-house library. This strategy was added to the design when Jick noted that some employees were visiting the library, seeking information (recent news reports, company memos) to relieve anxiety about their uncertain future. Jick named this procedure the anxiety "thermometer."

Analyzing the quantitative and qualitative results, Jick noted a good deal of convergence and was able to identify the specific events that were most anxiety producing, as well as the conditions under which the anxiety was attenuated. Interestingly, Jick also noted some divergent results stemming from the different methods. This divergence is an important clue to the researcher, and as Jick (1983) notes, "When different measures yield dissimilar results, they demand that the researcher reconcile the differences somehow. In fact, divergence can often turn out to be an opportunity for enriching the explanation" (p. 143).

Working from the divergent results, Jick went back to the drawing board and conducted additional interviews. These new interviews uncovered important new information that, once integrated into the developing picture, yielded a clear answer to his research questions. Let's now move to another multimethod study in a different field of applied psychology.

Blustein et al. (1997) studied the school-to-work transition for work-bound high school students. Their sample consisted of 45 employed young adults (ages 18-29) who were quite diverse in terms of race, gender, and place of employment. The researchers developed an interview protocol that included both open-ended and structured segments. The open-ended probes led subjects to tell their "own stories" (personal narratives) of how they moved from high school to work. The narrative probes tapped the subjects' personal, educational, and career development.

The interviews were tape-recorded and transcribed, and a grounded theory approach (Strauss & Corbin, 1990) to interpreting the data was used. During the open coding process, many basic themes emerged. Supplementing the qualitative interviews, the researchers incorporated quantitative procedures. First, they measured participants' career congruence and job satisfaction by using well-respected quantitative instruments. Next, they quantified the many themes that emerged from the qualitative interviews. The variables were generally quantified along a 3-point continuum that attempted to capture the extent to which a subject evidenced a particular attitude. For example, the general extent to which subjects exhibited "work motivation" was quantified as *very little* (1) to *high* (3).

The next step involved conducting correlation analyses by using the quantified themes and the two standard variables noted earlier—career congruence and life satisfaction. The purpose of this procedure was to winnow down the list of significant variables to allow subsequent focus in analyzing the transcripts. With the most significant correlations between the quantified themes and the standardized variables noted, Blustein et al. (1997) proceeded to identify low- and high-scoring groups on the two standardized variables—congruence and job satisfaction. With these participants selected, the research team then went back to the transcribed qualitative interviews and, using the AQUAD qualitative computer program (Huber, 1995), identified and extracted all passages from the inclusive participants that dealt with the significant variables identified in the earlier correlations. By examining the relevant passages from high and low scorers, the authors "sought to illuminate the critical differences in the experiences of those who had made an adaptive transition [to work] from those who had not" (Blustein et al., 1997, p. 374).

The Jick (1983) and Blustein et al. (1997) studies were very different in specific method and procedure, yet both used a multimethod approach to study the phenomena of interest. These studies, in our opinion, highlight the successful complementarity of quantitative and qualitative methods. We believe that the studies also effectively demonstrate both the intensity and the amount of work that go into a well-designed, carefully thought-out multimethod investigation. To be successful in this venture, the researcher must have adequate command of both methods, including knowledge and understanding of the underlying philosophy of the particular methods, and specific skills in conducting and interpreting each type of study. In the next section, we move to strategies for developing true multimethod competence.

DEVELOPING A MERGED RESEARCH IDENTITY

Throughout this chapter, we have been conceptualizing the quantitative-qualitative distinction as a cross-cultural conflict. Our bias has been clear: that just as being bicultural and bilingual in society is advantageous, similarly being "bicultural" in research identity is valuable and enriching. One assumption in this chapter is that most applied psychologists and students are more familiar and comfortable with the natural science, or quantitative, paradigms. Let's consider some empirical research that addresses this assumption. Keeley, Shemberg, and Zaynor (1988) examined all dissertation abstracts in clinical psychology in the years 1965 and 1985 and classified them as classes of traditional and nontraditional research methodologies. The qualitative procedures that parallel our definition in this chapter (refer back to column 2 of Table 5.1) were labeled by Keeley et al. (1988, p. 219) "descriptive/interpretive." They found that, of 249 abstracts identified in 1965, only 2 (or 0.8%) used descriptive/interpretive methodologies and that, of the 641 abstracts located in 1985, 23 (or 3.6%) used such methods. Thus, we conclude that, during the 20-year period of the study, qualitative methods increased slightly in usage.

In a much more recent study using counseling psychology as the applied psychology base, Kopala, Suzuki, Goldman, and Galdi (1997) surveyed 181 participants who received their doctorates in 1991-92. They found that roughly 15% of respondents used qualitative methods (which include interviews, case studies, and/or participant-observation procedures). Also of interest in this survey was the finding that 49% of respondents indicated that qualitative methods were taught as components of other research methods courses, and 31% noted that a separate course was offered on qualitative methods (the authors did not indicate whether this course was optional or required). It does appear that, during the 9-year period that separated the Keeley et al. (1988) and Kopala et al. (1997) studies, qualitative methods in applied psychology, at least in the counseling psychology domain, became more accepted and popular.

Despite the positive qualitative trend indicated by Kopala et al. (1997), we believe that it is fair to say the majority of applied psychology students and graduates have been socialized into the natural science (quantitative) paradigm. Developing a merged, or bicultural, identity for these individuals rests therefore on developing the human science (qualitative) component of their identity. How is this achieved?

First, we believe that it is not sufficient to rely on proposed graduate curricula (e.g., Hoshmand, 1989; Stabb, chap. 8, this volume) to meet the bicultural socialization needs and competencies we are recommending. Think back to your Spanish or Italian 101 course in high school or college. Did that course make you truly bicultural or fully bilingual? Probably not. Developing a merged research identity means immersing yourself in the "new culture," the one you had not been socialized into; in this case, that is the qualitative culture and worldview.

To frame our recommendation here, let's draw on a valued qualitative method known as *biography* (see Smith, 1994). A noted authority in the field of qualitative research (particularly using grounded theory methods) is David Rennie, who, incidentally, provides the opening chapter to this text. Some of his writing (e.g., Rennie, 1996) includes autobiographical accounts of his developing research identity. Let's use him as a model of a quantitatively trained scholar who, over time, incorporated a qualitative identity. Rennie received his Ph.D. in clinical psychology from the University of Missouri at Columbia, where his dissertation focused on observational learning. He notes, "[I] published enough to win the [faculty] appointment at York University [Canada]. Once there, the application of natural science methodology to research on counsellor [British spelling] training, in collaboration with Shake Toukmanian, was sufficient to win tenure" (Rennie, 1996, pp. 318-319).

Rennie was soon disillusioned with his program of counselor training research and wanted to move into studying the clients' experience of counseling through first-person accounts. During the next 5 years, Rennie began contemplating and reading about qualitative methods. At this point, he adopted the grounded theory approach and began to interview his first clients.

Rennie's (1996) research development closely parallels our own path as quantitatively trained researchers growing to embrace qualitative methods. Initially socialized into a natural science research worldview, we became somewhat disillusioned with the limits of the quantitative paradigms. We all thought that, through qualitative methods and direct face-to-face contact with research participants, a deeper, richer understanding of basic psychological processes would emerge.

An integration of Rennie's (1996) career as a researcher with our own led us to believe that developing a research identity that includes qualitative affiliations is a process that unfolds over time. It begins with disillusionment and/or frustration with the quantitative paradigm, followed by a lengthy period of reflection and study of qualitative methods (5+ years) and then proceeding to an actual qualitative research program and the ongoing refinement of our qualitative positions and preferences.

Again, this journey parallels the journey of becoming bicultural/bilingual. For example, an individual may live abroad for 3 years and learn the host culture and language. At times, acculturation conflict may occur as the person feels "caught between" two cultures. Similarly, a scholar can be torn between approaching (or integrating) a research question from a positivist or constructivist stance or both (see discussions of challenges of multimethod research in Brewer & Hunter [1989] and Trend [1979]). In the end, the scholar with a bicultural research identity and multimethod competence can deftly attack a research problem with varying methods over sequenced studies, or as demonstrated by Jick (1983) and Blustein et al. (1997), with varied methods in the same study.

SUMMARY

This chapter conceptualized the qualitative-quantitative distinction within a cross-cultural context. Faithful ties to a particular paradigm are understood within a socialization process that engenders a particular research worldview and identity. We suggest that quantitative-focused researchers consider embracing qualitative paradigms and incorporate them into a merged research identity. Specific examples illustrating the compatibility of both qualitative and quantitative methods in sequenced studies, or even within the same study, were presented. Finally, a road map for developing qualitative method competencies was delineated, and the strengths of developing a merged research identity were highlighted.

REFERENCES

Atkinson, D. R., Brown, N. T., & Casas, J. M. (1996). Achieving ethnic parity in counseling psychology. *Counseling Psychologist, 24,* 230-258.

Blustein, D. L., Phillips, S. D., Jobin-Davis, K., Finkelberg, S. L., & Rourke, A. E. (1997). A theory-building investigation of the school-to-work transition. *Counseling Psychologist, 25,* 364-402.

Brewer, J., & Hunter, A. (1989). *Multimethod research: A synthesis of styles.* Newbury Park, CA: Sage.

Denzin, N. (1978). *The research act: A theoretical introduction to sociological methods* (2nd ed.). New York: McGraw-Hill.

Denzin, N. K., & Lincoln, Y. S. (Eds.). (1994). *Handbook of qualitative research.* Thousand Oaks, CA: Sage.

Filstead, W. J. (1979). Qualitative methods: A needed perspective in evaluation research. In T. D. Cook & C. S. Reichardt (Eds.), *Qualitative and quantitative methods in evaluation research* (pp. 33-48). Beverly Hills, CA: Sage.

Hoshmand, L. T. (1989). Alternate research paradigms: A review and teaching proposal. *Counseling Psychologist, 17,* 3-79.

Huber, G. L. (1995). *Analysis of qualitative data with AQUAD Four.* Desert Hot Springs, CA: Qualitative Research Management.

Ibrahim, F. A., Ohnishi, H., & Wilson, R. P. (1994). Career assessment in a culturally diverse society. *Journal of Career Assessment, 2,* 276-288.

Jick, T. D. (1983). Mixing qualitative and quantitative methods: Triangulation in action. In J. Van Maanen (Ed.), *Qualitative methodology* (pp. 135-148). Beverly Hills, CA: Sage.

Keeley, S. M., Shemberg, K. M., & Zaynor, L. (1988). Dissertation research in clinical psychology: Beyond positivism? *Professional Psychology: Research and Practice, 19,* 216-222.

Kopala, M., Suzuki, L. A., Goldman, L., & Galdi, L. (1997). *Dissertation research in counseling psychology: Topics, methods, and qualitative training.* Paper presented at the annual meeting of the American Psychological Association, Chicago.

Kuhn, T. (1970). *The structure of scientific revolutions.* Chicago: University of Chicago Press.

LePage-Lees, P. (1997). Exploring patterns of achievement and intellectual development among academically successful women from disadvantaged backgrounds. *Journal of College Student Development, 38,* 468-478.

Linton, R. (Ed.). (1945). *The science of man (women) in the world crisis.* New York: Columbia University Press.

Patterson-Stewart, K. E., Ritchie, M. H., & Sanders, E. T. W. (1997). Interpersonal dynamics of African American persistence in doctoral programs at predominantly white universities. *Journal of College Student Development, 38,* 489-498.

Patton, M. Q. (1990). *Qualitative evaluation and research methods* (2nd ed.). Newbury Park, CA: Sage.

Ponterotto, J. G., Burkard, A. W., Yoshida, R. K., Cancelli, A. A., Mendez, G., & Wasilewski, L. (1995). Prospective minority student perceptions of professional psychology application packets: A qualitative study. *Professional Psychology: Research and Practice, 26,* 196-204.

Ponterotto, J. G., & Casas, J. M. (in preparation). *Handbook of racial/ethnic minority counseling research* (2nd ed.). Springfield, IL: Charles C Thomas.

Ponterotto, J. G., Casas, J. M., Suzuki, L. A., & Alexander, C. M. (Eds.). (1995). *Handbook of multicultural counseling.* Thousand Oaks, CA: Sage.

Ponterotto, J. G., & Pedersen, P. B. (1993). *Preventing prejudice: A guide for counselors and educators.* Newbury Park, CA: Sage.

Rennie, D. L. (1996). Fifteen years of doing qualitative research on psychotherapy. *British Journal of Guidance and Counseling, 24,* 317-327.

Smith, L. M. (1994). Biographical method. In N. K. Denzin & Y. S. Lincoln (Eds.), *Handbook of qualitative research* (pp. 286-305). Thousand Oaks, CA: Sage.

Strauss, A., & Corbin, J. (1990). *Basics of qualitative research: Grounded theory procedures and techniques.* Newbury Park, CA: Sage.

Taylor, S. J., & Bogdan, R. (1984). *Introduction to qualitative research methods: The search for meaning.* New York: John Wiley.

Trend, M. G. (1979). On the reconciliation of qualitative and quantitative analysis: A case study. In T. D. Cook & C. S. Reichardt (Eds.), *Qualitative and quantitative methods in evaluation research* (pp. 68-86). Beverly Hills, CA: Sage.

CHAPTER 6

Ethics in Qualitative Research

Cori Cieurzo
Merle A. Keitel

Although researchers have a variety of qualitative methodologies from which to choose, this chapter focuses on participant observation and in-depth interviewing because these are the methods most often employed in psychological research. *Participant observation,* often referred to as *fieldwork,* involves the researcher entering into a preexisting social milieu and attempting to gather data unobtrusively about a group or social process (Ponterotto & Casas, 1991; Taylor & Bogdan, 1984). Participant observation provides the researcher with a firsthand understanding of the area of interest, whereas in-depth interviewing involves gaining a secondhand account from others. In addition, the interviewer is not enmeshed in a natural setting, but rather establishes a situation specifically designed for the purpose of research (Taylor & Bogdan, 1984).

Qualitative approaches have gained increased popularity in the field of psychology, but more attention must be paid to the ethical issues unique to this methodology. This chapter examines ethical issues pertinent to qualitative methodologies in general and then highlights those specific to participant observation and in-depth interviewing.

GENERAL ETHICAL CONSIDERATIONS
IN QUALITATIVE RESEARCH

Numerous characteristics distinguish qualitative methods from quantitative methods. It is not the purpose of this chapter to elaborate on these, but for informative discussions the reader is referred to Bogdan and Biklen (1982) and Taylor and Bogdan (1984). Two aspects of qualitative research—that it is inductive and involves taking a humanistic perspective—are particularly germane to this discussion of ethics.

The Inductive Aspect of Qualitative Methods

The inductive nature of qualitative methods involves the researcher using initial behavioral observations to formulate tentative hypotheses. These hypotheses are then further tested, and more solidified hypotheses are posited. Clearly, the emergent design of qualitative research produces significant ethical ramifications in terms of informed consent (Cassell & Wax, 1980; Daly, 1992; Punch, 1994; Rosenblatt, 1995; Thorne, 1980; Wax, 1980). As is elaborated later in this chapter, participants cannot be fully informed about the potential consequences of the research or even the particular areas that will be studied because changes continually occur as the research process unfolds.

Taking a Holistic and Humanistic Perspective

A qualitative researcher studies individuals or groups within their own environments in an attempt to experience reality from the participants' personal frames of reference (Bogdan & Biklen, 1982; Bresler, 1995; Ponterotto & Casas, 1991; Taylor & Bogdan, 1984). Bresler (1995) described conducting qualitative research as "more like having a meaningful relationship than signing a contract" (p. 29). When the researcher becomes involved in intimate relationships with the individuals participating in research, she or he ultimately becomes morally involved and placed in situations of ethical tension (Cassell & Wax, 1980). Therefore, dealing with multiple roles becomes an ethical issue for qualitative researchers (Rosenblatt, 1995).

Particularly in field situations, the researcher is the tool, and her or his perceptions are shaped not only by interactions with those being researched but also by the researcher's personality, personal experiences, interpretations, and political agenda (Daly, 1992; Punch, 1994). The ethical dilemma raised is that researchers are now providing a voice for others and framing the social reality of the research participants from the researchers' own projections. The inevitable struggle for qualitative researchers is to navigate between "the illusion of objectivity and the borders of subjectivity" (Fine, 1994, p. 75).

PARTICIPANT OBSERVATION AND
IN-DEPTH INTERVIEWING

Participant observation studies require that researchers immerse themselves into a group or situation and acclimate themselves both physically and socially to the surroundings (Wax, 1980). Historically, ethical dilemmas in fieldwork have been associated with covert research efforts in which participants were deceived, such as Stanley Milgram's (1963) study on authority. Although ethical guidelines for research have been formulated since Milgram's infamous study, questions remain regarding the applicability of such guidelines to participant observation. Understanding the unique ethical issues in participant observation is difficult because researchers shy away from actually describing the ethical conflicts and conflict resolution strategies they encountered in the field (Price, 1996).

In-depth interviewing is also associated with ethical dilemmas because of the intensity and flexibility of this qualitative approach. Taylor and Bogdan (1984) described in-depth interviewing as "repeated face to face encounters between the researcher and informants directed toward understanding informants' perspectives on their lives, experiences, or situations as expressed in their own words" (p. 77). The interview process is not an interrogation session, but rather a conversation in which the interviewer is the research tool. Other interviews, however, are conducted in a structured manner in which a set of predetermined questions is established. May (1991) indicated that there is no typical pattern by which qualitative interviewing takes place and that this factor makes it difficult to assess adequately the ethical issues that arise because the nature of the issues are dependent on contextual factors.

ETHICAL ISSUES IN QUALITATIVE RESEARCH

Researchers using qualitative methods are collecting data through human interaction, and inherent in this process are the risks associated with any type of human interaction, such as embarrassment, anger, violation of privacy, misunderstandings, and conflicts in opinions and values (May, 1991). In addition, painful topics can emerge in both participant observation and in-depth interviewing. Because of the nature of the "give-and-take" relationship between researcher and participant, researchers are better able to navigate sensitively the ethical issues that arise by following the participants' preferred style in dealing with ethical dilemmas (Rosenblatt, 1995).

Various ethical dilemmas may occur in the following aspects of qualitative research: recruiting participants, informed consent, confidentiality and anonymity, protection from harm, deception, dual roles of researcher and therapist, and interpretation and ownership. It is important to note that participant observation methods and in-depth interviewing share many ethical considerations and that some ethical issues are more relevant to one than the other. A case example of a researcher using in-depth interviewing is used below to highlight these potential ethical considerations.

Dee Deporto-Callan (1996), a doctoral student in counseling psychology at Fordham University, investigated the types, forms, levels of severity, and contextual factors specific to sexual abuse suffered by battered women. She developed and then conducted semistructured interviews that were emotionally charged for both the interviewees and the researcher. The findings revealed that oral sex was the most frequent type of forced sexual act, that forced sex occurred under threat of punishment, that verbal abuse was often sexually related and perceived by women to be degrading and humiliating, and that pregnancy was a time in which sexual abuse seemed to escalate. We use this study to illustrate specific ethical dilemmas common to qualitative research because of the sensitive and personal nature of the topics discussed and the critical importance of ensuring that the research experience was in no way exploitative of participants.

Recruiting Participants

Gaining access to individuals is a difficult task for qualitative researchers. Although research is authorized by institutional review boards (IRBs) and this can be a difficult process, gaining access to organizations after receiving IRB approval is another obstacle to qualitative research. The process of recruiting subjects often involves convincing gatekeepers of the relevance of the research and of minimizing potential harm to participants (Price, 1996). The nature of the organization the researcher attempts to access and the extent to which the organization values research are often crucial factors in recruiting participants. The recruitment process can raise ethical issues because of the vague information often presented to gatekeepers. To gain access to private spheres, it is sometimes necessary to keep the presentation of one's research proposal somewhat ambiguous (Taylor & Bogdan, 1984).

Researchers conducting qualitative research have used advertisements as a recruitment device (Rosenblatt, 1995). Yet this process also raises ethical concerns. It is expected that participants are volunteering for the project and that coercion is not used in gaining access to them. Rosenblatt (1995) indicated, however, that when studies are advertised, participants are often recruited by family members and friends. Although participants may not directly say no to participating in the study, they may not have volunteered if not for the pressure from significant others in their lives. Therefore, even if nondeceptive practices are used, is it considered coercion if researchers interview individuals who did not directly refuse to participate but who under different circumstances may not have volunteered?

In the case example, gaining access to battered women for the purpose of conducting a qualitative study was not free from difficulties and involved intellectual, philosophical, and emotional reflection on the part of the researcher. The researcher used her connection as an assistant director of a grassroots, feminist-based counseling service for battered women to gain access to participants. Colleagues questioned the research because of the feminist nature of the organization and because the realm of scientific research was not considered consistent with feminist doctrines. In addition, the researcher's association with academia also led colleagues to question whether the purpose of the research was to advance the researcher's career or to empower battered women. After many discussions with colleagues, the researcher was permitted to conduct the study by agreeing that colleagues be involved in the research process and by making findings available to a variety of centers that deal with issues associated with battered women.

Informed Consent

The principle of informed consent requires that the researcher provide participants with sufficient information about the research so that they can make informed decisions regarding participation. In addition, informed consent indicates that participation is knowledgeable and voluntary and that participants can withdraw from the research at any time (LaRossa, Bennett, & Gelles, 1981; Thorne, 1980). On the basis of the ad hoc nature of the methodology, however, LaRossa et al. (1981) indicated that because a qualitative researcher is not able to offer specifics about what will emerge during the course of the investigation, participants giving informed consent are not truly informed (Price, 1996; Rosenblatt, 1995). In addition, although participants may be receptive to the information provided at the time of informed consent, questions remain regarding participants' retention of the information over time (Crabtree & Miller, 1992). In the light of the lengthy nature of qualitative studies, this ethical dilemma is of particular concern.

Researchers involved in participant observation studies have questioned the utility of informed consent in relation to the methodology (Thorne, 1980; Wax, 1980) and have argued that, in many ethnographic studies, it is inappropriate to gain consent because the activity of interest cannot be interrupted (Punch, 1994). Thorne (1980) indicated that it is rare for fieldworkers to divulge fully the nature and purpose of their work to potential participants, with many researchers providing information regarding only the most innocuous aspects of the study. This is not to suggest that deception is rampant in participant observation studies, but rather that the inductive nature of the methodology and the researcher's flexibility regarding the research questions make informed consent relatively uninformed (Cassell & Wax, 1980; Punch, 1994). It is unclear how much information needs to be provided for participants to make a knowledgeable decision and when a choice to participate is voluntary and responsible. In addition, often the assumption is that because a researcher's presence is tolerated, consent has been granted (Thorne, 1980).

As with participation observation, attaining informed consent is somewhat problematic in in-depth interviewing (Daly, 1992; LaRossa et al., 1981; Price,

1996; Rosenblatt, 1995). Researchers involved in in-depth interviewing can engage in several types of interviewing styles, such as unstructured, semi-structured, and structured interviewing (Ponterotto & Casas, 1991). Issues with informed consent appear to vary, depending on the type of interview style adopted. For instance, when structured and semistructured interviews are con-ducted, the researcher has an informed perspective about the area being studied and therefore can provide explicit information about the study to potential participants. When unstructured interviews are conducted, however, the direc-tion of the interview is determined by the interviewee, and the areas that emerge are difficult, if not impossible, to predict in an informed consent form (LaRossa et al., 1981; Rosenblatt, 1995). In addition, it is difficult to anticipate partici-pants' reactions prior to conducting the interview; this implies that participants cannot be fully informed about what their experience in the research study will be like (LaRossa et al., 1981; Rosenblatt, 1995).

Therefore, qualitative researchers have started to view informed consent as a process, rather than as a one-time event (Cassell & Wax, 1980; Price, 1996; Wax, 1980). Thorne (1980) indicated that because of the long-term nature of qualitative research, consent needs to be renewed as the setting changes and the relationships between the observer and the observed change. Offering multiple opportunities for participants to evaluate their comfort with the direction of the research allows for a more sensitive approach to the participants and the informed consent issue.

The case example used semistructured interviews, and the researcher was very clear on the general areas that would be explored in the interview. The researcher's knowledge of the population of battered women and anecdotal experiences were pivotal to her ability to skip the unstructured format and use a semistructured interview protocol. Despite the explicit nature of the study, the informed consent form and the sensitivity with which the information was presented were crucial to the researcher recruiting participants. The researcher described the areas that would be discussed in detail and how the findings would be used to improve the care provided to battered women. Moreover, individuals who agreed to volunteer for the study met with a counselor at the agency to discuss further the purpose and procedures of the research and to assess the current safety issues, dual roles, and trust and betrayal.

Confidentiality and Anonymity

The debate regarding the applicability of informed consent in participant observation research is intricately related to the issue of confidentiality. As is true for quantitative research, one responsibility of investigators is ensuring the confidentiality of participants (Punch, 1994). When individuals sign informed consent forms, however, their confidentiality is jeopardized. Especially when research is investigating illegal, immoral, and stigmatizing activity, informed consent forms can link individuals with these activities (Price, 1996). Moreover, inquiry records are not privileged materials under law and, therefore, are subject to subpoena (Price, 1996). This issue becomes even more complex when individuals engaging in reproachable behavior cannot be held accountable for their actions because of the need to uphold confidentiality privileges. Thorne (1980) suggested that if immoral behavior is involved, researchers need to assess carefully when rights to privacy apply. Ethically, this becomes a difficult issue in terms of who is to determine what behavior is reprehensible and when confidentiality rights should be revoked. Thus, researchers are assuring participants of confidentiality even though this promise may be compromised.

Additional ethical dilemmas are raised regarding the publication of qualitative research. Punch (1994) suggested that participants may not be completely aware that findings from the study may be published. In addition, when individuals agree to participate in a study, they are not necessarily giving consent to be quoted (Price, 1996). It is important that the researcher obtain explicit consent from participants to have their words published. Furthermore, participants should be given an opportunity to review the material before it is published so that they can correct, if necessary, the representation and interpretation given to their words by the researcher. If they are uncomfortable with the material, they should have the right to ask that the material pertaining to them be removed.

Although researchers conceal the identities of participants when findings are published, in many instances participants' identities have been discovered. Moreover, when the research involves renowned institutions or public figures, it is difficult for researchers to assure anonymity (Punch, 1994). Price (1996) suggested that when a researcher is confronted with these ethical issues, the well-being of participants should not be compromised, but rather the research should be altered.

Protection From Harm

In all forms of research, the welfare of participants is crucial. This ethical responsibility becomes more obscure in qualitative research, however, because of the inductive nature of the methodology. No guideline assists researchers in determining what should be considered public or private, what constitutes harm, and how beneficial the attained knowledge will be (Punch, 1994). The premise in protecting participants from harm involves weighing the costs and benefits of the research. In qualitative research, however, it is difficult to assess adequately the potential harm versus good of the research prior to conducting the study. When is it appropriate to intervene in situations of exploitation, abuse, and harm to subjects (Bresler, 1995)?

Balancing the costs and benefits of publication may be particularly problematic (May, 1980). Publications of participant observation studies reveal the beliefs and vulnerabilities of those being observed and are based on the perspective of the researcher (Bresler, 1995). How can a researcher discern whether these data will be misused by outside individuals? Moreover, when researchers are immersed in another culture, understanding what is potentially harmful to participants becomes an even more complicated ethical issue (Jacobs, 1980).

In-depth interviewing has two major areas of potential harm: public exposure of private issues and self-exposure. Although researchers assure confidentiality and anonymity, it is sometimes difficult to mask the identities of those being studied, and having one's life scrutinized and objectified could be potentially harmful for participants (Fine, 1994; LaRossa et al., 1981). In addition, because of the self-reflection and considerable self-disclosure that interviewees engage in, constant appraisal of the well-being of participants is crucial (May, 1991). If risks to participants are not feasible to predict prior to the study, it is suggested that researchers continually monitor the risks as the research progresses (Daly, 1992; LaRossa et al., 1981; May, 1991) to protect the welfare of participants.

When in-depth interviews focus on painful topics, another area of concern becomes the harm versus good for participants when disclosing emotional material. The inherent power differential between the researcher and the inter-viewee may promote unanticipated self-disclosures that could be potentially harmful for participants. In addition, when in-depth interviewing is conducted in an informal setting, participants may disclose more than they had planned (Daly, 1992; May, 1991). The question becomes, Does a researcher have a right to carry out an interview that causes emotional pain for the participant? Rosenblatt (1995) argued that hurting can be an antecedent for healing, yet acknowledged that there are limits to the pain that interviews should cause for participants. When interview questions seem to instigate acute pain, it is important for researchers to move away from the painful matters and to engage in more abbreviated interviews (Rosenblatt, 1995). However, who is to determine what is too painful and when participants are suffering too much?

In the case example, battered women were asked to discuss intense and often painful material. The researcher needed to be cognizant of the participants' emotional and psychological status, as well as her own emotional responses to the information presented. As the interviews were conducted, the researcher was empathic to the participants' emotional states and consistently assured participants they could withdraw from the interviews at any time. Not only was the researcher aware of the participants' experiences during the interviews, but after completion of the interview participants were debriefed by their primary counselor at the agency.

One way that qualitative researchers approach the cost versus benefit issue deals with the nature of the relationship between observer and participants. The perspective in the field is that the relationship is reciprocal and that it is the researcher's obligation to give something back to participants (Cassell & Wax, 1980). Qualitative research is often performed with the hope of promoting social change. The notion of giving back to those being studied is especially applicable when working with disenfranchised and marginalized groups. In the case example, the researcher shared the results of her investigation with centers involved with battered women to increase understanding of the nature and extent to which battered women experience sexual abuse. As Ponterotto and Casas (1991) indicated, "focusing solely on the prevention of harm while ignoring the provision of benefits is no longer ethically acceptable" (p. 143).

Although qualitative researchers have been increasingly more sensitive to the needs of individuals being studied, the inherent nature of the relationships formed during the research process can be potentially harmful to participants. For example, the researcher observes and participates in people's lives for an extended period of time or repeatedly interviews people and then exits when the research is completed, leaving behind those who were studied. Although researchers are committed to their roles during the investigation, their departure could lead to feelings of abandonment and betrayal (Punch, 1994; Taylor & Bogdan, 1984). Taylor and Bogdan (1984) suggested that slowly decreasing the frequency of visits and maintaining telephone and mail contact with participants may ease the difficulty of breaking attachments with the researcher. Referrals for counseling services could be offered to individuals having a particularly difficult time with the researcher's departure. Therefore, as with any other form of research, it is crucial for researchers to reflect on whether participants can be potentially harmed and the capacity of the researcher and the research to benefit adequately and specifically those being studied (Bogdewic, 1992).

Deception

Qualitative researchers have conflicting ideas regarding the justifiability of deceptive practices in participant observation. Punch (1994) contended that researchers tend to use some form of disguise and deception in participant observation research and that, therefore, some deception is inevitably involved. The reality of conducting participant observation seems to be that researchers cannot be explicit in their descriptions of the research because of the difficulty associated with accessing groups and organizations (Punch, 1994; Taylor & Bogdan, 1984). To gain access to groups, it is often necessary for researchers to get consent from gatekeepers. Taylor and Bogdan (1984) suggested that, when describing research to gatekeepers and informants, researchers be "truthful, but vague and imprecise" (p. 25). To gain access to organizations and groups that engage in deceitful and coercive practices, it is necessary to be vague when describing research to gatekeepers (Punch, 1994).

As Price (1996) indicated, the use of secrecy allows researchers to gain access to powerful groups that want to obscure their practices, and this becomes a conflict between established rules and moral principles (Thorne, 1980). The way secrecy is incorporated into participant observation research tends to be determined by the context of the situation being studied and how researchers are going to identify themselves (Thorne, 1980). Researchers may be explicit in describing their research, yet they should never break promises made to participants (Punch, 1994).

One area of controversy surrounds the debate between covert and overt research methods (Taylor & Bogdan, 1984). Although some researchers denounce the use of covert methods because of the potential harm to participants (Spradley, 1980) and the negative ramifications for social research as a whole (Warwick, 1975), the use of deception in participant observation studies allows researchers to gain knowledge about important social phenomena that would not be obtainable by other means (May, 1980; Punch, 1994). As with overt research, however, it is crucial that the researcher engaging in deception be aware of the balance between the benefits of knowledge and the potential harm (Punch, 1994). Yet as mentioned previously, balance is difficult to assess accurately, and the publication of research findings can further impinge on the rights of those being studied because of anonymity issues. It is clear that when researchers are deciding between overt/covert and open/less-than-open research methods, they need to evaluate the consequences for the participants, the profession, and themselves (Punch, 1994).

Dual Roles: Researcher or Therapist?

One major issue facing individuals conducting in-depth interviewing is the conflict between roles. The emotional content revealed during the interview process can create a moral and ethical dilemma for researchers. Where are the boundaries between therapy and research? When does providing the necessary emotional support cross the line into therapeutic interventions? The way researchers describe their obligations to interviewees often seems related to the therapeutic relationship. For instance, May (1991) indicated that when interviews are conducted over a long period of time, it is the moral and ethical responsibility of the researcher to terminate the relationship effectively and to provide a sense of closure for the participant. Although it is important for researchers to be sensitive to the needs of individuals participating in the interview process, it becomes a thorny ethical issue when the boundaries between therapy and research are obscured.

Rosenblatt (1995) indicated that boundaries may get blurry when individuals become emotionally distraught during their interviews and the researcher attempts to intervene therapeutically. The ethically appropriate approach to dealing with individuals needing therapeutic support is to provide a referral. Yet intrinsic to in-depth interviewing is the use of basic counseling skills, such as listening, avoiding being judgmental, bracketing personal reactions, supporting, knowing when to back off, and realizing when something has been misunderstood (Rosenblatt, 1995). Fine (1994) addressed how researchers struggle with "the ethics of involvement and the ethics of detachment, the illusions of objectivity and the borders of subjectivity, and the possibilities of collaborative work and the dilemmas of collusion" (p. 75).

Moreover, participants may enter the research process with the expectation that the researcher is going to provide advice regarding the specific problem under investigation (Daly, 1992). Although it is important to acknowledge that the relationship between interviewer and interviewee is based on a fair exchange, researchers should only respond to requests for advice on the basis of their training and competence in this area. The clear risk for the researcher overstepping professional boundaries is evident in the lack of differentiation between in-depth interviewing and therapy (Daly, 1992; Rosenblatt, 1995). Although in-depth interviewing is conducted for research purposes, participants commonly experience therapeutic effects (Daly, 1992; May, 1991; Rosenblatt, 1995). Overall, the standard for in-depth interviewing should be that the needs of the respondent take precedence over the needs of the research (Rosenblatt, 1995).

In terms of the study on sexual abuse in battered women, the researcher was torn between providing therapeutic interventions and sticking to the interview protocol. The researcher's training in counseling and her own work with this population exacerbated the difficulty she experienced with respect to dual roles. One way this issue was addressed was to certify that no participant was currently or previously treated by the researcher in a therapeutic capacity. This ensured that the participants were clear on the researcher's role of interviewer rather than therapist. To establish rapport and create an environment in which the women felt comfortable disclosing, however, the use of therapeutic strategies was necessary. In addition, the debriefing sessions were designed to provide the participants appropriate therapeutic support. As part of the research project, the researcher was also supported by colleagues and monitored by close supervision.

Interpretation and Ownership

Several issues are related to interpreting the findings obtained through in-depth interviewing, such as researcher bias (Daly, 1992; Price, 1996) and the validity of participants' responses (Ponterotto & Casas, 1991; Rosenblatt, 1995; Taylor & Bogdan, 1984). Especially when research is published, the tendency is for the researcher not to take ownership of her or his interpretation, and this inevitably marginalizes and betrays participants (Fine, 1994; Price, 1996). A compelling perspective on researchers' interpretation of data is provided by Fine (1994):

> No need to hear your voice when I can talk about you better than you can speak about yourself . . . only tell me about your pain. I want to know your story. And then I will tell it back to you in a new way. . . . I am still the author, authority. I am still the colonizer. (p. 70)

It is important to note that the nature of in-depth interviewing is limiting in the sense that not only can the researcher's personal biases affect data interpretation, but the interviewees can also distort and exaggerate experiences (Ponterotto & Casas, 1991; Taylor & Bogdan, 1984). Because in-depth interviewing involves self-report and does not offer the researcher observation of actual behavior, the data need to be understood and interpreted in the light of these limitations. Moreover, the researcher's own experiences can affect the line of questioning pursued and the interpretation of the findings. Daly (1992) indicated that, in qualitative family research, the researcher's own family experiences can affect the choices made about what to study, whom to ask, and how to ask it.

Although the case example presented has not been published, the findings were written up and presented to colleagues. The researcher was attentive to her role in shaping the findings and cautioned others to evaluate the findings tentatively. The researcher carefully interpreted her results on the basis of the small sample size and used triangulation to clarify findings. The nature of the findings was particularly heartrending, and the researcher acknowledged her own responses to the women's experiences and alluded to how her perceptions shaped the findings. Finally, the researcher acknowledged how the semistructured interview limited the findings because of the possibilities of distortions, exaggerations, and misperceptions.

CONCLUSION

Qualitative research is a powerful tool for accessing the personal experiences of individuals. Researchers invested with the power inherent in qualitative research, however, need to be attentive to the ethical issues that arise from the methodology and the population being studied. Although ethical guidelines seem inappropriate to this form of research because of the wide range of issues that can emerge specific to each study, researchers need to acknowledge important ethical considerations prior to the research endeavor, during the research process, and after the research is completed.

Qualitative researchers need to reflect on the potential harm the research process could cause for participants and to recognize how their own presence, personal experiences, and biases can affect research findings. Sensitivity to the experiences of those being studied should not be an afterthought, but rather an important consideration at the beginning of the research process. The notion of giving back to others will benefit not only the people being studied but also the researcher and the profession as a whole.

REFERENCES

Bogdan, R. C., & Biklen, S. K. (1982). *Qualitative research for education: An introduction to theory and methods.* Boston: Allyn & Bacon.

Bogdewic, S. P. (1992). Participant observation. In B. F. Crabtree & W. L. Miller (Eds.), *Doing qualitative research: Research methods for primary care.* Newbury Park, CA: Sage.

Bresler, L. (1995, Fall). Ethical issues in qualitative research methodology. *Bulletin of the Council of Research in Music Education, 126,* 29-41.

Cassell, J., & Wax, M. L. (1980). Editorial introduction: Toward a moral science of human beings. *Social Problems, 27,* 259-264.

Crabtree, B. F., & Miller, W. L. (1992). *Doing qualitative research: Research methods for primary care.* Newbury Park, CA: Sage.

Daly, K. (1992). The fit between qualitative research and characteristics of families. In J. F. Gilgun, K. Daly, & G. Handel (Eds.), *Qualitative methods in family research* (pp. 3-11). Newbury Park, CA: Sage.

Deporto-Callan, D. (1996). *A qualitative examination of sexual abuse: Types, forms, and contextual factors as experienced by battered women.* Unpublished manuscript.

Fine, M. (1994). Working the hyphens: Reinventing self and other in qualitative research.. In N. K. Denzin & Y. S. Lincoln (Eds.), *Handbook of qualitative research* (pp. 70-82). Thousand Oaks, CA: Sage.

Jacobs, S. E. (1980). Where have we come? *Social Problems, 27,* 371-378.

LaRossa, R., Bennett, L. A., & Gelles, R. J. (1981). Ethical dilemmas in qualitative family research. *Journal of Marriage and Family Counseling, 43,* 303-313.

May, K. A. (1991). Interview techniques in qualitative research: Concerns and challenges. In J. M. Morse (Ed.), *Qualitative nursing research: A contemporary dialogue* (pp. 188-201). Newbury Park, CA: Sage.

May, W. F. (1980). Doing ethics: The bearing of ethical theories on fieldwork. *Social Problems, 27,* 358-370.

Milgram, S. (1963). Behavioral study of obedience. *Journal of Abnormal and Social Psychology, 67,* 371-378.

Ponterotto, J. G., & Casas, J. M. (1991). *Handbook of racial/ethnic minority counseling research.* Springfield, IL: Charles C Thomas.

Price, J. (1996). Snakes in the swamp: Ethical issues in qualitative research. In R. Josselson (Ed.), *Ethics and process in the narrative study of lives* (pp. 207-215). Thousand Oaks, CA: Sage.

Punch, M. (1994). Politics and ethics in qualitative research. In N. K. Denzin & Y. S. Lincoln (Eds.), *Handbook of qualitative research* (pp. 83-97). Thousand Oaks, CA: Sage.

Rosenblatt, P. C. (1995). Ethics of qualitative interviewing with grieving families. *Death Studies, 19,* 139-155.

Spradley, J. P. (1980). *Participant observation.* New York: Holt, Rinehart & Winston.

Taylor, S. J., & Bogdan, R. (1984). *Introduction to qualitative research methods: The search for meanings* (2nd ed.). New York: John Wiley.

Thorne, B. (1980). "You still takin' notes?": Fieldwork and problems of informed consent. *Social Problems, 27,* 284-296.

Warwick, D. P. (1975). Social scientists ought to stop lying. *Psychology Today, 8,* 38, 40, 105-106.

Wax, M. L. (1980). Paradoxes of "consent" to the practice of fieldwork. *Social Problems, 27,* 272-283.

CHAPTER 7

The Internet and Qualitative Research

Opportunities and Constraints on Analysis of Cyberspace Discourse

Patricia O'Brien Libutti

The Internet has transformed the research terrain for qualitative researchers with the availability of text-based computer-mediated communication. The bottleneck of costly transcriptions of field notes and interviews, the ease of access to data, and the evasion of the political hassles of doing fieldwork are seemingly resolved. Currently, researchers can use Internet discussion archives for qualitative research, as well as for finding like-minded fellows in on-line communities. Each possibility raises new avenues for imaginative research applications, as well as ethical concern in studies of business, academic, recreational, and support group cultures. This chapter, intended for the beginning qualitative researcher, examines the pragmatic issue of availability of researchable text in concert with ethical issues inherent in research on the Internet.

Using computers for analysis of qualitative research data has been a practice since the mid-1960s. Renata Tesch (1991) noted that the first software program that allowed researchers to analyze text was termed the General Inquirer, designed by MIT developers for content analysis. It took more than 15 years, however, for programs to be developed for narrative analysis. These early applications by pioneering qualitative researchers are described in the special issue of *Sociological Methods and Research* (1991).

Another milestone in the use of computers for qualitative research was the advent of the personal computer in the mid-1980s, followed by an exponentially increasing application of programs developed by academic researchers for qualitative use alone. Tesch (1991) concluded her article with a listing of programs available at that time. Richards and Richards (1994) continued the updating of evaluation of computer programs for qualitative researchers, often focusing on the occurrence of new analytical possibilities using computer-assisted data analysis. For more information regarding current software packages for qualitative data analysis, the reader is referred to specific texts focusing on the issue (see, e.g., Weitzman & Miles, 1995).

Since the mid-1980s, researchers have used communications networks to connect with others interested in the development of qualitative methodologies. This extension of computer use has had profound implications beyond the individual researcher's data analysis. Internet access has provided researchers with textual material for studies on business, academic, recreational, and support group cultures. Several components of the Internet (Web sites, listservs, newsgroups, e-mail, chat, and multiuser dimensions) have presented the qualitative researcher with choices for participation, information access, and responsibility for the use of information. The proliferation of such published studies has accompanied growing concerns about the ethics of using Internet-accessible content.

ACCESS TO DISCOURSE ON THE INTERNET

Electronic journals and 'zines have sprung up in many subject areas, many providing discussion forums for the topics contained in each issue. Multiuser dimensions (MUDs) are part of many people's extended social contacts (Reid, 1996; Turkle, 1995). Listserv and newsgroup postings are generally available in archives, usually through contact with a listserv moderator. Access to materials in any of these formats is logistically possible, as Vento (1997) notes in the introduction to *H.R. 98: The Consumer Internet Privacy Protection Act* (http://rs9.loc.gov/cgi-bin/query/z?r105:E07JA7-165). Other venues may be closed in nature and require application to join, such as MUDs in which application is made to get a "character" (Reid, 1996; Turkle, 1995). The content of a MUD session, in which role playing is done and logged, is not uniformly available. Elizabeth Reid (1996) reports that the MUD she joined as a researcher did not have the sessions available in a public archive. Web sites are possibly the clearest about expected access by the public: They are mounted for public access, and papers, site links, proceedings, and so on are intended for reading.

Electronic Mail

No method is more involved or "private" than the use of e-mail: One initiates or receives direct contact. Consequently, the electronic missive is considered a private letter, and researchers need permission to use the content of such a communication. This "privacy" is illusory. It is possible to gain access to e-mail, as noted in the explanatory text of *H.R. 98: Consumer's Electronic Privacy Protection Bill.* The one-to-one connection using e-mail has provided the "invisible college" with means of rapid exchange. E-mail has proved to be valuable in qualitative research; logs of participants, questionnaires, and replies to calls for information have figured in qualitative research (Workman, 1992). E-mail has also been the focus of linguistic analysis, such as the structure of "conversations" (Herring, 1996a).

Listservs

The active forums for discussion (listservs and bulletin boards) have been the focus of study of "virtual community," as well as of debate over what constitutes a community in cyberspace. Judith Preissle's compilation of major listservs (discussion forums) of interest to qualitative researchers can be found at http://ualberta.ca/jrnorris/forum962.htm.

Lists vary in intimacy of focus, norms for discourse, and nature of boundaries for joining or not joining the discussion forum. Some lists, such as Q-METHOD (Q-METHOD@LISTSERV.KENT.EDU), are not moderated and simply provide a convenient way to be added to the discussion distribution mailing list. Other lists, such as QUALS-R, are moderated, which ensures that a certain level of screening and occasional redirection of a conversation thread may occur.

A listserv demonstrates social characteristics, and these have been examined by qualitative researchers. Because listserv discussions are often archived, a researcher can follow threads of discussions, note unfolding variants on themes, and do textual analysis on discourse by participants. Although researchers can and have done such analyses, numerous considerations have just begun to emerge in both list discussion and electronic journal articles (Herring, 1996a; King, 1996; Reid, 1996; Thomas, 1996).

Discussants in a large list who focused on a recent issue of exploration of their list varied in reaction, including discomfort with researchers "lurking" on the list. Participants reported that they felt "watched," some noting that the presence of researchers was linked with feelings of discomfort. Herring (1996b) examined language structure on the Internet by using academic lists. She asserted that harm comes least when the structure of a list, rather than the participants themselves, is being examined.

MUDs (Multiuser Domains)

What effect does research on MUD sessions have on the members of the MUD? Reid (1996) noted that she was originally welcomed as a participant-observer but that later participation and subsequent publication caused adverse effects to at least one MUD she was observing. She had joined a MUD focusing on sexual abuse issues and described her quandaries and resolutions of ethical issues. One imaginative method was to have her character carry a tape recorder, a notebook, and so forth to indicate the activity.

The same kind of role play/reality juxtaposition was reported by Turkle (1995) in the MUD she was studying/participating in. She observed that a character named "Dr. Sherry" was handing out questionnaires and interviewing participants. Because Dr. Sherry was not her character, she wondered about the identity behind the role. Later, Turkel found that the character was actually two psychology students doing a paper on MUDs.

The presence of a great variety of behaviors in Usenet cultures has been the focus of many researchers (see, e.g., McLaughlin, Osborne, & Smith [1995], as well as a quantitative perspective of the same material in Smith [1997]). This combination of qualitative and quantitative perspectives may well be a trend in future research on Net cultures, but at this time the methodologies are rarely combined. Ponterotto and Grieger (chap. 5, this volume) provide a more in-depth examination of merging methodologies in a research identity.

Web Sites

Individual qualitative researchers, university departments, and software companies have constructed and mounted Web sites containing a vast array of resources for the interested researcher. A gateway to many available sites can be found at http://www.nova.edu/ssss/QR/qualres.html. These sites span geographic boundaries and provide the researcher with snapshots of different cultures' understandings and research areas. A researcher can use a computer to gain access to Web sites that include, as possible content publications, data archives of past qualitative studies, drafts of papers, journals, and archived discussions from listservs.

Journals. Several on-line journals with a primarily qualitative research focus have a presence on the Internet; most have a 2-year run archived for inspection or subscription. Examples of such journals are *The Information Society, Sociological Research Online, Computer-Mediated Communication Research,* and *Qualitative Report.* An example of an article readily available through Internet linking is "The Performance of Humor in Computer-Mediated Communication" (Baym, 1995b). The phenomenon of increasing electronic publication reflects trends seen in social science disciplines, in which electronic journals are receiving attention both by contributors and by increasing audiences. Discussion forum opportunities are included in some of these electronic publications, such as *The Information Society*'s (1996) special issue on ethics of Internet research. Archives of the discussions of the issue are available at http://www.soci.niu.edu/archives.

Archives/Conference Proceedings. The lack of geographic boundaries inherent in the application of the Internet makes it possible for conferences to be held on-line, as well as for archives of past conference proceedings to be available. The American Educational Research Association (AERA) is one professional organization that makes past papers from annual conferences available (http://aera.net/). Others of interest to the qualitative researcher are the Qualitative Users Interest Group annual conference papers (http://www.coe.uga.edu/quig/) and the PARnet archive of action research articles (http://www.PARnet.org/parchives/). These archives present a rich source of material for the researcher who wishes to conduct language analysis of qualitative studies.

Data Archives. Another kind of archive presents the researcher with past qualitative analyses. Qualidata archives the data from past qualitative research for future interpretation (available: http://www.essex.ac.uk:80/qualidata). This databank may provide a resource for beginning researchers in which their own interpretations can be seen alongside one previously completed. Differences in coding, theoretical construction, and interpretation can then be an area of inquiry itself. Recent deposits in Qualidata are Robert Dingwall's Child Protection Study (1977-82), which includes case studies, interviews, and participant observations on child protection.

Papers. Archives of individual papers are obviously intended for reading. Several major collections of individual papers are on the Internet, such as Ron Chenoil's assemblage (http://www.nova.edu/ssss/QR/text.htm) and Judy Norris's QualPage (http://www.ualberta.ca/jrnorris/qual.html). Some papers demonstrate technologies that make it possible for a reader to follow the hypertext in a nonlinear manner. Preparation of papers using this technology has yet to be assessed by researchers for impact of nonlinear presentation on the reader's perceptions of the author's communication.

Yet the presence of linking papers opens a compelling possibility for exploration of presentation of results. Coomber's (1997) paper, for instance, links supporting papers and references in the text. The paper was hyperlinked with Paccagnella's (1997) (available: http://207.201.161.120/jcmc/vol3/issue1/paccagnella.html).

Syllabi. The contribution of information to the field is furthered by the knowledge "canon" constructed by professors willing to mount their syllabi on the Web. Several gathering sites contain such information: Course syllabi can be linked at http://www.nova.edu/ssss/QR/qualres.html, as well as in individual researchers' home pages. Today, syllabi and courses in qualitative research are an important part of the wealth of resources accessible to anyone with a computer, modem, and Internet service provider. Classes, courses, and seminars—sometimes free, sometimes for a fee—are part of the spectrum of opportunity.

Researchers' Home Pages. Researchers compose Web sites that archive personal publications, links of interest to others, syllabi, and contact information (see http://www.nova.edu/ssss/QR/text.html for examples of researchers' home pages). Prominent in the array of individual Web sites is one maintained by Jim Thomas (1995) devoted to the ethics of research on the Internet, available at http://www.soci.niu.edu/jthomas. Other examples of papers mounted on researchers' home pages are *The Art Lovers: Studying the Visitors of the Metropolitan Museum of Art* (Anna Dong Sun, Queens College) and *Computer-Mediated Soap Talk: Communication, Community, and Entertainment on the Net* (Baym, 1995a).

ETHICAL CONSIDERATIONS AND INTERNET "ARTIFACTS"

The use of text from any of the formats reviewed earned attention when the practices violated common societal assumptions, such as privacy, or when practices generated fearful concerns. Ethical considerations on research using the text of Internet postings may well have been shaped by two prominent cases in which basic ethical norms were prominently violated. Finn and Lavitt's (1984) case study of victims of sexual abuse included the participants' postings in their entirety. Identifying headers, e-mail addresses, and content were included without the permission of the posters.

The user of a Web site obviously needs to be aware of attribution, as well as take cognitive responsibility in information use: verifying that the contents obtained are accurate. For instance, although papers are in a public archive accessible through an Internet address, many are labeled by the researcher "not for citation or quotation," "obtain permission before citing or quoting," or "working paper—not for citation." The intentions of the Web authors vary: In some cases, papers have been labeled chapter drafts; in other cases, no such explanation beyond the prohibition was included. According to a legal expert retained by Gurak (1996), these labels need to be taken seriously.

Ethical considerations for the maintainer of a Web site that need articulation include the responsibility for the accuracy of resources, as well as concern about the quality of content being assembled. Web maintainers can track the behaviors of site users. Although some Web sites do maintain voluntary guest books (which are simple counters) to estimate Web site activity, the "cookie" technology (embedded software that reports back to the Web maintainer each instance of visitation by the explorer) is found most often at commercial sites. Academics, however, are using cookies (check E. Trauth's page, Trauth, 1998). For a fuller explanation of what information can be gathered about Web site visitors, check http://anonymizer.cs.cmn.edu:8080/prog/snoop.pl.

Rimm's study of pornography on the Net has been the focus of numerous analyses of ethical violations, ranging from doubtful methods of gathering data to the nature of the sponsoring institution's involvement, such as the amount of pornography a child may be able to access. The Rimm case files are archived at http://www.soci.niu.edu/jthomas.

Lobbying groups, such as the Electronic Privacy Information Center (http://www.epic.org), developed as citizens became concerned with adverse effects of the technology. Currently, legislation presented in the House (*H.R. 98: Consumer Internet Privacy Protection Act*, Vento, 1997, available at http://rs9.loc.gov/cgi-bin/query/z?r105:E07JA7-165) reflects this growing interest in this arena.

Informed Consent

Informed consent of participants on a listserv, a MUD, or a bulletin board is exceptionally difficult to obtain. Many participants do not sign on regularly to such a source and may miss notices or announcements of ongoing research. Further, it has been suggested (Jones, 1994) that informed consent affects the phenomena being studied. Several researchers have tried participant observation, with the noted consequence of possibly "going native" (Patterson, 1996). Others have interviewed several participants "off-line" (Giordano, 1996). Reid's (1996) outline of the perils involved in obtaining informed consent and what the differing meanings of informed consent may be to participants over time is cautionary reading.

Privacy

For lists, newsgroups, and bulletin boards, many researchers consider the content of discussions to be public (Braddlee, 1993; Giordano, 1995; Patterson, 1996; Turkle, 1995), and it has been interpreted as such by a legal expert (Gurak, 1996). Issues of ownership of the files, however, confound this "private/public" distinction. It is possible that copyrights may extend to the postings.

Copyright

Opinions on whether the content of a posting is automatically protected by copyright lack uniformity (Gurak, 1996; Patterson, 1996). If the postings are in the public domain, one can quote them and give full attribution. Yet such a practice is seldom followed because of concerns for the privacy of the individual and the sensitive matter of some of the lists (Braddlee, 1993; Giordano, 1995). Several dissertations examined by using qualitative research methodologies with Internet texts (Usenet groups, Listserv archives) reported concerns being handled cautiously. Braddlee (1993), in his study of GayNet texts, specified that discussions by their very nature are public and suggested that a model for the text on lists and newsgroups is Oldenberg's (1991) *The Great, Good Place; Cafes, Coffee Shops, Community Centers, Beauty Parlors, General Stores, Bars, Hangouts, and How They Get You Through the Day.* Braddlee did not publish any e-mail addresses or individual names in his examples, but used pseudonyms or first names only. Patterson (1996), in her study of AGM (newsgroup: alt.goodmorning), went beyond observation: She participated in the group and met participants socially. She also considered the privacy of the individual by using several methodologies, including obtaining individual permission from the posters. She also mounted numerous postings of notice of the study to the group, sent out a questionnaire, and involved participants in the choice of their pseudonyms. She conducted follow-up interviews with participants by e-mail as part of the study.

Patterson (1996) considered posts public domain. Privacy in a newsgroup was guaranteed only to those characterized as lurkers—that is, readers who do not contribute to the discussions. She held that the copyright issue of postings has not yet been settled. Similarly, Giordano (1995), studying the themes of a menopause support group list, considered the postings in the public domain, yet she asked permission for including postings in her dissertation.

Perhaps most illustrative of the multiple approaches used both to report accurately and to protect privacy is Sherry Turkle's (1995) outline of her procedure:

> In this book, I follow a consistent policy of disguising the identities of all my informants . . . I have invented names, places (virtual and real), and some elements of personal background. Of course, I try to invent a disguise that captures what seems to me to be the crucial variables of life history. In reporting cases of people who have part of their identities on the Internet, I follow the same policies as for other informants: I protect confidentiality by disguising identities. This means that among other things, I change MUD names, character names, and city names. In the case of The WELL, there is a clear community norm that "You Own Your Own Words," I have asked contributors to WELL discussions how they wish to be identified. Different people have made different choices. When I use materials from publicly archived sources, I simply indicate the source. (p. 324)

The literature on computer-mediated communication is replete with many studies on the effects of such examination. It is often confusing, and researchers, such as Herring (1996a), note that protocols evolved. John December's (1993) annotated and classified bibliography on computer-mediated communication provides a background to examine this issue further.

Ethics Policy Statements

Elsewhere in this book, ethics and the qualitative researcher have been examined thoroughly (Cieurzo & Keitel, chap. 6, this volume). The primary issues of informed consent, protection of the subject from harm, and privacy, however, are currently being stretched in application to textual data gleaned from the Internet. Numerous researchers (Boehlefeld, 1996; Herring, 1996b; King, 1996; Thomas, 1996) have difficulties with the ethical standards in current applications. Some assert that the guidelines in place by professional groups, such as the American Psychological Association (APA, 1997) or the

American Sociological Association (ASA, 1996), are not sufficient in specificity (King, 1996) or are in conflict with other guidelines treating the same phenomena with differing perspectives (Herring, 1996b).

Herring reviewed two new proposals for using text from Internet groups in her studies. She noted that one claim proposes all sources need to be cited specifically and that the second proposes any identifying information be removed to ensure no harm to the person. Both of these guidelines are rooted in differing ethical considerations, pitting the right of privacy against the honesty of attribution.

APA (http://www.apa.org/ethics/code.html) and ASA (http://sun.soci.niu.edu/sssi/ethics/ecoderev.html) guidelines for ethical research have been applied in qualitative work on Internet-based studies. The APA's *Ethical Principles of Psychologists and Code of Conduct* (1997) does not include specific passages about data gained from databases, but the ASA's (1996) draft contains the following:

11.05. Confidentiality and Use of Technology

(a) Sociologists protect the confidentiality of research participants, students, employees, clients or others when collecting information through electronic technology. . . .

(b) Sociologists are attentive to the problem of maintaining confidentiality and control over sensitive material and data when use of technological innovations, such as public computer networks, may open their professional and scientific communication to unauthorized audiences. (http://sun.soci.niu.edu/sssi/ethics/ecoderev.html)

It remains to be seen whether the language in the passage above is deemed sufficient for researchers calling for revision of existing guidelines. It is likely that many groups whose members focus on computer-mediated communication will develop similar, and perhaps stronger, guidelines as the boundaries now in place are stretched repeatedly.

SUMMARY: IMPACT OF INTERNET INFORMATION AVAILABILITY ON FUTURE QUALITATIVE RESEARCH

The implications of the availability of so much information and participation opportunities for the individual researcher can change the ways scholars publish and convene. No longer is there necessarily an "invisible college"; even beginners will be able to have contact with sources of information once available only through a network of scholarly colleagues. The maintenance of contact with rapidly changing developments is both stimulating and straining. It is likely that specialization of interest in the field will develop at a faster rate than in times when communication was in person and through journals.

Beyond Ease of Access

A researcher faces issues demanding considered judgment, including standardization by professional organizations of ethical considerations on the use of data gathered from communities on the Internet. The competing concerns of privacy and attribution are, at this point, not resolved and will most likely play into continued debate that affects practice. The technical possibilities raise issues about the privacy of the individual using Internet sites. Should such data be available without a participant's consent? A well-developed resource on these issues is Rob Kling's (1996) textbook *Computerization and Controversy: Value Conflicts and Social Choices.* The fact that such material is now entering the educational stream of information professionals is encouraging; however, the same attention needs to be paid to these issues by all qualitative researchers using text-based computer communication for study.

Presentation of Results as Part of the Evolution of Qualitative Studies

The possibilities of presentation of findings that use advanced computer technology could enrich the chain of communication. It also is possible that such presentation could weaken the conceptual flow of the reader through a document, as well as incorporate material into the publication that is less well prepared than the initial document. Coomber's (1997) paper had numerous hyperlinks to both references and papers related to his passages. Currently, the fields of communication and information access behavior are evaluating this method of presentation.

The studies examined for the basis of this chapter spanned several disciplines. Awareness of qualitative research strategies used by researchers of differing professional persuasions can only enrich efforts within a discipline. For instance, psychologists can gain much from the current work being done in the communications field on language structure and social correlates (Baym, 1995a, 1995b; Herring, 1996a). Psychological studies can inform communication and linguistic examinations with in-depth perspectives on motivation, self-presentation, and so on. The growing interest of management and business analysts in qualitative research is seen in studies of work culture (e.g., Simonsen & Kensing, 1997). Variants of this study can be seen in research on group interaction in virtual conferences (e.g., Murray, 1997).

THE FUTURE: ORIGINALITY AND RESPONSIBILITY

Tomorrow offers richer possibilities, with image, voice, and animation transfer being integrated into the communication of findings to the qualitative research community. The technology is already in place for such realities; for example, Netscape's Communicator software (Netscape Communications Corporation,

1997) offers conferencing capacities replete with a "whiteboard" for image sharing and mark-ups. Researchers have shown substantial interest in the impact of technology on learning, with a base of qualitative studies already having been completed. Given the advent of such new technologies, the use of qualitative research is warranted for assessment of unique learning opportunities. The chance for original analyses of work, recreational, and learning environments should be rewarding for both the researchers and the society being reflected through new lenses.

REFERENCES

American Psychological Association (APA). (1997). *Ethical principles of psychologists and code of conduct.* Available: http://www.apa.org/ethics/code.html

American Sociological Association (ASA). (1996). *Draft of the proposed new ASA code of ethics.* Available: http://sun.soci.niu.edu/sssi/ethics/ecoderev.html

Baym, N. K. (1995a). *Computer-mediated soap talk: Communication, community, and entertainment on the Net.* Available: http://pluto.mscc.huji.ac.il/mscmc/elib/asynch/baym.txt

Baym, N. K. (1995b). The performance of humor in computer-mediated communication. *Journal of Computer-Mediated Communication, 1*(2). Available: http://shum.cc.huji.ac.il/jcmc/vol1/issue2/baym.html

Boehlefeld, S. (1996). Doing the right thing: Ethical cyber-research. *Information Society, 2,* 141-152 [On-line serial].

Braddlee. (1993). *Virtual communities: Computer-mediated communication and communities of association.* Unpublished doctoral dissertation, Indiana University (DAI, Vol. 54-04A, 1134).

Coomber, R. (1997). Using the Internet for survey research. *Sociological Research Online, 2,* 2. Available: http://www.socresonline.org.uk/socresonline/2/2/2.html

December, J. (1993). Selected readings in computer-mediated communication, communication theory, computer networks, and the Internet. Available: http://www.december.com/john/papers/cmcbib93.txt

Finn, J., & Lavitt, M. (1994). Computer-based self-help groups for sexual abuse survivors. *Social Work With Groups, 17*(1/2), 21-46.

Giordano, N. A. (1995). *An investigation of the health concerns of the menopause discussion group on the Internet.* Unpublished doctoral dissertation, Columbia University Teacher's College.

Gurak, L. J. (1996). The multifaceted and novel nature of using cyber-texts as research data. In T. M. Harrison & T. D. Stephens (Eds.), *Computer networking and scholarly communication in the 21st century.* Albany: State University of New York Press.

Herring, S. (Ed.). (1996a). *Computer-mediated communication: Linguistic, social, and cross-cultural perspectives.* Philadelphia: John Benjamins.

Herring, S. (1996b). Critical analysis of language use in computer-mediated contexts: Some ethical and scholarly considerations. *Information Society, 12*(2), 153-168 [On-line serial].

Jones, R. A. (1994). The ethics of research in cyberspace. *Internet Research, 4*(3), 30-35 [On-line serial].

King, S. (1996). Researching Internet communities: Proposed ethical guidelines for the reporting of results. *Information Society, 12*(2), 119-127 [On-line serial].

Kling, R. (1996). *Computerization and controversy: Value conflicts and social choices* (2nd ed.). San Diego: Academic Press.

McLaughlin, M. L., Osborne, K. K., & Smith, C. B. (1995). Standards of conduct on Usenet. In S. Jones (Ed.), *Cybersociety: Computer-mediated communication and community* (pp. 90-111). Thousand Oaks, CA: Sage.

Murray, P. (1997). Using virtual focus groups in qualitative research. *Qualitative Health Research, 7*(4), 542-548.

Netscape Communications Corporation. (1997). Netscape communicator [Computer software]. CITY?: Author.

Paccagnella, L. (1997). Getting the seat of your pants dirty: Strategies for ethnographic research on the Internet. *Journal of Computer-Mediated Communication, 3*(1). Available: http://207.201.161.120/jcmc/vol3/issue1/paccagnella.html

Patterson, H. (1996). *Computer-mediated groups: A study of a culture in Usenet.* Unpublished doctoral dissertation. Available: http:www.sci.tamucc.edu/hollyp/pubs/dis/

Reid, E. (1996). Informed consent in the study of on-line communities: A reflection on the effects of computer-mediated social research. *Information Society, 12*(2), 169-174 [On-line serial].

Richards, T. J., & Richards, L. (1994). Using computers in qualitative research. In N. K. Denzin & Y. S. Lincoln (Eds.), *Handbook of qualitative research.* Thousand Oaks, CA: Sage.

Simonsen, J., & Kensing, F. (1997). Using ethnography in contextual design. *Communications of the ACM, 40*(7), 82-88.

Smith, M. (1997). *Measuring and mapping the social structure of Usenet.* Paper presented at the 17th Annual International Sunbelt Social Network. Available: http://www.sscnet.ucla.edu/soc/csoc/papers/sunbelt97/

Tesch, R. (1991). Introduction [Special issue]. *Qualitative Sociology, 14,* 225-243.

Thomas, J. (1995). *The ethics of Carnegie-Mellon's "cyber-porn" study.* Available: http://www.soci.niu.edu/jthomas

Thomas, J. (1996). Introduction: A debate about the ethics of fair practice for collecting social science data in cyberspace. *Information Society, 12*(2), 107-117 [On-line serial].

Trauth, E. M. (1998). Homepage. Available: http://www.cba.neu.edu/etrauth/

Turkle, S. (1995). *Life on the screen: Identity in the age of the Internet.* New York: Simon & Schuster.

Vento, B. F. (1997, January 7). H.R. 98: Consumer's Electronic Privacy Protection Bill. Available: http://rs9.loc.gov/cgi-bin/query/z?r105:E07JA7-165

Weitzman, E. A., & Miles, M. B. (1995). *Computer programs for qualitative data analysis: A software sourcebook.* Thousand Oaks, CA: Sage.

Workman, J. R. (1992). Use of electronic media in a participant observation study. *Qualitative Sociology, 15*(4), 419-425.

CHAPTER 8

Teaching Qualitative Research in Psychology

Sally D. Stabb

This chapter presents a very personal view on teaching qualitative research in psychology. I don't pretend to be a national expert on either pedagogy or qualitative research, and frankly I started this project in the same way I began learning about and then teaching qualitative methods themselves—with a moderate degree of background, a moderate degree of experience, and a lot of enthusiasm and interest. I attempt to present a picture of what I do in my qualitative research course and to explain why I do what I do. Also included are verbatim quotes from students who have taken and evaluated the course. The course syllabus is incorporated as well.

What I know about qualitative methodology is largely self-taught. I had never even heard of qualitative methods in graduate school, much less had a course in the area. Perhaps it started with my reading of Kuhn's (1970) *Structure of Scientific Revolution* in my first doctoral course. I recall finding it controversial, which I enjoyed. On reflection, however, I did little with it at the time and continued in a relatively traditional course of research and statistics training. I was, however, exposed to ideas about process research, such as stochastic chain analysis, that got me thinking that life was probabilistic rather than discreetly quantifiable. It occurs to me, too, that my undergraduate and master's training, which was strongly cognitive-behavioral, also probably generated an acceptance of small-n designs, case studies, and going into the field to look at actual behaviors, albeit from a different perspective than qualitative work. Other contributors might have been doing needs assessment research with gay and lesbian students on internship (Buhrke & Stabb, 1995), where I found quantitative methods so frustrating in generating "acceptable" data (I knew I'd never get a random sample!). Maybe my frustration stemmed from feeling overwhelmed by the inadequacy of experimental methods to address the complexity

I saw in doing therapy. Maybe it came from Garfield and Bergin's (1984) sobering *Handbook of Psychotherapy and Behavior Change,* in which literally thousands of quantitative studies emerged with a remarkable lack of specificity (all therapies are effective but none more than others, and we still don't really know why) or with mixed/inconclusive results. (Bergin & Garfield [1994] is now in its fourth edition, but the basic conclusions above still hold!)

After earning my degree in Counseling Psychology in 1988, I began my first teaching job in a rather traditional Counseling Psychology program. I know that during this time I gained my first exposure to qualitative methods, probably via Hoshmand's (1989) seminal article in the *Counseling Psychologist,* "Alternate Research Paradigms." I remember thinking that perhaps this was the kind of paradigm shift Kuhn (1970) was talking about—or if not a paradigm shift, a major wake-up call to the profession about expanding our methodological perspective. In combination with my personal propensity to enjoy shaking up the status quo (unresolved adolescent issues, no doubt), I was hooked. In addition to reading, talking with colleagues, and so on, I also started my first two qualitative research projects: One was an archival study of African American men's concerns as presented to a university counseling center (Stabb & Cogdal, 1991); the second was a study of attributions in couples therapy (Stabb, Brockman, & Harber, 1997).

These two projects, the latter in particular, taught me a lot about doing qualitative work. I learned firsthand about the time commitments and the labor-intensive rigor of developing, refining, and applying a coding system to transcribed data. The major lesson I learned from those first two projects is one I try to build into my current course: Get hands-on experience. No amount of content acquisition (reading or talking about doing it) can even bring a researcher close to having an idea of what is involved. This sentiment is echoed by students who have taken the qualitative course:

> I really like the way you broke it down into pieces and had us practice little pieces, all the way through the semester. You got familiar with the work by doing a little piece of it.

> The actual experience, hands-on, instead of just reading about it or hearing about it.

> I would agree with that. I don't know that you can learn this stuff without doing it. And the variety of learning tasks . . . having us do different aspects of qualitative work: Reviewing, coding, observing.

> Make sure people go out and look for articles to critique. I saw the syllabus and I thought, "Oh, I'll just zip over to the library." But going through journal after journal, it got pounded into me, "Hey, this really is a problem!" Especially in our field. I had to go over to the sociology journals. So I think that's important. To have that experience ourselves.

After 2 years in my first job position, I moved to Texas Woman's University (TWU), where I remain. Since my arrival here, my interest and involvement with qualitative work have grown. I expect that the strong emphasis on family systems and feminism in my department has nurtured this expansion. Both disciplines have respected qualitative advocates, who at the very least push for diversified methods (e.g., Bray, 1995; Moon, Dillon, & Sprenkle, 1990; Reinharz, 1992). I incorporated the paradigm/methods debate in the doctoral level course I teach here at TWU, Research in Counseling and Family Psychology (basically, a survey of process and outcome literature plus some research issues/philosophy of science stuff). Students and faculty had encouraged me to develop and teach a course devoted to qualitative methods. Still, it was 4 years before the idea became a reality. Meanwhile, I was continuing to read and talk with others (including peers in sociology and women's studies programs) about qualitative research, as well as to conduct my own research.

Finally, I was able to offer a "special topics" course on qualitative research methods in the summer of 1994. The summer session is 5 weeks long. I don't recommend this! The more time you have, the better. I now teach the course in a regular fall semester (16 weeks). The Sociology Department at TWU teaches a two-semester sequence: theory the first semester, practical application/hands-on the second semester. I wish we had the resources to do this in the Psychology Department, but we are constrained by all the usual time and money factors.

Nevertheless, in that first 5-week course, the students and I did our best to cram the basics into two 4-hour class sessions each week. I used Patton's (1990) text *Qualitative Evaluation and Research Methods* as a basis and supplemented with handouts from Lincoln and Guba (1985, 1986) and some of my own materials previously developed for a presentation at APA on the fit between qualitative research methods and feminist psychology (Stabb, 1991).

The "basics" covered understanding the philosophical underpinnings for qualitative methods and the paradigm debates (qualitative vs. or combined with or complementary to quantitative? Do we have a paradigm in psychology at all, anyway?), as well as comparing and contrasting inductive and hypothetico-deductive ways of knowing. These discussions were integrated with material on professional socialization and the realities of the research process in terms of time, money/funding, publication, attitudes, gate keeping via editorial policies, and so on. We also covered the range of qualitative inquiry in an attempt to have students grasp that there isn't one qualitative method, that there are a whole range of methods, often with disciplinary roots outside psychology. We worked on understanding the language and vocabulary of qualitative methods, most of which were totally new to students. Following this, we moved into specific methods for sampling, data collection, analysis, and establishing the trustworthiness and credibility of designs and data. Presentation of a final product was also discussed on the basis of the often multiple constituencies involved. These basics remain the framework for my current, revised course.

The ways I have expanded and elaborated on the basics have evolved considerably, however.

The first time I taught the course, I had collected many texts on qualitative methods that I hadn't had time to examine; I built this into the course and let each student review and evaluate a text for its usefulness in teaching qualitative methods to other students; and when students found particularly useful sections in their books, we often made xerographic copies of these and shared them with the class. Other than this, however, students reported that this was the least useful aspect of the course, and I dropped it in further refinements. What did work the first time around were such tasks as having students find qualitative articles in journals and apply the concepts as they were learning them to a critique of these articles, having students go out and engage in participant observation in a setting of their choice and write this up with personal reactions, having students share and discuss their experiences as they occurred, and having students design and execute a small qualitative project.

I taught a slightly modified version of this course in the summer of 1995 but did not have the opportunity to get past the 5-week format until the fall of 1996. In tailoring the course to a full semester, I greatly expanded the experiential component of the class. In addition to article reviews and participant observations, I had each of the students tape-record three 20- to 30-minute interviews with persons of her or his choice on a topic of her or his choice (with appropriate consents, and so on). Students then transcribed their tapes. Following this, we rotated transcripts among students and had each student code her or his own interviews plus one set of another student's interviews. We then compared the cross-coded results in class and attempted to construct models (done on the chalkboard) from the data for each student's work. To gain depth in qualitative analysis, I added Miles and Huberman's (1994) text on qualitative data analysis. This was used to facilitate both exercises and the final class projects.

Both transcribing and cross-coding experiences were very well received; students had many "Aha!" experiences as they learned firsthand about the time, trials, and tribulations of recording and transcribing data, as well as insights about the interviewing process itself. The cross-coding exercise brought life to the ideas of triangulation and multiple perspectives:

> It particularly worked in getting an understanding and grasp on the results of our interviews, in that we did the coding individually and then cross-coded, and how we came up with the different categories. And at first, it didn't seem to make a lot of sense, but then having that experiential piece of having it all come together into a global understanding worked best for me.

> It's certainly implanted in my brain that you need to have analyst triangulation and member checks, you know, participants. It's just in there now. I could never do a study or explore a question without doing that now. It's anchored. As much as I hated it—I know you can code things and work with that material without transcribing—but I recommend transcribing.

Yeah, as much as I hated the time involved, I sure became an advocate for transcription. I sat there thinking, Not only would the transcription stuff be great for the research, in terms of really understanding a client, I think I learned a lot from this that would be really useful to apply in therapy.

I built in more time for discussion and in-progress reports of students' qualitative projects. The additional time granted by a full semester allowed students to have more complete products and to develop and refine their work. Projects are presented at the end of the semester and constitute the main assignment of the semester. I give no exams. Class participation is weighted heavily, as contributions to other students' projects are essential.

In general, I try to teach the course from a feminist pedagogical position (Brown, 1992; Hughes, 1995; Poplin, 1992; Ropers-Heilman, 1995; Ryder, 1994; Thompson & Gitlin, 1995; Wakai, 1994). Without going into the substantial debate about what constitutes such a position, for me, regarding qualitative research, this means (a) focusing on a critique of traditional, Western, linear, patriarchal, competitive, quantitative science; (b) encouraging topics that give voice to women and other oppressed minorities and thereby raise the consciousness of all class participants; (c) encouraging personal reactions to qualitative inquiry, validating these reactions, and incorporating them into discussions and write-ups of qualitative projects—which fits nicely with the method's focus on the researcher as a tool in analysis and interpretation; and (d) running the classroom with a maximum degree of collaboration and a minimum degree of power differential and competitive evaluation. I also try to model a feminist pedagogical stance by keeping the classroom environment as open as possible to critique of my own teaching methods, by recognizing multiple viewpoints, and by having the content of the course acquired via relational, emergent processes rather than through lecture, note taking, and exams. These feminist principles are, I hope, in evidence in this chapter as well.

Regarding their experiences with their basic exposure to the critique of the traditional, hypothetico-deductive model of science and to the quantitative/qualitative debate in general, students noted:

Naturalistic inquiry provides me with discrepant information. And I've decided even though it's emotionally difficult to let go of a worldview, or a particular idea, even for a moment, when you get discrepant information it's essential because it's exactly how we get entrenched into paradigms . . . it's the freedom to find things that don't fit with current paradigms.

I liked what [another student] said about a continuum—and you presented that too—it's not qualitative is always better than quantitative or vice versa. I was thinking about the field of counseling—we're constantly taught that certain interventions work better with certain clients, or in Multicultural we're taught to adjust to the client and where they're at and use different interventions, but in our research, we've always been taught quantitative is the way to do it. So it seems almost hypocritical in a sense, that we can be so broad [in therapy], but realize we need to adjust in our research. We're not following suit.

I've been moving in this direction for a long time now, and this is a big relief to me to talk about this as a legitimate approach.

I think a great deal of respect should be had for this class. It's one thing to crunch numbers, get a critical value, or two factors and it means this and that's it. But it's more complex when you work with feelings and trying to interpret those.

I identify with the statement [by another student] about freedom . . . coming to this class after that class [Research Techniques—our basic quantitative methods course], it was really freeing. I've gone through an evolutionary process.

We're all talking about how freeing this experience has been, and I wonder what my experience would have been like if I had taken this before my "Research Techniques" course. I think I'd be real resistant to that course after this . . . I'd feel like I was sitting on my hands a lot.

I appreciated too was your being up front with the controversy over qualitative in the field. And sort of preparing us for that, "If you're planning on doing this for a dissertation, be prepared, you'll have to deal with this."

In fact, I do recommend that students have completed our traditional, quantitative methods sequence before enrolling in my class, for just the reason mentioned by the student above. I have not made it a prerequisite, however; I talk with prospective students about the pros and cons of the possible sequences. As students become exposed to the range of qualitative inquiry and their unique ways of producing viable data, they become able to articulate clearly a qualitative position.

[I was surprised by] the vastness of the topic. And the criticisms of it as weak or [it] can only be used for exploratory purposes. I'm surprised at the number of counterarguments I have for that now. Because done correctly, I think it can hold its own with quantitative.

It has the best of being rigorous and being creative both. It is hard work and you need to be exacting to come up with those matrices you did and apply those concepts, but there's many right ways to do that, or many effective ways to interpret.

In keeping with the feminist goal of giving voice to women and other marginalized populations, I try to emphasize throughout the course that qualitative methods may, in some cases, provide a better fit for research questions on multicultural or feminist topics or both. Both of these areas are emphasized in our doctoral training program, and numerous critiques have been available for some time regarding the shortcomings of traditional/quantitative research approaches involving these two domains (e.g., Buhrke, BenEzra, Hurley, & Ruprecht, 1992; Gergen, Gulerce, Lock, & Misra, 1996; Iijima Hall, 1997; Ponterotto, 1988). Students expressed their understanding of this compatibility in several ways, particularly in relation to such ideas as in-depth personal knowledge of participants, accessibility to people in their communities, personal emotional involvement, and a collaborative approach to learning/ research.

[These students conducted an archival study of elderly women in bankruptcy court using audiotapes from court that are now in the public domain.] One of the parts I did like was, even though we didn't meet our participants in person, that I think I have a lot more respect than if I'd just done a survey about the process. By doing it the way we did it, I had a lot more respect for their situation—an appreciation for their worldview.

One of the things I really like about the qualitative approach is you get really close to your participants. They're not "subjects," they're people . . . and it seems like with the other way you can't really ever know the feelings of the participants.

[Male student upon hearing verbatim descriptions of sexual abuse] . . . it was really good for me . . . it kind of threw me for a loop when she read that graphic description, it made me stop and think, because you can read a lot of quantitative articles about sexual abuse, but just that one little piece that [another student] read was descriptive, it just kind of threw me back.

This kind of research emphasizes getting to know the participants and the shared meaning of the group. That's one thing I'll remember from it, if I go out and this kind of study again, that'd be one of the goals I'd strive for—is to get to know the participants.

I have a real sense of wanting to hang on to these two people here [other students], because I know we know it together, and the rapport that's grown between the group here, that's really been nice.

When we did our individual studies, I thought, "Oh, I won't be able to do that, I don't have the feedback of the group." Because in that moment, I thought, "This is great! This is research team at its best!"

. . . and knowing that you can explore topics you could approach that there's no way to approach with another methodology . . . there's no way you could get that kind of information.

It's a much richer experience. I found myself even getting some personal revelations out of this. Confronting fear. And I'm not sure that would have come up. I have had to do this. The difficulty doing this project . . . I think that this project enabled me to get in touch with a side of me that I wasn't willing to [This was a female, white, middle-class student who interviewed a male, Hispanic, ex-gang member.]

And then for me, I found, the last thing: Be prepared to be emotionally moved by the whole experience.

In terms of topics, the focus on women has included projects on elderly women in bankruptcy, family influences on women's career choices, Muslim women's attitudes about counseling in relation to acculturation and sex roles, the experiences of women who are first identified as gifted in middle age, adolescent girls' experiences of anger, lesbian women who chose to parent, and the mentorship experiences of women in management. In addition to those projects focused on lesbian women and Muslim women, topics relating to other marginalized persons have included homelessness, the strengths of African American families living in challenging urban environments, and Native American (Potowatami) heritage.

At the end of the semester, I ask students what advice they would have for other students about doing qualitative research or about taking the qualitative research class. I believe that these quotes are the most telling of all in terms of how to teach the course. The absolute number one consideration is having enough time. And that means a lot of advance planning by the instructor not only for the course structure itself but also in helping each student organize, set boundaries ("bound"), and think through her or his qualitative project. I suppose my hope is that those instructors who read this chapter will let their students read what these students have said because, try as I might, I have been unable to convey just how time-intensive qualitative work is. It is quite possible that other instructors are better at it than I, but I suspect that peers will be more successful at it than any professor!

In terms of the research project, confining it was so hard! There was so much. We kept finding things . . . it could get bigger and bigger.

We had the same experience [as two other class members]—that there were all these people to interview, and data, data, data!

And maybe the advice is, when you take this course, don't take one of those other real time-consuming courses.

It's a process, and you really need to collect your data early enough to have a lot of time to think about it. [Me: "There's a lot of incubation time."] Yes. Absolutely. I can't emphasize that enough. And you tried to give us fair warning of how much time it would take, but none of us really believed you! Unfortunately! You get into your old, bad habits of how you finished out every other class, and you can't do it in this class.

Yeah, I made a list of things. Number One: Get organized. Number Two: Allow for time, time, time. Third thing: The member checks and the cross-validation are absolutely invaluable. And the fourth one: Set a stopping place and stick to it.

Another thing that occurred was our project planning meetings were crucial, because that really helped me define and bound it from the beginning. I was having real trouble doing that, and just getting other people's feedback gave me a sense of what was realistic to accomplish.

There's not enough time. Even if you plan for time, there are going to be differences. Just even an exercise, one thing, like the person I was interviewing— it took me 12 hours to transcribe it, and you wouldn't plan for that.

I would say, any time limits they give you in textbooks, multiply by three!

And along with time too, there was that issue of bounding it. Because it was so tempting to keep going and going. It was really hard to stop and place boundaries on the project.

Also in keeping with feminist pedagogy —as well as qualitative member checks— I had students critique and evaluate the course as a group to give input about possible changes, improvement, deletions, and so on. Some of their ideas and conflicts are noted below. I am currently wrestling with how much of this feedback to incorporate into the course for next time and how to do so.

It would be nice to tie some of the exercises into this major project, because I found myself doing a whole semester's work in a short amount of time.

Maybe condense it a little harder and faster at first, so that the back end of the semester had a little more time. There was a lot of reading, so there was a lot to absorb . . . so its something to be careful about.

I'm also wondering if some of the Miles and Huberman stuff could come after we've started collecting some of our data. For me, it would have made more sense if I already had some data to think about. Its real crucial reading, I just think, for me, the timing could have come later.

In general, it seemed as though students wanted the most technical aspects of Miles and Huberman's book (1994) to be covered concurrently with some already obtained data and to move the whole course sequence up a bit to allow more time for projects during the semester. I hope these students' experiences, along with the description of the course and the syllabus (at end of this chapter), will assist others in planning their qualitative courses. Teaching qualitative methods is a complex task involving understanding, philosophical foundations, and specific methods, as well as the importance of practical applications in training. This chapter has documented the evolution of one faculty member's journey in developing a qualitative course.

REFERENCES

Bergin, A. E., & Garfield, S. L. (1994). *Handbook of psychotherapy and behavior change* (4th ed.). New York: John Wiley.

Bray, J. H. (1995). Methodological advances in family psychology research: Introduction to the special section. *Journal of Family Psychology, 9*(2), 107-109.

Brown, J. (1992). Theory or practice: What exactly is feminist pedagogy? *Journal of General Education, 41,* 49-63.

Buhrke, R. A., BenEzra, L. A., Hurley, M. E., & Ruprecht, L. J. (1992). Content analysis and methodological critique of articles concerning lesbian and gay male issues in counseling journals. *Journal of Counseling Psychology, 39*(1), 91-99.

Buhrke, R. A., & Stabb, S. D. (1995). Gay, lesbian, and bisexual student needs. In S. D. Stabb, S. Harris, & J. E. Talley (Eds.), *Multicultural needs assessment for college and university student populations* (pp. 173-195). Springfield, IL: Charles C Thomas.

Garfield, S. L., & Bergin, A. E. (1984). *Handbook of psychotherapy and behavior change* (3rd ed.). New York: John Wiley.

Gergen, K. J., Gulerce, A., Lock, A., & Misra, G. (1996). Psychological science in cultural context. *American Psychologist, 51,* 496-503.

Hoshmand, L. S. T. (1989). Alternate research paradigms: A review and teaching proposal. *Counseling Psychologist, 17,* 3-101.

Hughes, K. P. (1995). Feminist pedagogy and feminist epistemology: An overview. *International Journal of Lifelong Education, 14*(3), 214-230.

Iijima Hall, C. C. (1997). Cultural malpractice: The growing obsolescence of psychology with the changing U.S. population. *American Psychologist, 52,* 642-651.

Kuhn, T. (1970). *The structure of scientific revolutions.* Chicago: University of Chicago Press.

Lincoln, Y. S., & Guba, E. G. (1985). *Naturalistic inquiry.* Beverly Hills, CA: Sage.

Lincoln, Y. S., & Guba, E. G. (1986). But is it rigorous? Trustworthiness and authenticity in naturalistic evaluation. In D. D. Williams (Ed.), *Naturalistic evaluation: New directions for program evaluation* (No. 30, pp. 73-84). San Francisco: Jossey-Bass.

Miles, M. B., & Huberman, A. M. (1994). *Qualitative data analysis* (2nd ed.). Thousand Oaks, CA: Sage.

Moon, S. M., Dillon, D. R., & Sprenkle, D. H. (1990). Family therapy and qualitative research. *Journal of Marital and Family Therapy, 17*(4), 327-348.

Patton, M. Q. (1990). *Qualitative evaluation and research methods.* Newbury Park, CA: Sage.

Ponterotto, J. G. (1988). Racial/ethnic minority research in the *Journal of Counseling Psychology:* A content analysis and methodological critique. *Journal of Counseling Psychology, 35*(4), 410-418.

Poplin, M. S. (1992). We are not who we thought we were. *Journal on Excellence in College Teaching, 3,* 69-79.

Reinharz, S. (1992). *Feminist methods in social research.* New York: Oxford University Press.

Ropers-Heilman, B. (1995, April). *Negotiating knowledge and knowing: Philosophies of teaching and learning in feminist classrooms.* Paper presented at the annual meeting of the American Educational Research Association, San Francisco.

Ryder, P. M. (1994, March). *Giving or taking authority: Exploring the ideologies of collaborative learning.* Paper presented at the annual meeting of the Conference on College Composition and Communication. Nashville, TN.

Stabb, S. D. (1991, August). *Qualitative and quantitative designs in feminist research.* Paper presented at the annual conference of the American Psychological Association, Boston.

Stabb, S. D., Brockman, D., & Harber, J. (1997). Therapist attributions and gender bias in couples therapy: A process investigation. *Journal of Marriage and Family Therapy, 23*(3), 335-346.

Stabb, S. D., & Cogdal, P. A. (1991). Black males in personal counseling: A 5-year archival study. *Journal of College Student Psychotherapy, 7*(1), 73 86.

Thompson, A., & Gitlin, A. (1995). Creating spaces for reconstructing knowledge in feminist pedagogy. *Educational Theory, 45*(2), 125-150.

Wakai, S. T. (1994, November). *Barriers to and facilitators of feminist pedagogy in college and university teaching.* Paper presented at the annual meeting of the Association for the Study of Higher Learning, Tucson, AZ.

Addendum: Syllabus for Qualitative Research Methods

COURSE OBJECTIVES AND SCOPE:

This course is designed to give students an introduction to the philosophical, conceptual, and practical basis of qualitative methodologies. The course will survey the most common types of qualitative inquiry and their theoretical roots, differences between qualitative and quantitative methods, techniques of data collection and analysis, integration of qualitative and quantitative methods, and current debates regarding qualitative inquiry. Students will also become familiar with published qualitative work in the discipline of psychology. Additionally, students will begin to explore the practical aspects of qualitative inquiry via the design and implementation of a small qualitative project. The course is considered highly exploratory.

COURSE SCHEDULE AND ASSIGNMENTS:

Date:	Assignment/Topics:
Week 1	Introduction and Course Overview
Week 2	The Nature of Qualitative Inquiry The Context of Controversy P: CH. 1 & 9
Week 3	Overview of Qualitative Methods: Themes and Variety in Qualitative Inquiry P: CH. 2 & 3; M & H: CH 1

AUTHOR'S NOTE: I thank the students who contributed in so many ways both to the development of this course and to my own development as a teacher of, and a researcher using, qualitative methods. First, let me thank my "guinea pigs" from that crazy, initial 5-week class: Marcia Bendo, Deborah Cox, Winona Bryant, Judy Cocks, Peter Kahle, and Evelyn Parker. Second, I thank the Fall 1996 class: Cheryl Inmon, Becky Lindecamp, and Lisa Weschler. These two classes provided the quotes you have read. Third, I thank those students who took the qualitative course with me in Summer 1995 or who worked with me over the last 5 years or so via independent study and/or thesis/dissertation. These students include Betsy Campbell, Sally Hill, Sabrina Houser, John Hoper, Monica Pilarc, Cathy Macgregor, Asra Haque-Khan, Diane Myers, Bonnie Osmon, and Trina Davis. I have learned a lot from all of you!

Week 4   Appropriate Applications and Examples
                P: CH. 4
                JOURNAL ARTICLE 1 DUE & PRESENTED

Week 5   Designing Qualitative Studies: Methods of Sampling and
                    Data Collection—I
                P: CH 5 & 6; M & H: CH 2

Week 6   Designing Qualitative Studies: Samples and Data
                    Collection—II
                P: CH 7; M & H: CH 3
                JOURNAL ARTICLE 2 DUE & PRESENTED

Week 7   Project Discussion—I
                PARTICIPANT OBSERVATION DUE & PRESENTED

Week 8   Qualitative Data Analysis—I: Overview & Coding
                    Procedures
                P: CH 8; M & H: CH 4
                TAPES w/TRANSCRIPTS DUE

Week 9   Qualitative Data Analysis—II: Within Case Displays
                M & H: CH 5 & 6
                CROSS-CODING DUE

Week 10   Qualitative Data Analysis—III: Cross Case and Matrix
                    Displays
                M & H: CH 7-9

Week 11   Presenting Qualitative Reports
                M & H: CH 10-13

Week 12   Project Discussion—II

Week 13   (THANKSGIVING VACATION)

Week 14   PROJECTS DUE & PRESENTED

TEXTS:

Miles, M. B., & Huberman, A. M. (1994). *Qualitative data analysis* (2nd ed.). Thousand
  Oaks, CA: Sage.
Patton, M. Q. (1990). *Qualitative evaluation and research methods.* Newbury Park, CA:
  Sage.

EXPLANATION OF COURSE ASSIGNMENTS:

1. *Journal Articles:* Bring in two articles during the semester. Be prepared to discuss
   them in relation to the content covered prior to their due dates. Write up a 2- to
   3-page (double spaced) summary of your integration, impressions, and critique.
   Include things you found helpful/enlightening/good additions to the course and
   things you found boring/unclear/useless. Include a copy of the article when you turn
   in your paper.

2. *Naturalistic/Participant Observation:* Go out somewhere—anywhere—of your
   choice and practice observation for 30 to 60 minutes (minimum). You may take notes
   or tape-record your impressions (and then present the tape or a transcript of the tape).
   You will be asked to hand in your actual notes and/or tape, as well as a 1- to 2-page
   write-up of your reactions to the exercise. Be prepared to discuss/present your
   experiences in class.

3. *Tapes and Transcripts:* Tape three 20- to 30-minute interviews on a topic of your
   choice with three different people. Transcribe the tapes. Hand in FIVE COPIES of
   your transcripts, the original tapes (1 copy), and a 1- to 2-page reaction paper
   (1 copy) to doing this assignment. Make sure to retain a copy of your transcripts for
   yourself.

4. *Cross-Coding:* Develop a rough coding system for your own transcript and one for
   ONE OTHER PERSON'S transcript (I'll handle the distribution aspects). You only
   need to bring in one copy of each to turn in at this class period. Discrepancies
   between coders will be explored in class.

5. *Project and Project Reports:* This assignment entails each of you discussing and
   developing a small, qualitative project you might like to do, either as an individual
   or in a small group or pair. Group discussion is to clarify, refine, brainstorm, and so
   on regarding topics, methods, analyses, write-up, rationales, justifications, and so
   on. Then you carry out the project, write it up, and present it to the class.

6. *Participation:* This will be a CRUCIAL element of this course.

COURSE GRADES:

Article 1	25	90-100% = A = 270-300
Article 2	25	80-89% = B = 240-269
Observation	25	70-79% = C = 210-239
Tape Transcripts	25	
Cross-Coding	25	
Project	100	
Participation	75	
Total	300	

CHAPTER 9

Designing Qualitative Research Reports for Publication

Constance T. Fischer

To maximize chances that a qualitative report will find its way into print, its author should observe traditional standards for reporting research and take special care in describing qualitative methods and findings. These steps will also assist readers in understanding the text as the author intended. Colleagues who serve on editorial boards have affirmed my experience that many qualitative research manuscripts are rejected, not because of methodology, but because of poor research design, weak reflective rigor, and inadequate discipline in preparation of the report. Hence, I review standard advice about manuscript preparation, along with my own suggestions for preparing qualitative research reports for journal publication. My suggestions are consonant with the "evolving guidelines" developed by Elliott, Fischer, and Rennie (in press), which were refined with feedback from colleagues who represented a wide range of qualitative research methods. This chapter is intended to be useful for first-time authors of qualitative reports while also serving as a resource for thesis and dissertation supervisors.

CONSIDER THE EDITOR'S PERSPECTIVE

An editor is responsible to the journal's sponsoring organization for publishing contributions to an evolving, coherent body of knowledge, along with related controversy. In accordance with that responsibility, the editor, with the advice of reviewers, selects the best of the received manuscripts for the next issue of the journal. Selected manuscripts are judged to be of archival (enduring) value or of specific relevance to current debate. Exploratory studies and piecemeal reports are rarely accepted.

Many completed dissertations require follow-up studies before their findings are appropriate for publication. In the meantime, *Dissertation Abstracts,* conference presentations, and Internet postings allow other researchers to reflect on the possible relevance of the preliminary findings for their own work. These prepublication disseminations also provide occasions for feedback, much of which furthers the author's thought and contributes eventually to a publishable report.

Background Preparation

Before drafting a manuscript, the savvy author reviews copies of several target journals. He or she consults the statement, usually printed on the inside cover, about the sponsoring organization's purposes and the range of content for that journal. He or she takes notes about actual content and about intended audiences across articles—various theorists, researchers, practitioners. The interests represented by the board of consulting editors also provide clues to what a journal might value. Finally, an author may record data for each prospective journal about the greatest and average number of pages for articles (and the ratio of printed page to manuscript pages), frequency of publication (e.g., monthly, quarterly, annually), prestige of the journal, number and probable characteristics of subscribers, publication lag, and an estimate of likelihood of acceptance. Then prospective journals can be rank-ordered in accordance with the author's goals. Unlike book manuscripts intended for commercial publication, journal manuscripts may be submitted to only one outlet at a time.

Editors are allocated limited pages per issue; they value efficient, economical manuscripts. Editors and reviewers also want the journal to be widely read and respected and accordingly value text that respects readers through clear organization and writing. Before writing, most authors find it useful to assign page limits for each section of their outline. Attempts to miniaturize a dissertation into a journal manuscript are frustrating and usually unsuccessful. Generally, it works better to put that opus aside and determine which aspects of it one would like to share with a particular readership. Such a tactic allows for a streamlined, coherent presentation. Similarly, efforts toward precision and brevity of expression usually sharpen the writer's own understandings. In that not all worthy manuscripts can be accommodated within limited journal pages, authors best serve their interests by crafting the best possible reports of their work. That endeavor includes writing clear abstracts, discussions, and summaries that make the significance of the work explicit.

Disciplined Presentation

Editors and reviewers, who usually lead demanding professional lives, are not paid for this work. They do not appreciate the unnecessary time and labor entailed by premature submissions and are likely to respond with brief judgments about the work's unsuitability for publication. Editors and reviewers do appreciate carefully thought-out reports that respect the work of other authors and that make a clear contribution to the field's integration of findings and understandings. Manuscripts that fall in the latter category are likely to evoke helpful, contribution-enhancing comments from reviewers, whether they recommend resubmission after revising or submission to a more appropriate outlet.

The editor first glances through the document to determine whether its content is appropriate for the journal and whether it is well enough executed to forward to reviewers. The latter judgment is based not only on the apparent quality of the research but also on whether the journal's instructions (usually printed on inside covers) for style, format, and submission have been followed. The American Psychological Association's (APA) style manual (1994) includes helpful suggestions for writing, along with its style requirements (e.g., punctuation, spelling, headings, reference format). Editors and reviewers assume that careless physical preparation typically predicts careless research and reflection. Otherwise worthy work may be rejected outright, sometimes many months after submission. Even revisions requested for an otherwise accepted manuscript can require considerable time. I once calculated that, from initial submission to a journal, publication of my own work averaged 15 months, with the range being 6 months to 28 months. Time aside, when the author has not taken great care in initial writing, much to his or her chagrin, some less than satisfactory features may show up in print.

In short, authors serve themselves well by taking extra care in preparation of their initial reports. This care maximizes chances that the editor will send the manuscripts out for review, that reviewers will be favorably impressed and will put in time and effort to provide constructive and tailored suggestions, that the works will find their way into print, and that readers will appreciate the works as intended.

RESPECT PERSPECTIVES; SITUATE THE STUDY

A major stumbling block for qualitative research publication is that its philosophical and methodological frameworks are not understood by mainstream professionals in psychology. Unlike experimental research, with its long-standing procedural and statistical analysis traditions, qualitative methods and procedures may vary creatively from study to study. To be understood and respected by mainstream editors, reviewers, and readers, the qualitative researcher must take into account the probable framework of these colleagues and, accordingly, provide trail signs, translations, and clarifications to help them travel through the research report with an open attitude. Even when writing to fellow qualitative researchers, the psychologist should likewise provide guideposts and clarifications that allow the reader to follow the researcher's particular journey.

Conventions

In most circumstances, it is best to organize the research report with the customary format and headings: (a) a content-oriented title, (b) an informative abstract, (c) reasons for undertaking the study, (d) the general method, (e) specific procedures, (f) information about the research participants ("subjects"), (g) findings, (h) discussion, (i) conclusions or summary or both, and (j) references. This conventional format allows the reader to anticipate the general development of the report and to locate details within the article.

The traditional purpose of the report's literature review is to explain how the study is intended to contribute to a discipline's body of knowledge. This "statement of the problem" reviews what is known about the topic and then presents the gaps, anomalies, or critiques that occasioned a new study. Anticipated implications for theory, policy, and/or practice are spelled out. Most qualitative researchers would speak of "*understandings* integrated from various perspectives," rather than of a "body of *knowledge*" (as though it were a collection of truths about a world separate from its knowers). We, too, however, will contribute most systematically through a presentation of the reasons for the study. Of course, the qualitative researcher must also explicate the choice of a *qualitative* approach to the topic, usually in terms of the desirability of exploring the ways individuals endow situations with meaning.

Collegiality

What with meaning-making, in one way or another, being our subject matter, we cannot fall back on operational definitions nor otherwise assume that our terms are widely agreed on. "Qualitative research" occurs in many forms in divergent specialized communities that have not yet agreed on shared language. For now, it is especially incumbent on an author to meet probable readers where they are and to assist them in understanding his or her qualitative research terminology.

More particularly, throughout the research report, from the initial statement of its purposes through the summary, "respecting and situating" require bearing in mind in which journal and hence with which audience one has chosen to speak. Terms should be explained accordingly as they appear. For example,

> By *lived world*, I mean how one experiences and navigates one's daily situations, influencing and being influenced en route.

Because we want to be read and understood by a range of colleagues, it is important to imagine a readership somewhat beyond the target journal's regular readers. Respecting readers by writing clearly and to the point so that their time and effort are well spent encourages readers, in turn, to consider the research report respectfully. Helpful clarifications that anticipate readers' questions enhance the chances that the entire report will be read.

Similarly, one's contributions are more likely to be regarded as such when one's stance toward others' research is collegial. It is considerate and usually accurate to say, for example,

> John Jones's research, undertaken from such-and-such a perspective, yielded *x*, *y*, and *z* findings useful for *a*, *b*, and *c* purposes. The present study, undertaken from so-and-so perspective, is intended to yield findings useful for *m*, *n*, *o*, and *p* purposes.

Respect, as I mean it, does not imply agreement. It implies recognizing that we are all situated differently and that all of our efforts are necessarily perspectival. Note that etymologically, *regard* and *respect* mean to look back, to look again. To reach another, so that he or she can turn to gaze from his or her own stance, requires acknowledging the power and value of perspective. So, beyond good manners and promoting shared community, I'm talking about gaining reciprocated respect.

Anticipating Misunderstandings

Let me elaborate an earlier point about anticipating misunderstanding. Because most qualitative research is undertaken from a philosophical framework that is foreign to the majority of North American psychologists, communication is enhanced through proactive clarification. In my own writing, I do not regard this tactic as being defensive about my qualitative work, but rather as "taking the wind out of the sails" of readers who might be on their way toward "cutting me off." For example, I might mention that this qualitative method is most appropriate for studying my particular subject matter but that it does not work for the subject matter of laboratory psychology. I might say explicitly that I do not seek to "generalize" my findings as one seeks to do in a controlled study, but rather that I would expect further local studies to yield some commonalities. I might acknowledge that my findings are indeed subjective in that they require my reading of meanings, which is intrinsic to the philosophy of science that grounds my method. I would then also say that my findings are not "merely subjective" and that, to be credible, they must also be "intersubjective": Other researchers and readers must be able to arrive at similar findings through my data and method. Potential critics see that I am, after all, familiar with their positions and then are more likely to remain on course through the report.

Acknowledging the study's limitations, as all proper scientists do, also heads off potential challengers. This acknowledgment is appropriate in both the section introducing the study and its method and in the discussion section. It is not an apology, but rather a sophisticated specification of what the study does and does not accomplish. For example,

We limited the study to suburban residents who reported nonviolent crimes to their township police. This decision allowed us to investigate experience not overshadowed by violent incidents. From this study, however, we cannot address the experience of the urban dweller or the repeatedly victimized citizen.

To one degree or another, these suggestions promote effective communication, no matter whether the journal is mainstream or dedicated to qualitative research. Indeed, in either context, we often find that we refine our own thoughts as we try to be clear to others. Again, these suggestions serve the interests both of getting published in the first place and then of being understood as intended.

DESCRIBE THE METHOD, HELPFULLY

Methodology refers to the study or nature of method. This term is appropriate for an introduction of the philosophical foundations, for the history of a particular method, and for a discussion of its selection for the particular study. At this stage of psychology's unfamiliarity with qualitative research, at least brief mention should be made of the author's adoption of a method appropriate to the study of the lived world, meaning-making, or whatever. What the author means by *hermeneutic, ethnographic, grounded theory, phenomenological, case narrative,* or other method should be specified. This specification serves two purposes. First, it provides an understandable definition for readers unfamiliar with that approach and its philosophy. Second, the specification indicates to which researchers the author's philosophical approach and methods come closest and how they differ (if they do). Care should be taken not to appropriate terms loosely. For example, one would not say that a phenomenological method was used when all that was meant was that experience was attended to, or that grounded theory was used when all that was meant was that three sources of data were used. This care is in the dual interest of respect for the efforts of professionals working within various frameworks and of scholarly, systematic development of philosophical foundations, methods, and findings.

First Person, Active Voice

I prefer to write the entire manuscript in first person, active voice, for the sake of clear writing and as a continual reminder that our understandings are developed by actual individuals, not by an automated procedure. For example: "We selected instances to illustrate each theme," in contrast with "Examples were listed for each theme"; or, "In Table 2, I characterize how each subject's protocol contributed to the general structure," in contrast with "Each subject's contribution to the general structure is characterized in Table 2." Although the APA style manual (1994) encourages writing in first person, unfortunately even qualitative research authors sometimes succumb to trying to appear scientific by writing anonymously and in passive voice ("A transformation to third person, past tense, was performed"). Use of first person, however, is *not* meant just to be personal or casual. Rather, writing in first person serves as an implicit reminder that qualitative researchers are themselves research "instruments." First person references also remind us that researchers are individuals, not mechanical instruments.

Method;

Contexts

Following a methodology section, a "Method" heading indicates that the specifics of a particular method will now be described. Beyond naming the general method and specifying how one adapted or expanded it from cited touch-point work, the author describes the research circumstances adequately for a reader to have a sense of the contexts in which data were gathered and of the participants' situations. "Contexts" includes environments, like "the Pittsburgh airport McDonald's, on weekdays between 2:00 and 4:00 a.m.," or "crowded (standing room only) waiting room of a private practice pediatrician." The researcher's multiple interests in the subject matter are also part of context. One might say, for instance, "My interest was in providing examples and descriptions that would challenge the prevailing conception of anger as force" or "We hoped to demonstrate that qualitative study could make a crucial difference for understanding and thereby changing patients' noncompliance with their health programs."

Two sets of participants are to be described: the subjects and the researchers. The latter group is ignored in traditional research reports; in qualitative research reports, we may include a "Researchers" subheading before or after the subjects section to specify the perspectives through which data were identified, collected, and analyzed. Examples:

Undergraduate students enrolled in a methods course received extra credit for submitting typed accounts of "finding myself frustrated"; they then participated in a collaborative analysis group.

The interviewer was a married Caucasian mother, about 10 years older, on average, than the single Hispanic mothers.

Later, the discussion section can mention the ways research features seem to have given rise to aspects of the data and findings. Throughout a qualitative research report, one specifies whatever one knows about one's access to data and understandings in recognition that researchers, and not just their subjects, are meaning-makers. These specifications serve as reminders that, in contrast with traditional efforts to control-out variability, we instead point to how findings were situationally constituted—how they came into being in the particular situation.

The second set of participants is the persons who provide actions or verbal accounts or both for the study. "Who" these subjects are is part of the research situation. In qualitative accounts, however, the goal is not to identify moderator or intervening variables or even limits to "generalizability," but rather to evoke for readers the circumstances out of which subjects approached the research task. The implication is that we might expect similar findings in similar circumstances.

Procedures

The level of detail with which the remaining procedures are described depends on the probable readers' familiarity with them. The major purpose is to help readers see how the findings became apparent. Readers can then check whether their impressions are similar to the author's as they try out the procedures, either with the data provided or with their own examples. Differences in understandings of the subject matter can then be related to formal procedure, researcher interests, participants' circumstances, and/or researcher sensitivity and reflective discipline.

When a manuscript is written for a journal that specializes in a particular qualitative approach, a brief methodological description may suffice. Even then, one should cite published work that fully illustrates the general method. One should also mention any innovations, refinements, or deviations from the cited work.

Nevertheless, for the sake of communicating helpfully across qualitative research traditions, technical terms usually should be explained. For example, instead of simply reporting

> Standard memo procedures recorded and documented the analysis.

one might add

> That is, as I reread each cluster of statements for each client, I dated my reflection on identified themes and cross-referenced notations of similar themes. The cross-reference scheme was as follows: . . .

Instead of reporting only

> A general structure was then generated from the situated descriptions.

one could say,

> I had maintained an informal log of themes that were recurring across my summaries of each boy's account of having been bored. Now I set up a working table of themes, with excerpts from each summary that illustrated that theme. Often, I returned to the original transcript for greater detail; sometimes that return

led me to modify an overly abstract or forced characterization. Thus, the steps were not unidirectional, but rather followed a version of the hermeneutic circle of reviewing prior understandings in the light of new ones. Table 3 shows the current form of the themes and illustrative instances for each boy.

The preceding description of procedural steps shows that, in qualitative research, interpretation is not mechanical, but indeed is contingent on the researcher's perspective. For some readerships, it is helpful to acknowledge this point further by mentioning that insights about the data come, not just while sitting before it, but also while reading a novel, discussing the research with a colleague, musing while driving to work, and so on.

It is always advisable to specify any request made to participants, such as, "Please describe an instance when you were angry at yourself." Similarly, the queries the researcher posed to the data should be specified. Examples:

What is essential to this account being an instance of anger at self?

What is being said here about the person's relation to self, world, and others, and to past, present, and future?

How does this account differ from Fischer's structure of becoming angry (toward another)?

Such specification is not just a matter of method, but also qualifies the character of the ensuing findings.

Within the method section, one also describes the various steps followed to ensure that all available data were taken into account, that one did not impose prior meanings on data but rather allowed the data to "coauthor" meanings, and that other parties were involved in agreeing on consensual descriptions or overall agreement. As mentioned earlier, it is advisable not to evoke notions of validation, which in turn evoke a positivist or other correspondence paradigm that too readily takes some readers out of the study's frame of reference. Again, the "wind out of sails" tactic can be helpful. One might mention in a sentence that current readers may contribute helpful qualifications, felicitous phrasings, disagreements, and so on through which the research may be furthered. One may footnote how the interested reader may obtain, at cost, copies of original accounts, intermediate analyses, and so on. Overall, the author conveys the disciplined, rigorous nature of the reflective work.

In the manuscript's next section, the presentation of findings (a term I prefer to *results,* which can be confused with a mechanically processed product), the author takes care to allow a second rigor to be evident—that of faithful representation of what the researchers found (Fischer, 1994). Readers can more readily appreciate the empirical nature of the study and the researcher's disciplined attitude when examples are provided of researcher assumptions that were discovered during the analysis of data and then were either put aside or acknowledged as perspectival access to the subject matter. Example:

> Along the way, we realized that we had been assuming that "being impatient" was a negative state; as we looked more closely, we saw that, in their impatience, participants were concerned about their failed responsibility.

Another example:

> In the process of comparing our analyses of the crime victims' reports, we realized that my political science background and valuing of community had shown up in my analyses. Because we then readily found that dimension in all the accounts, we retained it in our findings but specified the value through which it became evident.

CRAFT ALTERNATIVE PRESENTATIONS OF FINDINGS IN ACCORDANCE WITH THE PURPOSES OF REPORTING THE STUDY

Qualitative research findings are indeed crafted—shaped with care and ingenuity. Organization, word choice, juxtapositions, and data excerpts are all calculated to represent and evoke the subject matter—the event or situation as it was lived by the participants. The presentation should resonate with the readers' own experiences, say more than its printed lines, evoke implicit connections and depth, and be credible in the reading, all the while respecting the ambiguity inherent to human understandings. First, of course, the findings must have been well enough developed to be of archival value. Although there is always more to learn, the account of the subject matter must be coherent and tell a full story with no unidentified gaps in understanding.

Again, the intended readership should influence the level of findings and the forms of reporting one chooses. To illustrate this choice, I draw extensively from a research report by Fischer and Wertz (1979), "Empirical Phenomenological Analyses of Being Criminally Victimized." We presented six forms of our study's findings to illustrate research phases and to demonstrate that the findings of each phase can serve a different purpose for different audiences. The original data were transcribed descriptions, provided by 50 victims, of what was going on prior to the crime, what it was like to go through the event, and what happened after that.

Individual Case Synopsis

To develop this form of finding, we asked the transcription, "What reveals and is essential to this person's experience of being criminally victimized?" We wrote in the person's words or in close approximations. This was our first step in developing our general findings (general condensation). The synopses also serve as a first form of findings. Here is the first tenth of one case synopsis:

> Upon returning home from a family outing shortly after Christmas, the R. family noticed that the bottom panel of the front door was broken, the glass shattered. Mr. R. thought that children must have been playing.
>
> When he went inside, he saw the candy dish on the floor rather than on stereo as usual. He looked around and saw a pair of pants lying on the steps and thought the house might have been ransacked. He walked into the living room and when he saw the stereo gone, he was in disbelief. He knew robbing existed but felt "it would never happen to me." He screamed out to his wife, "Don't come in," thinking someone might still be there, but Mrs. R. had already gone inside. . . .

Exemplar (Post General Condensation) Case Synopsis

Here, we asked the individual case synopsis, "How does this person's experience exemplify what is true for all our victims of crime?" That is, "What is most evocatively representative of each theme in the general condensation" (presented below, after the exemplar synopsis)? Again, we wrote in the person's words or in close approximations. This form is necessarily more succinct than the original synopsis because only those features that illustrate what was true for all the subjects are preserved. Here is the first fourth of an exemplar case synopsis:

> Mrs. K. is walking through the shopping center parking lot with her children. She holds her purse lightly and pays little attention to the sound of kids running. Suddenly, these blue-jeaned black kids grab her purse, which she finds herself releasing for fear of injury. She yells for several minutes for help and for her children to stop chasing the thieves. She grows both increasingly furious and frightened for her children. There is no one to help, only an old lady getting into a car. As the shock wears off, Mrs. K. goes to Hornes, and for 10 minutes looks for a policeman to whom to report the details. She doesn't expect much help or recovery of the purse, but they're who you turn to. . . .

Case synopses provide readers with concrete examples that reverberate with their own lives, thus intimating the full structure of being criminally victimized. The briefer exemplar synopsis is useful when time or space is limited, as in journal articles to introduce concrete instances of the topic under study, or when readers must develop a quick sense of the phenomenon if they are to become interested in reading further, as in reports to legislators or in grant applications. The richer detail of the longer case synopsis foreshadows the general findings less succinctly but more vividly. These longer accounts have been used with criminals by counselors, and we used them in community workshops on crime problems to encourage sensitivity to the individual victim's plight.

General Condensation

Here, we asked the individual case synopses, "What is essential to all these personal meanings? How do they reveal the existential (including social) meaning of being criminally victimized?" We wrote in general terms that collapsed/gathered the concrete expression of earlier findings, and we organized the account temporally. Here is the first fourth of the general condensation.

> Being criminally victimized is a disruption of daily routine. It is a disruption that compels one, despite personal resistance, to face one's fellow as predator and oneself as prey, even though all the while anticipating consequences, planning, acting, and looking to others for assistance. These efforts to little avail, one experiences vulnerability, separateness, and helplessness in the face of the callous, insensitive, often anonymous enemy. Shock and disbelief give way to puzzlement, strangeness, and then to a sense of the crime as perverse, unfair, undeserved. Whether or not expressed immediately, the victim experiences a general inner protest, anger or range, and a readiness for retaliation, for revenge against the violator.
>
> As life goes on, the victim finds him/herself pervasively attuned to the possibility of victimization—through a continued sense of reduced agency, of the other as predatory, and of community as inadequately supportive. More particularly, one continues to live the victimization through recollections of the crime, even worse imagined outcomes, vigilant suspiciousness of others, sensitivity to news of disorder and crime, criticalness of justice system agents, and desires to make sense of it all.

The usefulness of the general condensation is its provision of a succinct sense of the phenomenon, a form of the findings that can be kept in mind by a wide readership. Its compact, temporal form (not fully evident above) allows quick comparison of the phases of the experience. The limitation of this condensed version is that it does not retain the richness of the lengthier versions—their concreteness and variations within general themes.

Illustrated Narrative

Here, we selected excerpts from the original transcripts and presented them under themes that characterized all victims, again organized temporally, under the headings "Living Routinely," "Being Disrupted," "Being Violated," "Reintegrating," and "Going On." Our first version was 15 double-spaced typed pages (see Fischer, 1984, for a full published version). Here are two segments:

> [from "Being Violated"] where the victim is subject to recurring crime, the indignation or outrage additionally vacillates with despair, hopelessness, resignation. "Sometimes you wonder, you feel like because there don't seem to be nothing that will solve this nonsense . . . you don't enjoy your home anymore . . .

You can only take so much stuff . . . You just feel like putting your house for sale and getting out of here"; "I'm sorry that I even helped my mother to move here . . . I really feel bad about it. When I move out I want her to go someplace that's going to be safe too . . . I'm scared to death because I don't know . . ."

[from "Reintegrating"] The victim begins to assimilate and overcome the violation by "doing something" to protect against future intrusions. "I've got different locks on my house now but maybe I should really be thinking about a burglar alarm type of thing. Because you don't want that uncertainty, that disruption of what is taking place"; "I had everything in my purse. But I cleaned out my purse since then and I leave very little of that stuff in there [pay check, phone numbers]."

This form of finding retains the temporal unfolding of the experience while combining both general and concrete aspects of being criminally victimized. Diverse populations have readily understood it, and implications have been drawn for a range of policy decisions. For example, safety counseling is useful when police arrive, but personal counseling is not useful until later in the social sense-making phase. The disadvantage of this form of findings, of course, is its length, which cannot be accommodated by many publication formats.

In addition to the above forms, the Fischer and Wertz (1979) chapter also presented Fischer's condensed, one-paragraph structure of being criminally victimized and segments from Wertz's (1985) general psychological structure, which addressed the psychological organization of the experience of being criminally victimized, highlighting the previously implicit horizons and structural interrelations of its essential constituents. My point in presenting these excerpts is to emphasize that one can choose the depth, generality/abstraction, and concreteness with which to present findings to different readerships. For some purposes, one could compose a narrative, such as a journalist might write, with illustrations.

DISCUSS THE FINDINGS: SPELL OUT THE "SO WHAT?"

Qualitative research findings are so rich and yet so difficult to convey in limited space that some authors seem to peter out in this section, leaving the findings to stand on their own. At this point in the manuscript, however, one ought to spell out the study's implications. The discussion should return to the description of the study's purposes (the "statement of the problem") and highlight what the findings imply for that domain. The significance of having used a qualitative approach and the advantages and disadvantages of one's particular method, given the findings, are presented here. Differences that procedural variations in method seem to have made are discussed. Philosophical, theoretical, content, and methodological implications are presented. In short, this section of the research report presents one's claims about the significance of the project's findings.

Acknowledging the study's limitations is good scholarship, part of the qualitative researcher's task of situating the study and its findings. Reporting surprises and newly discovered relevance of other authors' work likewise testifies to scholarship. Indeed, the contribution of the qualitative study is made clearest when its connections with earlier understandings are indicated in a circumspect manner. Speculations are appropriate here so long as they are pertinent to the report's story line and are clearly identified as speculations. Suggestions for future research design also are appropriate.

REVIEW THE DRAFT

English 101

Here are some reminders about clear writing, which we tend to forget when we are caught up in content. Reading a manuscript aloud helps us realize where text is unclear and where shortening a sentence or otherwise changing punctuation would clarify meaning. Be mindful that written communication works best when it adheres to conventional grammar and style. Excise all nonessential words, phrases, clauses, sentences, and paragraphs (see Zinsser, 1976).

My list of the most frequently encountered sources of unclear writing includes (a) passive voice, (b) unduly long sentences (anything beyond three lines is suspect), (c) out-of-order clauses (which clauses modify which other parts of the sentence?), (d) undefined terms, (e) unclear referents (do not use the word *this* as a noun), (f) the word *data* used as singular, (g) inconsistency in number (e.g., "this person, they"), and (h) nonparallel construction (e.g., "the researcher numbers each unit *to* indicate its initial location and *for* checking for inclusion").

Multiple Readers

Be your own reader. After putting the draft away for a few weeks or so, review your draft for that strong story line. Standard advice about checking for consistency across the introduction, method, findings, and discussion sections holds for qualitative research too. Redundancy that helps keep the reader on your course is positive. A summary and an abstract should both recapitulate the study (the author should ask him- or herself, If either portion is all a reader looks at, given the constraints of brevity, will that portion have adequately represented the study?).

It is a very good idea to ask several colleagues to read the draft both for clarity and for style. Different colleagues will note different areas that could be cleaned up. You will revise your own text with each of many readings.

Designing and crafting one's report with these considerations in mind enhance the chances that editors and reviewers will provide useful comments and recommend publication of a revision. This same care also assists readers in understanding one's work as intended and increases its contribution to psychology's evolving body of understanding.

REFERENCES

American Psychological Association (APA). (1994). *Publication manual of the American Psychological Association* (4th ed.). Washington, DC: Author.

Elliott, R., Fischer, C. T., & Rennie, D. L. (in press). Evolving guidelines for the publication of qualitative research studies in psychology and related fields. *British Journal of Clinical Psychology.*

Fischer, C. T. (1984). Being criminally victimized: An illustrated structure. *American Behavioral Scientist, 27,* 723-738.

Fischer, C. T. (1994). Rigor in qualitative research: Reflexive and presentational. *Methods* (annual edition), 21-27.

Fischer, C. T., & Wertz, F. J. (1979). Empirical phenomenological analyses of being criminally victimized. In A. Giorgi, R. Knowles, & D. Smith (Eds.), *Duquesne studies in phenomenological psychology* (Vol. 3, pp. 135-158). Pittsburgh, PA: Duquesne University Press.

Wertz, F. J. (1985) Method and findings in a phenomenological psychological study of a complex life-event: Being criminally victimized. In A. Giorgi (Ed.), *Phenomenology and psychological research* (pp. 155-216). Pittsburgh, PA: Duquesne University Press.

Zinsser, W. (1994). *On writing well: An informed guide to writing nonfiction.* New York: HarperCollins.

APPLYING QUALITATIVE METHODS IN PSYCHOLOGY

CHAPTER 10

Exploring Multicultural Issues Using Qualitative Methods

Lisa A. Suzuki
Maria Prendes-Lintel
Lauren Wertlieb
Amena Stallings

Qualitative methods in research provide an appropriate means to examine multicultural settings and diverse populations. Understanding the lived experiences and meanings of events to the lives of research participants is often a focus in qualitative study. Although it is difficult to generalize multicultural themes in relation to the use of qualitative methods across studies, we illustrate for the reader some concerns and provide recommendations that have arisen from our work. This chapter highlights some issues that can confront the qualitative researcher as she or he undertakes the complex process of accurately capturing and understanding the experiences of diverse individuals within a cultural context. Although many factors may be considered multicultural in

AUTHORS' NOTE: The Cuban Pedro Pan was funded by a New York University School of Education Research Challenge Fund grant.

nature, this chapter focuses primarily on conducting research with various racial/ethnic minority community members. The issues presented here may have implications for the study of cultural topics in different contexts (Asher & Asher, chap. 11, this volume, on conducting qualitative research with lesbian populations).

Material from a qualitative study of unaccompanied Cuban refugee children and adolescents now in adulthood are used here to illustrate various cultural issues. Results of this study were examined by using a constant comparative theme analysis. This chapter discusses the importance of the following: (a) understanding the researchers' interest and investment in the project; (b) comparing interview skills; (c) developing a collaborative relationship between the researcher and the community; (d) retaining the complexity of the multicultural context (history, influences of demographic variables, multiple sources of information); (e) integrating and processing affective content; (f) identifying emerging themes and coding for meaning; (g) writing up the thematic results; and (h) integrating psychological theory.

THE PEDRO PAN STUDY

To illustrate the complexities of using qualitative methods in the multicultural context, we focus on our study of Cuban unaccompanied children and adolescents now in adulthood. Operation Pedro Pan was developed to help Cuban parents send their children, unaccompanied, to the United States to avoid Communist indoctrination. The unaccompanied group that participated in this study came to the United States between 1960 and 1962 during Operation Pedro Pan, which began shortly after Castro established his socialist government in 1959. This relocation movement was organized primarily under the auspices of the Catholic Church in conjunction with government agencies in the United States.

By 1962, 14,048 unaccompanied Cuban children and adolescents had arrived in the United States. Approximately half of the children were met by family members; most of the others were reunited with their families when the freedom flights from Havana to Miami began on December 1, 1965. Some of the children and adolescents remained in the refugee camps until their parents arrived. Others were relocated throughout the United States in Cuban group homes, orphanages, or foster homes under the Cuban Children's Program. For the majority of the children and adolescents, the separation lasted approximately 3 to 4 years (Walsh, 1971). A few of the parents were not allowed to leave Cuba or decided to remain and never relocated to the United States.

In this study, information obtained from the Pedro Pans and their parents and offspring revealed a great deal regarding the transgenerational impact of these refugee experiences. This project has implications for other communities because nearly all refugee groups relocating to the United States include unaccompanied children (B. Walsh, personal communication, November 2, 1995).

This research project can contribute to an understanding of the transgenerational impact of these events. It should be noted that the majority of the interviews were conducted by telephone. The team did meet with members of the Cuban unaccompanied community in person at their reunion gala in Miami, Florida.

Understanding the Researcher's Interest and Investment in the Project

In conducting qualitative research on multicultural populations, it is important for the researcher, the participants, and the readership to understand the motivations that inform the project. Qualitative researchers are participant-observers of the phenomena they study. Therefore, it is imperative to acknowledge and explore how a researcher's personal perspectives shape the research experience. This includes guidelines for interview questions, participant selection procedures, interactions between participants and investigators, data collection procedures, and interpretation of results.

The originators of the Cuban study conceptualized the initial project while discussing their frustration and dismay at how "minorities" were so misunderstood in the literature and how their classroom experiences and texts often neglected to mention the rich histories and experiences outside the "mainstream" culture. In addition, they thought the field often failed to acknowledge members of minority communities who had achieved high educational attainment and socioeconomic status.

In this context, one team member shared that her "dream" was to study a group of unaccompanied Cuban refugee children and adolescents who were now in adulthood. It was a group she knew well because she was one of them. She recounted her journey as part of a group of children who arrived in the United States from Cuba in the early 1960s. Not much had been written about this group since their arrival. She described how the group had fared well and were not demonstrating pathology or problems. The team thought someone needed to document these experiences to ensure that the history and experiences of this group were not forgotten. Given this initial agenda, the study conducted had a nonpathological focus. The interview opened with a general prompt—that is, "Tell me about your refugee experience. What comes to mind?" Follow-up questions explored coping strategies, relationships, support systems, dramatic life changes, acculturation, current impact of experience, and so on. Stories of strength and resilience were obtained, as well as stories that revealed a negative impact of the refugee experience on the particular participant.

Although the researchers believed that they were coming from a "strength"-oriented perspective, they learned through the interview process that some of their questions implied a negative impact of events. For example, one question was asked about how the refugee experience affected the refugees' "current sense of stability." When phrased in this way, participants hesitated to answer and often responded with a question: "What do you mean?" It appeared that the term *stability* implied a somewhat negative connotation, especially because the question was asked at the end of the interview. The stability question was revised to use more neutral language: "How does the refugee experience affect you now?"

As new members joined the research team already in progress, it became apparent that some training was needed to assist them in understanding not only the context of the Cuban study experience but also the agenda for the project. At times during team meetings, new members who were not involved in the interviewing but primarily in transcribing tapes had more pathological interpretations of the interview material. Other team members who had been involved with the community responded by pointing out the historical and cultural context in which the events occurred. It appeared as though two perspectives existed: (a) that of the interviewers (more experienced team members) focusing on cultural context and (b) that of the transcribers (new team members) focusing primarily on the content of the interview. Discussions within the research team were important as a cross-check on the data analysis procedure. It became clear that the process of coding the data and understanding the thematic codes must be flexible enough to encompass various interpretations, and in some cases themes were modified on the basis of discussion.

Comparing Interview Skills

In discussions with other qualitative researchers focusing on the experiences of diverse groups, it became apparent that the ability of the research team member to engage the participant was imperative. As one colleague put it, "Not everyone is a good interviewer." Listening to the tapes and reading the transcripts reflected different levels of interview skills and motivation in the project. For example, some team members were able to engage a participant in an almost conversation-like interview experience as the discussion flowed naturally from one area to another. Awareness of multicultural constructs, such as racial identity, acculturation, and marginalization, informed the interview process. The interviewer picked up subtle cues from the participant to move the interview into various areas on the basis of the information shared. This led to richer stories, a more "personalized" interview, more data for analysis, and new foci for interpretation. Other interviewers stuck strictly to the guiding questions, and the interview tended to flow less smoothly and with briefer responses.

Developing a Collaborative Relationship
Between the Researcher and the Community

Bridging and forging a connection with the community under study is imperative in conducting qualitative research with diverse populations. Qualitative research involves an important consensual component with the community being studied (Hill, Thompson, & Williams, 1997). Although the importance of this may seem obvious in conducting all types of research, this issue is even more pronounced in a qualitative framework. To obtain entry into the community, one is confronted with a variety of concerns. In the case of the Cuban study, one principal investigator was a member of the community, whereas the other members were not. Potential issues of mistrust were based on a perceived lack of knowledge of the experiences facing the group, and questions were raised about why the team members were invested in the topic and for what purpose the results were being used. Research team members were frequently asked, "What is your interest in this study? How did you come to know about Pedro Pan?" Answers often centered around their relationship with the team member who was a part of the community and the agenda to document these important events. Given the history of racial/ethnic conflict in the United States, prior to visiting the Cuban community at their reunion gala in Miami the principal investigators also had serious discussions regarding how research participants would view team members from different racial/ethnic and cultural backgrounds (Japanese American, African American, and European American).

In addition, during the interview it was not uncommon for the interviewers to be asked about their racial/ethnic backgrounds. Often, comments from participants during the telephone interviews were based on the surnames of the interviewers—for example, "Suzuki, is that a Japanese name? Are you a Pedro Pan? What is your interest in Pedro Pan?" Again, responses to these questions focused on reiterating connections with the member of the community on the research team in a leadership position. This seemed to be imperative to gaining the trust of the group. As one team leader put it, there was "entry and trust by association."

This reliance on the community member of the research team created a sense of dependency on this one person. As one researcher wrote:

> I am reluctant to view myself as anything more than a mouthpiece to the experiences of this group. I am constantly humbled at the level of trust this group has given me over the years. I recall telling Maria [community member] that I felt my job was coming to an end with this Cuban group. In the beginning there was not much out there being written or studied with regard to this group. Now members of the community like Maria are beginning to focus their attention on documenting this important piece of history. I believe my hesitancy is based upon the assumptions that I have made with regard to my belief that members of the community possess a depth of understanding that cannot always be captured by an outsider.

Although this research team member recognized that her thoughts regarding this project stemmed from a personal agenda, it was important to discuss these issues with the team. In discussing the importance of collaboration, the community team member (Maria) noted the following:

... we [insider] cannot see the forest from the trees. We can't always see what fits and what can't fit. You (outsider) can see transcultural things and make connections. It's like they say, as qualitative researchers we are the instruments ... but we [insiders] can contaminate things ... we try to be objective but we can't always ...

When I look at our data my "heart tugs." I want to include everything ... people further removed [outsiders] see pretty much the same thing as I do but I can get stuck in the data ... I can't always condense things into thematic categories.

The importance of the depth of understanding mentioned by the outsider team member was also noted by the insider:

At times I felt that they couldn't understand because they weren't a part of it ... then it would strike me ... she's got it.

Qualitative research methods emphasize collaborative relationships and the importance of all members of the team in identifying and communicating the "meaning" of participants' experiences. Establishing a true collaboration is imperative so that issues may be discussed in an informed and open manner.

Retaining the Complexity of the Multicultural Context

Understanding Historical Context. Understanding history is imperative in multicultural research using any methodology. People of color have been inappropriately pathologized at times because of a lack of understanding of the context in which the participants existed. In the case of the Cuban study, team members had to be wary of interpreting results according to a deficit model. For example, understanding the refugee context and the "desperation" of the times is imperative for appropriate interpretation of the responses of participants.

Demographic Influences. It is important to consider multiple factors that may influence participants differentially. For example, demographic variables such as age, socioeconomic status of family prior to arrival, socioeconomic status of family once reunited in the United States, gender, and religion appeared to affect the adjustment of the Cuban refugee children and adolescents now in adulthood. Including these variables in the interpretation process is imperative to understanding more fully the meaning of their experiences. For example, one important source of coping that came through in the interviews was religion. God was described by some as a "universal parent"; others reported they sought comfort and solace through prayer.

Multiple Sources of Information. In conducting research with multicultural populations, data can be obtained from multiple sources in addition to interviews with community members. These include historical documents (e.g., articles, films), interviews with community leaders, visitation to field sites, and observation of community activities. In the Cuban study, information was obtained through documentaries, meetings with a relocation organizer, field trips with community members to refugee camps, and exposure to various events in the Cuban community (e.g., reunion gala, tours of centers of Cuban life). As the project progressed, the team came into contact with a supportive network of other researchers, many of whom were part of the Cuban community, exploring aspects of adjustment of the unaccompanied group. It was helpful to discuss findings with them to consider new and alternative interpretations and validation of the team's own observations. In addition, the research team experienced a "snowball effect" as interviewees shared lists of additional people to contact who had been part of this unaccompanied group.

Integrating and Processing Affective Content

In identifying the meaning of experiences in peoples' lives, the emotional content of the stories informs the researcher regarding the impact of the experience. In our study of Cuban refugees, the individuals' affect during the interviews coincided with the amount of information or description or both of their personal accounts of relocation to the United States. Some interviews began with a distant and removed stance of the interviewees as evidenced by responses like, "I don't remember much . . . " or "It was not that bad." Often, as the interviews progressed, the interviewees appeared to connect more to the memories of their experience, and changes in tone of voice and degree of openness combined to bring the interviews to a deeper level. As one team member wrote, there seemed to be "an obvious need to tell their story."

Other interviewees were forthcoming as they told their stories yet appeared to be emotionally disconnected from the words they were speaking. These individuals would use words like *traumatic* in describing their relocation sites, abusive situations, or degree of fear or loneliness they remembered feeling. At times, many of these stories were told with what appeared to be a lack of emotion during the interview. This often coincided with the ways these particular interviewees discussed their coping styles during the time of relocation. As children and adolescents, they were often the ones who kept their fears and anger to themselves: "I just worked hard and kept busy." Others expressed their emotions in solitude: "I cried myself to sleep." It appeared that the emotional context expressed during the present-day interviews reflected to some degree the ways participants may have coped during the time of their refugee experiences.

The emotional tone of the interview was often not readily seen in the transcribed text. Research team members decided that, on completion of the transcript, one member of the team would go back and listen to the tape again and code for emotional content. This additional procedure was time-consuming but yielded very important information.

Observations during meetings with members of the community and field trips also yielded a great deal of affective data. For example, during the visit to the refugee camps, the researchers gained information as participants walked through the camp, recalling stories of their experiences based on what they saw. The Cuban member of the research team, tears rolling down her face, walked through the camp, saying only, "I remember." The power of this experience deeply affected the other team members.

Therefore, it is important to integrate the emotional reactions of the researchers in this process. At particular points during the Cuban study, research team members discussed how they were being affected by their involvement in the study. Feelings ranged from connection and empathy with participants to isolation and being clearly outside this community.

Identifying Emerging Themes and Coding for Meaning

As the research team entered the phase of coding transcripts, the importance of working collaboratively was clear. Initially, the team worked collectively on identifying general thematic areas based on the interview transcripts they had reviewed. On the basis of these general themes, each team member independently coded the same transcript. Meetings were held to discuss intercoder reliability. It was interesting that the general themes held up fairly well across coders, but the level of subcoding varied. Some team members wished to have more detailed coding schemes; others wished to keep it general. Themes were modified on the basis of discussion. The Cuban member of the research team served as an auditor checking the data trail. As the coding became more consistent, the team was divided into pairs. Each transcript was coded by two members of the team independently and then audited by a third member.

Writing up the Thematic Results

Initially, the writing of the actual paper was difficult. So many stories each had so much importance. Two team members took primary responsibility for writing up the initial text. The team then met to discuss the write-up. It was interesting to observe the process as people identified with particular stories or wanted particular pieces of a transcript added to bolster a part of a thematic discussion.

Integrating Psychological Theory

Integrating existing psychological theories in interpreting the various themes can provide important linkages in understanding meaning from one's qualitative data. For example, in the Cuban study, understanding trauma, resilience, and acculturation provided potential theoretical frameworks in connection with the information shared by participants.

For example, interviewees often used the word *traumatic* to describe their experiences of leaving Cuba without their parents, of uncertainty and fear of the unknown on arrival in the United States, of isolation because of language and cultural barriers, and at times of maltreatment at their relocation sites. Trauma has been defined in the literature as "the effects of external events impinging upon the individual—events that are beyond the usual expectation of what life should be" (Apfel & Simon, 1996, p. 6). The experiences of the Cuban group clearly fit within the trauma domain.

Results of the Cuban project were also informed by studies on resiliency that point to many factors that may have contributed to fostering the achievements of this group. One factor is resourcefulness, which calls to action a child's ability to "make something out of nothing . . . and extract some amount of human warmth and loving kindness" (Apfel & Simon, 1996, p. 9). The majority of interviewees in this study recalled relationships with peers, siblings, and adult caretakers as creating a loving and supportive atmosphere. Another important factor of resiliency is the ability to recognize "an experience not only as a personal travail but as a phenomenon affecting others as well" (Apfel & Simon, 1996, p. 10). This can be seen in the interviews as participants recalled that "it was just as bad if not worse for others" or "my friends [at the orphanage] made it bearable."

The above-mentioned issues are only a few of many that contribute to the development of resiliency under traumatic conditions. These factors most likely accumulate during a traumatic experience and continue to manifest themselves throughout one's life. Garbarino and Kostelny (1996) discuss ameliorating factors leading to resiliency and coping. These factors could be applied to understanding the widespread professional and personal success within the Cuban unaccompanied population. Cognitive competence was discussed as a way children could gain mastery over their environment. Many members of this Cuban refugee population have received high levels of education and hold advanced degrees. Emphasis on education was mentioned by participants as a value they held both in Cuba and in the United States. It could be ascertained that this need for intellectual competence served an important purpose during the time of relocation and continues to act as a driving force in their adult lives. Similarly, experiences of self-efficacy and corresponding self-confidence are described as responses to stressful experiences that could increase one's capacity for resiliency. This may also be seen as characteristic of many participants in this study who emerged as successful and goal-driven individuals.

Some participants also noted the value of acculturation and at times assimilation as they adjusted to the U.S. culture. Many mentioned the importance of learning the language and of focusing on school achievement as a means to get ahead. One described learning English as a "do or die situation." Some recalled experiences of assimilation in their attempts to fit in and of rejecting everything that was Cuban; others acculturated and felt that they were bicultural: "I feel comfortable going in and out. I can be in both cultures."

Given the initial perspective of the research team to focus on coping, the theoretical applications that appeared to fit were those linked to coping with traumatic circumstances, resilience, and cultural adjustment. Despite this orientation, it was important for the team to discuss alternative theoretical considerations in particular cases (some interviewees had not made good adjustments and shared ongoing problems they believed stemmed from their early experience).

SUMMARY AND CONCLUSION

Through usage of a qualitative method, the unique experiences of multicultural groups can be studied. As illustrated through the Cuban refugee study, each participant within a community may have a unique story to share. In investigating the impact of the refugee experience on individuals, it was clear that degrees of coping styles, adjustment, as well as protective and defensive efforts on the part of the children during this time varied. Qualitative methods enabled a diversity of perspectives to emerge for a richer documentation of this important historical event. Stories and reactions to the relocation experience depended, in part, on the age of the child during the time of relocation, the amount of preparation by parents for the separation and the information provided by parents prior to leaving Cuba, the quality of life at the relocation site, as well as the amount of time the children were separated from their parents before reunification. As noted in this chapter, the motivations and investments of the researcher clearly affected the qualitative procedures from the recruitment of subjects to the determination of interview guidelines.

Integrating various factors (e.g., history, demographics, multiple sources of information, emotional content) enabled the researchers to understand better the complexities of perceptions and experiences within the Cuban refugee group. Application of psychological theories also provided an important framework for conceptualization. For example, despite what many participants reported as a "traumatic" experience during childhood, this population has emerged as quite successful (e.g., socioeconomic status, occupation, education) in their adult lives. Answers to questions about how this diverse group of individuals endured these traumas and what enabled them to do so can only be captured through a qualitative method.

REFERENCES

Apfel, R. J., & Simon, B. (Eds.). (1996). *Minefields in their hearts: The mental health of children in war and communal violence.* New Haven, CT: Yale University Press.

Garbarino, J., & Kostelny, K. (1996). What do we need to know to understand children in war and community violence? In R. J. Apfel & B. Simon (Eds.), *Minefields in their hearts: The mental health of children in war and communal violence* (pp. 46-51). New Haven, CT: Yale University Press.

Hill, C. E., Thompson, B. J., & Williams, E. N. (1997). A guide to conducting consensual qualitative research. *Counseling Psychologist, 25,* 517-572.

Walsh, B. O. (1971). Cuban refugee children. *Journal of Inter-American Studies and World Affairs, 13*(3-4), 378-450.

CHAPTER 11

Qualitative Methods for an Outsider Looking In
Lesbian Women and Body Image

Nancy Salkin Asher
Kenneth Chavinson Asher

From 1994 to 1997, I conducted a qualitative study that investigated how lesbian women felt about their bodies and how their body images were affected by their lesbianism. The study focused on eight lesbians, all of whom shared with me their attitudes and opinions about such things as their bodies, eating and exercise behavior, and sexuality. Because I am not a lesbian, I anticipated some potential resistance or awkwardness in conversations about such personal matters. I expected to be asked, "Why are you so interested in lesbian attitudes?" Not only did I not know any of these women before I interviewed them, but I did not intimately know their culture either. If they had looked at me askance, I would not have been surprised. Before I began the project focusing on this minority population, I prepared myself for issues of disclosure—on both my part and my participants'.

In the end, the disclosure issue did not present a significant problem in this study. This and other potential issues were minimized mainly because of a conscientious adherence to the tenets of good qualitative methodology. But before explaining further, some background is in order.

Why was I interested in this minority population? In America today, a pervasive "culture-of-thinness" exists in which the reigning standard of female beauty is one of fitness and slenderness. In this dominant culture, larger women perceive themselves and are perceived to be less beautiful than smaller women.

AUTHORS' NOTE: Although the second author did not participate directly in conducting this study, he provided valuable assistance throughout the process. In addition, he actively contributed to the writing of this chapter.

This was the first premise of the study and was supported by ample research (Collins & Plahn, 1988; Jacobi & Cash, 1984; Wooley, 1984).

The study's second premise was perhaps implicitly suggested by the literature but was based primarily on my own personal feelings and observations: This thin beauty ideal was somehow created by, influenced by, or associated with the preferences of men. Support for this supposition can be found in some existing literature (Ewen, 1977; Martin, 1989; Seid, 1994).

Although several studies have shown that contemporary American women accept the current beauty ideal (believing that thin bodies are most attractive), it is readily evident that this is a heterosexually based definition of attractiveness (Garner, Garfinkel, Schwartz, & Thompson, 1980; Gray, 1993; Jacobi & Cash, 1994; Kilbourne, 1994). Men, therefore, could be seen as directly or indirectly implicated in this mainstream definition of female beauty. In the most obvious interpretation, heterosexual women might be striving for beauty and thinness to appear sexually attractive to men. Or at a subtler level, the behaviors of women might be influenced by a patriarchal order that controls the means of shaping popular tastes and standards (Hesse-Biber, 1989).

I was interested in finding out whether lesbians somehow escaped current pressures to look thin and beautiful and whether this cultural incubation somehow led to stronger, healthier body images. A few studies have indicated that the elimination of male-induced pressure can or should result in fewer body image disturbances (Dworkin, 1988; Gettelman & Thompson, 1993; LaTorre & Wendenburg, 1983; Mintz & Betz, 1986; Siever, 1994). Other studies, however, have shown lesbianism to have little effect on body image, pointing instead to at-large cultural pressures that bear on all women regardless of sexual orientation (Brand, Rothblum, & Solomon, 1992; Dworkin, 1988; Eldridge & Gilbert, 1990; Mintz & Betz, 1986).

The point of this study, then, was not to define a lesbian body image or to compare the body image issues of lesbians with those of heterosexual women. The goal of the investigation was to illuminate how some lesbians experience these expectations and how the lesbian culture may contribute to or mitigate body image pressure.

Research that considers the relationship between lesbianism and body image is meager. Although a few studies have found that lesbians seem to have a more positive body image than heterosexual women, little research explains why this is the case. Most research on this topic primarily asks women to rate their eating habits, body image, and body parts in a questionnaire or survey (Berscheid, Walster, & Bohrnstedt, 1973; Wooley, 1984).

Because body image describes a complex relationship that may include identity, esteem, sexuality, cultural mores, and health issues, reductionistic surveys and context-independent questions seem to offer limited insight into the topic. Instead, a deeper understanding seemed to require a more exploratory methodology that would address more fully the reality of the relationship between lesbians and body image (Thompson, 1994). I wanted to conduct an investigation in the qualitative spirit that attempted to understand issues holistically and that assumed that nothing was trivial and everything had potential meaning (Lincoln & Guba, 1985).

An investigation of lesbian body image was particularly well suited for a qualitative approach for a variety of reasons, the first being the dearth of research on the topic. Before thinking about variables and instruments, it seemed crucial to focus on defining the issue itself. What is the nature of the relationship between lesbian women and their bodies? Do patterns or themes consistently show up? If patterns of thought or behavior exist, are they conscious, semiconscious, or subconscious? The first task in understanding this relationship was to begin drawing out the perceptions and attitudes of those involved.

This points to another reason why qualitative methodology was most appropriate: This investigation asked how a certain group of people view a particular aspect of their selves. It is an inquiry into belief, value, opinion, and attitude—human systems that are notoriously difficult to quantify. Thus, the study goes to the heart of the qualitative point of view, which values immensely the *description* (and not prediction) of the perceived reality of a select group of individuals. With minority populations like lesbian women, this commitment to the authenticity of the participants' point of view seems especially important.

How I was to recruit lesbian participants was one of my first challenges. I did not want to advertise the study, for fear of either too many respondents or a misconception of what I was trying to do. I decided to ask friends, colleagues, and acquaintances whether they knew of any lesbian women who might be willing to participate. In this way, the idea could be presented by a trusted individual and not an unknown researcher. After the first interviewees contacted other possible participants, I followed up with telephone calls and additional information. In this manner, each of the next six participants was recruited for the project.

This is how I began the study, and I continued the recruiting process by using the "snowball" method, the process whereby participants help solicit other potential participants (Taylor & Bogdan, 1984). After those first few interviews, the participants gave me the names of friends or acquaintances they thought might like to be interviewed as well. Participants would then casually brief their friends about the interview process, and shortly thereafter I would contact the potential participants to explain the focus and scope of the study. Each woman was told that participation was completely voluntary and that she could withdraw from the study at any time.

Obviously, the success of this recruiting method depended on the quality of the experience of the participants themselves. Thus, I used every means I could think of to make the participants as comfortable as possible and to facilitate a positive experience: The participants were told to choose the sites of the interviews, the time, their pseudonyms, and so on. I brought several audiotapes and allowed each interviewee to speak for as long as necessary—sometimes up to 3 or 3½ hours. I kept my interruptions to an absolute minimum and tried to maintain some levity throughout the interview process. Not only did these strategies help establish a comfortable and open dialogue, but they ensured that the interviews would be stimulating for the participants—increasing the likelihood of subsequent referrals for the study. In the end, recruiting was not an issue.

Nearly all participants had done substantial thinking about this topic prior to the actual interview, which eased the interview process significantly. Again, I attribute this to the snowball method of recruiting, which enabled a preliminary dialogue between potential participants and women who had already been interviewed.

The interview itself was based on a set of semistructured, open-ended questions that could elicit detailed information regarding each participant's interpretation of her body image. Throughout the interviews, I occasionally shared my own thoughts, feelings, experiences, and opinions, not to sway the participants, but to establish a trusting and open dialogue. I made a conscientious effort to diminish the power imbalance that is inherent in a researcher-participant relationship.

For instance, after a great deal of consideration, I decided that disclosing my heterosexuality at the start of each interview was important. I had been concerned that, as a cultural outsider, I might be received coolly and without the level of trust I needed to get the information I was looking for. This created considerable apprehension on my part. (This might be a common theme among researchers who study minority populations.) Fortunately, I received feedback from the first interviewees that this information was deeply appreciated; it seemed to assuage any suspicions about my motivations and quickly let the participants know a little more about me. By doing this at the beginning of the interview, it allowed for some purposeful banter prior to the interview itself and helped establish rapport. Most important, it sent a message that I was respectful of the participants' right to know who I was, why I was interested in them, and what I was willing to do to establish a forthright discussion. Each of the participants expressed acceptance and appreciation for the disclosure (although they told me of lesbian friends who might not have shared their graciousness).

Body image as a construct was purposefully left undefined. This was another deliberate move aimed at giving the participants a degree of control over the subject matter. Although my research had given me ample information on the body image construct, I did not present these findings to the participants. As it turned out, this was a productive decision. I believe that I got more information (and more authentic information) because I did not formally explain the body image construct. The literature review and my initial assumptions focused on the physical body itself (especially weight-related issues), but the participants actually spoke quite a lot about clothing, makeup, hairstyles, and other applied artifices that only indirectly had anything to do with the actual shape or size of their bodies. In addition, several participants did not distinguish between body and self. In other words, I learned that body image was often inherently bound to feelings and emotions, having little or nothing to do with the size, shape, or condition of the physical body itself. When they felt good in general, they felt good about their bodies.

I do not think this type of ambiguity made the body image construct less valid. Instead, I think it helped capture the complexity of the reality. The participants lived with this ambiguity. There was no reason for the study to smooth this over. The qualitative methodology was very helpful in recognizing and then relating this uncertainty, even if it added to the uncertainty of the results. Especially with minority groups, it seems crucial to me that investigators remain open to the richness and variety of experiences within that population. This is one way to avoid the stereotypes that are so easily attributed to minority populations. In this study, the wide-open body image construct helped me respect these differences.

It might also be the case that a minority group is not able to express or articulate a response because of a language barrier, a cultural misinterpretation, or an unfamiliarity with the subject matter. This study had no language barriers, but the subject matter was nevertheless difficult to communicate for many of the respondents.

I sometimes thought a participant was struggling to describe her body image, not because she questioned its existence, but because she could not nail down an absolute description for something that always seemed to be changing. I began to understand body image as an ephemeral construct—one that could fluctuate over years, months, or even days. It was not described as a fixed state, but as an elastic state of being highly dependent on a host of other influences that continually acted on it—for example, exercise, relationship status, work, and stress. Whether body image would be described in this way among a different group of lesbian women, or among straight women, or among men for that matter, was not clear to me.

In analyzing the information I was given, I also recognized an imbalance between commentary about tangible, concrete influences (e.g., mothers, exercise, friends, television commercials) and more abstract, implied, or subtle influences (e.g., culture, spirituality, politics, psychology). Although I do not doubt the validity of the former, I do wonder about the relative lack of discussion around the latter. It is entirely possible that abstract factors such as these may simply have been unimportant and therefore unmentioned. I also recognize that these factors are often more difficult to identify, elaborate on, and talk about. To illustrate this point, consider that all the participants talked about the desire to stay "fit" as a body image concern. Yet seldom did they mention the possibility that this desire might stem from a cultural expectation that fit women are somehow superior to out-of-shape women. Because deeper reasons such as these are subtly suggestive, inferred, or insinuated, the participants may not have fully accounted for their significance. This is no criticism; the whole point of subtle media manipulations and deep cultural mores, for example, is to influence societal members beneath the level of full consciousness. Without an interviewer who intentionally and carefully brings these issues to light, motivations such as these run the risk of going underreported. Even with this sample of bright, well-educated, and psychologically minded women, that possibility should be considered.

Throughout the interview process, I was also intrigued with the possibility that I was not getting to the bottom of all the issues—either because of information the participants did not want to reveal or because they did not know how to. One obvious example is the physical or sexual abuse that was a part of four participants' histories. Despite the fact that such abuse may have been extremely influential in their lives, it was not mentioned as a significant body image factor. This may have been for good reason: Perhaps the abuse had little effect on their body image. But if the abuse was viewed as important and the participants were unwilling to share these feelings with me, I had no way of knowing. I was therefore unable to account for this kind of potentially significant information.

To test best the conclusions I drew in the study, I once again turned to the participants themselves. Member checking gave the participants an opportunity to confirm the accuracy of my interpretations. This was another way to keep me on track, and it lent credibility to my interpretations.

One interesting aspect of this study was that the topic overlapped with an existing paradigm unique to the lesbian population. Lesbian "typology" (as defined in this study) referred to the butch/femme continuum—a method of typecasting that lesbians commonly use to conceptualize and talk about gay women's bodies, body images, and body attitudes. This presented a challenge to me, not because I was unfamiliar with the language, but because I did not have firsthand experience of the nuances of this subcultural practice. This issue was complicated by the ambiguous role that butch/femme typecasting plays in the lesbian community. The participants themselves could not precisely explain (let alone agree on) the meanings, definitions, uses, and shortcomings of the butch/femme terminology. Yet they all agreed that it was certainly an important factor in understanding and relating to the way many lesbians thought and felt about their bodies.

The butch/femme continuum has been a controversial part of lesbian culture for the past 100 years, so I was not surprised at the complexity of this issue (Soares, 1995). For example, two participants said the butch/femme typology was too limiting. One said:

> There are a lot of different groups living in the gay community. It seems like there's the butch dykes, you know, in the flannel shirts and jeans . . . definitely the femme—pretty lesbians, athletic dykes—there are those dykes that want to look like guys, grunge—the younger kids coming out. . . . you see a lot of androgynous, slick-looking gay women who have short black hair, piercings . . . k. d. lang wannabe's in a way. . . . you just see such a cross section, it's just amazing.

The simple butch/femme typology broke down for other participants for different reasons. One participant explained how she is considered masculine in heterosexual circles but quite femme in the lesbian world. It is easy to understand why her self-image and body image did not fit neatly into one or the other category. Another participant accepted that the typecasting existed but questioned how helpful the practice was when it came to body image issues.

A difficulty in studying this population, then, especially when using the qualitative approach, is the tendency to oversimplify issues like this one just to facilitate discussion. From the use of butch/femme terminology in the study, one may easily infer that certain types correspond to certain self-images and body images. Yet this correspondence doesn't seem to exist, or at least it didn't seem obvious from this particular study. Yet I could think of no way to conduct the interviews and no way to write up the research without using these terms.

This discussion leads to several questions about how to understand better the differences in the lesbian population. Six of the eight interviewees identified as femme lesbians. This was sheer coincidence, as I did not make any effort to balance the sample along these lines. In fact, given my recruiting method, I couldn't have done such a thing in this investigation. The study might have turned up different results if there were more self-identified butch lesbians or more of a balance. This issue of "hindsight" is particularly acute in studies like this one, in which patterns like these do not emerge until after the data have been collected. To me, this issue reinforces the importance of simultaneous data collection and analysis so that at least the researcher is aware of differences like these as the study progresses.

Other peculiarities specific to the lesbian population should be considered when conducting a study like this one. For instance, all eight women I interviewed were college educated. This was an intentional criterion for the study, but it may have skewed the results. Not only were these women extremely learned, but they also had been highly exposed to social and cultural ideas like feminism, patriarchy, and even the body image construct itself. Their ability to identify and reject the mainstream beauty myth must have been partially a result of this cultural refinement. A college education has the ability to open an individual's mind, not only to "book knowledge" but also to self-knowledge. This might improve a woman's body image.

Some participants explained that college offered the opportunity to develop intellectual and other nonphysical aspects of the self. Not only did this have the effect of diminishing the relative importance of beauty or other physical attributes, but it also offered alternative avenues to betterment or fulfillment that could have led to heightened esteem. These issues would seem applicable to all college students, not just to gay women. But college also provides a certain type of environment for the coming out process, which was a very important life event for all participants in the development of their body images.

The range of ages included in this participant group is another issue to consider. For this particular research, which was really aimed at giving voice to lesbian women about their body image concerns, the age range was intentionally broad. The aging process raises many body image issues, however, and a 40-year-old woman will have a different body (and body image) from a 20-year-old. Furthermore, the influences of social trends, political movements, changing cultural mores, and so on are also very age dependent. Thus, an alternative route to investigating lesbian issues would dictate sensitivity to age-related differences. Follow-up studies to this one could isolate lesbians who self-identified as feminists in the 1970s, for example.

One final issue to discuss is how my own beliefs, values, and biases may have influenced the research. As I have pointed out, I was not a passive receptor of information; during interviews, I happily agreed with some points raised by the participants and remained politely indifferent to others. Especially when told of body image attitudes that mirrored my own, I may well have subtly encouraged participants to emphasize or elaborate where they might not have otherwise. At other times, I am sure my heterosexual orientation kept me from a degree of understanding that might have benefited the study.

On the one hand, there must have been questions and insights that would have occurred to a lesbian investigator that did not occur to me. On the other hand, it was easy for me to remain neutral about certain issues (the role of butch/femme), whereas a lesbian researcher could have created more of an unwanted influence by way of her own opinions, attitudes, and biases.

Perhaps my original hypothesis that lesbian women are somehow less reliant on the popular definitions of feminine beauty than heterosexual women influenced the study as well. I did not share this belief with the respondents, nor did I base the study on this belief. Nevertheless, it probably influenced everything from the questions I asked to the expressions on my face during the interviews. Many, but not all, participants have experienced body image in much the same way I have. These participants may have been given more of my attention in both the interview and the analysis.

In hindsight, it is easy for me to see how the qualitative approach benefited both the process and the content of this investigation. By encouraging these women to give me the full range of their feelings about body image—however they defined it—I was able to get past the label of "lesbians." During the interviews, and indeed even within certain responses, these women took on the roles of mother and daughter, little girl and grown woman, self-fulfilling and self-deprecating, thin and fat, healthy and out of shape, feminist and nonfeminist, friend and lover, teacher and student. They were all of these things, and they were gay. Had I focused too much on their homosexuality, I would have missed the holism I was striving for.

Ironically, the two components of this study—body image and lesbianism—are nothing more than inexact labels that only broadly categorize a nexus of complicated interrelationships. Neither lesbianism nor body image can be easily understood as an isolated factor. Both terms are only meaningful when regarded within the complicated contexts in which they actually exist. Indeed, the combination of lesbianism and body image revealed a fascinating and complex tapestry of feelings, attitudes, perceptions, beliefs, and opinions. Hence, the differences among the participants, and even the ambiguity in each participant's own testimony, was as striking as their commonalties and consistencies. My belief is that in no way could this richness, this complexity, this dynamism have been reasonably captured using traditional quantitative tools.

REFERENCES

Berscheid, E., Walster, E., & Bohrnstedt, G. (1973, November). The happy American body: A survey report. *Psychology Today,* pp. 119-131.

Brand, P. A., Rothblum, E. D., & Solomon, L. J. (1992). A comparison of lesbians, gay men, and heterosexuals on weight and restrained eating. *International Journal of Eating Disorders, 11*(3), 253-259.

Collins, J. K., & Plahn, M. R. (1988). Recognition accuracy, stereotypic preference, aversion, and subjective judgment of body appearance in adolescents and young adults. *Journal of Youth and Adolescence, 17,* 317-334.

Dworkin, S. H. (1988). Not in man's image. Lesbians and the cultural oppression of body image. *Women & Therapy, 8,* 27-39.

Eldridge, N. S., & Gilbert, L. A. (1990). Correlates of relationship satisfaction in lesbian couples. *Psychology of Women Quarterly, 14,* 43-62.

Ewen, S. (1977). *Captains of consciousness: Advertising and the social roots of the consumer culture.* New York: McGraw-Hill.

Garner, D. M., Garfinkel, P. E., Schwartz, D., & Thompson, M. (1980). Cultural expectations of thinness in women. *Psychological Reports, 47,* 483-491.

Gettelman, T. E., & Thompson, J. K. (1993). Actual differences and stereotypical perceptions in body image and eating disturbance: A comparison of male and female heterosexual and homosexual samples. *Sex Roles, 29,* 545-562.

Gray, E. A. (1993). Women's body image: A multivariate study. *Free Inquiry in Creative Psychology, 21,* 103-110.

Hesse-Biber, S. (1989). Eating patterns and disorders in a college population: Are college women's eating problems a new phenomenon? *Sex Roles, 20,* 71-89.

Jacobi, L., & Cash, T. F. (1994). In pursuit of the perfect appearance: Discrepancies among self-ideal precepts of multiple physical attributes. *Journal of Applied Social Psychology, 24,* 379-396.

Kilbourne, J. (1994). Still killing us softly: Advertising and the obsession with thinness. In P. Fallon, M. A. Katzman, & S. C. Wooley (Eds.), *Feminist perspectives on eating disorders* (pp. 3-16). New York: Guilford.

LaTorre, R. A., & Wendenburg, K. (1983). Psychological characteristics of bisexual, heterosexual, and homosexual women. *Journal of Homosexuality, 9,* 87-97.

Lincoln, Y. S., & Guba, E. G. (1985). *Naturalistic inquiry.* Beverly Hills, CA: Sage.

Martin, J. E. (1989). The role of body image in the development of bulimia. *British Journal of Occupational Therapy, 52*(7), 262-265.

Mintz, L. B., & Betz, N. E. (1986). Sex differences in the nature, realism, and correlates of body image. *Sex Roles, 15*(3/4), 185-195.

Seid, R. P. (1994). Too "close to the bone": The historical context for women's obsession with slenderness. In P. Fallon, M. A. Katzman, & S. C. Wooley (Eds.), *Feminist perspectives on eating disorders* (pp. 3-16). New York: Guilford.

Siever, M. D. (1994). Sexual orientation and gender as factors in socioculturally acquired vulnerability to body dissatisfaction and eating disorders. *Journal of Consulting and Clinical Psychology, 62*(2), 252-260.

Soares, M. G. (1995). Images of butch/femme. In M. G. Soares (Ed.), *Butch/femme* (pp. 5-9). New York: Crown.

Taylor, S. J., & Bogdan, R. (1984). *Introduction to qualitative research methods: The search for meanings.* New York: John Wiley.

Thompson, B. W. (1994). *A hunger so wide and so deep.* Minneapolis: University of Minnesota Press.

Wooley, S. C. (1984, February). Feeling fat in a thin society: 33,000 women tell how they feel about their bodies. *Glamour,* pp. 198-252.

CHAPTER 12

Friendship Patterns Among Urban Adolescent Boys

A Qualitative Account

Niobe Way
Kerstin Pahl

Although the field of developmental psychology has its roots in methods that rely on qualitative interviews—from Piaget's studies of cognitive development to Kohlberg's studies of moral development—developmental psychologists have spent the last 20 years challenging the validity of such methods. Much debate has occurred over whether qualitative interviews adequately and objectively tap developmental processes. In this chapter, we present findings from a qualitative study with adolescent boys that reveals the ways semistructured interviews detect relational processes undetectable with more established and accepted quantitatively based research methods. We focus particularly on the quality of friendships among urban, ethnically diverse adolescent boys from low-income families and seek to indicate the ways qualitative interviews enhance our understanding of their relationships. Because our intent in this chapter is to reveal *through the data* the importance of conducting semistructured interviews in studies of human development, the primary focus of this chapter is on the interviews themselves.

As is evident in this volume, qualitative methods encompass a multitude of approaches. Qualitative approaches to data collection that have been most accepted among developmental psychologists and that, in fact, define the field are those involving systematic observations in a laboratory or in a natural environment. These observations are then coded, and numbers are created and statistically analyzed. Although the approach starts off being qualitative, the product is typically a quantitative assessment of the processes being observed. The methods that have been the least accepted among developmental psychologists involve semistructured or unstructured interviewing. The analyses of these types of interviews typically attempt to avoid reducing the qualitative material to numbers that can be analyzed through the use of statistics. The argument behind this approach is that much is lost when information is understood only through a quantitative lens. Such approaches to data collection and analysis are often accused of being too subjective and unsystematic to depict developmental processes accurately. During the past 15 years, however, semistructured and unstructured interview studies with adolescents and adults have repeatedly uncovered processes not found by using more quantitative approaches (see Brown & Gilligan, 1992; Fine, 1991; Gilligan, 1982). These qualitative studies have focused on listening to the voices of adolescents and discerned crucial turning points that occur at the edge of or during adolescence. As a result, our understanding of adolescence as a period in the lifespan has been radically transformed.

In the present study, we set out to listen to a group of adolescent boys to understand how they experienced their same-sex friendships. Quantitative research has typically concluded that adolescent boys have less intimate friendships than adolescent girls and that they are more interested in playing basketball with their friends than in talking with each other about their secrets and problems (Belle, 1989; Buhrmester & Furman, 1987; Caldwell & Peplau, 1982; Miller, 1991; Youniss & Smollar, 1985). These descriptions have emphasized the autonomy-promoting and activity-oriented aspects of boys' friendships. Few studies of boys' friendships, however, have listened to the ways boys perceive their friendships on their own terms. The qualitative research that has listened to adolescents speak about their friendships has typically found that such relationships are more complex and nuanced than the quantitative picture suggests (see Duff, 1996; Eder, 1986, 1991, 1993; Hey, 1997; Merten, 1997; Selman, 1980; Thompson, 1995; Way, 1996, 1998). For example, Way's (1996, 1998) qualitative, longitudinal study of urban adolescents indicated that although boys may be less likely *to have* intimate, same-sex friendships than their female counterparts, they are equally likely *to seek* such friendships during high school. By their latter years in high school, however, boys' desire for intimate male friendships appears to diminish as they increasingly discuss their lack of trust in their male peers. Although closed-ended questionnaires and surveys can assess what boys *have,* these methods cannot assess what boys *want* in their relationships. When Way listened to boys' stories of friendships, she detected a meaningful difference between these two components of experience.

Closed-ended questionnaires and surveys are also limited by their inability to explore the meaning of friendship experiences. We know a lot about how much support, intimacy, affection, or satisfaction adolescents experience in their friendships based on findings from questionnaires that examine such dimensions. We know little about what intimacy, support, or affection feels like or means for the adolescents in these relationships.

Our qualitative research on boys' friendships was prompted not only by the limitations of quantitatively based methods but also by a recent call by friendship researchers to conduct more descriptive research on adolescent friendships (Bukowski, 1997). The research on adolescent friendships has focused more on prediction than on description. We know more about what friendships predict (e.g., higher self-esteem) and what predicts the quality of friendships (e.g., family relationships) than we do about the quality of these relationships themselves. To understand the functions of friendships for adolescents, we need to know more about the friendship patterns that exist among them.

Motivated by these gaps in the research literature, we sought to understand the experiences of friendships among ethnically diverse adolescent boys from low-income families living in an urban environment. We wanted to know what types of friendships boys had, what types of friendships they wanted, how they experienced their friendships, and what they thought was important in their friendships. Our sample included 42 adolescent boys (8 Chinese American, 11 African American, 9 Puerto Rican, 9 Dominican, 1 Senegalese, 1 Columbian, 1 half Puerto Rican/half Dominican, 1 half Puerto Rican/half Irish American, 1 half African American/half West Indian) who attended an urban high school in New York City. The boys were all in the ninth grade at the time of the interviews and were selected from mainstream English classes (they were all fluent in English).[1]

Participants were individually interviewed by an ethnically diverse team of male and female graduate students in psychology who had been trained extensively in interviewing techniques with adolescents. Prior to beginning the interviewing process, interviewers spent considerable time in the high school, establishing rapport with students and teachers and acquainting themselves with the environment. We hoped this strategy would enhance the quality of the interviews. When they began their interviews, interviewers were not complete strangers to the adolescents or to the teachers who allowed us to interview their students during class time.

Over the course of a year, the interviewers on the team met on a weekly basis while the research was being conducted. We, the interviewing team, listened to the interviews each week and provided extensive feedback to each other concerning the interviewing process, particularly attuning ourselves to the extent to which follow-up questions were posed that clarified the adolescent's meaning. During these weekly meetings, we refined our listening skills and occasionally made minor changes to the interview protocol.

Although we originally thought that most of the boys should be interviewed by male interviewers, some of the boys expressed a preference for being interviewed by a woman rather than by a man. Consequently, we had women and men interview the boys. We also initially believed that each adolescent should be interviewed by someone from the same ethnic group as the adolescent. Therefore, many of our interviews were matched for ethnicity. Although an ethnic and/or gender match between interviewer and interviewee seemed to enhance the quality of the interviews at times—the adolescents seemed to share information that would not have been shared with someone from a different ethnic or gender group—at other times during the interviews the ethnic or gender match seemed to prevent the interviewer from asking important follow-up questions. The apparent familiarity of the interviewer (based on ethnicity or gender) with some of the experiences described by the adolescent made it difficult, at times, for the interviewer to hear when the meaning of a particular story was not clear. Interviewers who differed from their interviewees in terms of ethnicity or gender often had fewer preconceptions about their interviewees' experiences and, consequently, asked more questions and got richer and more detailed stories from them. Our interviewing experience suggested both strengths and weaknesses to matching the gender or ethnicity or both of interviewer and interviewee.

The in-depth, semistructured interview conducted with each adolescent in the study typically took 1½ hours and was audiotaped and professionally transcribed.[2] The interviews took place during the school day in a small private room in the school building. The interview protocol included such questions as, "How would you describe your closest male friend?" "What kinds of things do you like/dislike about this relationship?" and "What kinds of things are important in a friendship?" Although each interview included a standard set of questions, follow-up questions were based on the adolescents' responses. The goal of this semistructured approach to interviewing is to ask a core set of questions to each adolescent while also capturing the adolescent's own ways of describing his relationships. This method of interviewing explicitly acknowledges the interviewer's agenda (e.g., to understand a particular phenomenon or topic) and the interviewee's power (e.g., to introduce important new knowledge the interviewer had not anticipated). At the end of each interview session, interviewers audiotaped their impressions of the adolescent and of the interview process. The purpose of this task was to record aspects of the interview that cannot be captured from a transcript of the dialogue between interviewer and interviewee (e.g., the adolescent's appearance, affective tone, facial expressions, comfort with being interviewed).

To analyze the interview data, we first read the transcripts of all the interviews, with the aim of understanding and summarizing the story being told by each adolescent. These "narrative summaries" seek to condense the interview material into a shorter narrative that captures the essence of the story being told by each adolescent (see Miller, 1991). Following the creation of summaries, we read them *independently*, looking for key themes or concepts that seemed to play an important role in the stories (e.g., trust, protection). We discarded any concepts or themes that only one of us considered key or central to the stories. Following our detection of themes and patterns, we reread the original interviews (not the summaries), examining how these key concepts or themes related to the adolescents' stories of friendships. As a result of this repeated reading process, we detected three friendship patterns among the boys in the study. Each of these patterns represents a distinct group of boys. Variations and commonalities across and within each of these three groups of boys are the focus of this chapter.

Throughout our entire analytic process, we maintained an active awareness of how our own values, beliefs, and expectations may affect the themes or concepts we noted in the data. For example, when we began analyzing the interviews, we as women expected the boys' friendships to sound less close than girls' friendships (even though we were not analyzing girls' friendships). We assumed that many of the boys' friendships would seem superficial. Our awareness of our bias helped us stay attuned to when we quickly dismissed an activity or process as superficial or unimportant. Although we initially perceived talking and sharing secrets with a friend as the primary sign or indicator of a close friendship, we realized after reflecting with our research team and listening to the boys' interviews that we were not fully understanding the closeness that boys might experience when they play sports and video games with each other. We were being blind-sighted by our own preconceptions about the meaning of closeness in relationships. These types of insights were ongoing throughout the process of analyzing the interview data and deeply influenced the friendship patterns described in this chapter.[3]

BOYS' FRIENDSHIPS

Pattern 1: Sharing Secrets

Contrary to beliefs that boys' friendships are characterized by a paucity of emotional connection (Belle, 1989; Kilmartin, 1994), we found that over a third (38%, $N = 16$)[4] of the boys spoke about other boys with great warmth and intimacy. Using exceptionally affectionate and vulnerable language, these boys expressed strong feelings for their close male friends, setting a tone that conveyed an emotional depth to their friendships. Various meanings of closeness unfolded as these 16 boys described their same-sex friendships.

James, a 15-year-old African American[5] who spends most of his free time writing plays with his best friend, tells his interviewer that he has satisfying and trusting relationships with other boys. He believes that they know him well and that they can relate to him emotionally:

Interviewer: OK, can you tell me things that you like about your friends who are guys?

James: They understand how I am. They know how to make me feel better whenever I am feeling down. We all understand each other's feelings and, you know, if there's a home problem, we understand that.

Interviewer: How do you know that somebody else understands you?

James: They show it by their feelings, like, expressions.

Although James is an unusually creative boy, doing improvisational theater with his best friend on a regular basis, his sense of intimacy with his friends and the language he uses to describe it are not unusual. The boys in the first group told us that their best friends were their confidantes in a variety of matters, including which girls they liked, what problems they had in school, or what difficulties they experienced at home. They shared their most "private secrets," and they firmly believed that they could trust their closest friends to keep them confidential.

Talking together and listening to each other's problems were an important part of the friendships in this first group. Asked what he does with his best friend, Julio, a sensitive 15-year-old from Puerto Rico, tells his interviewer: "We hang out, we talk to each other about serious things, share some deep secrets." For Julio, whose mother is dying of AIDS at the time of the interview, it seems particularly important to be open with his best friend. Fortunately, his best friend and his other friends are quite empathic:

Interviewer: Do you think this particular friendship [with his best friend] has changed since you were younger?

Julio: It changed a lot. Just like my other friends changed a lot.

Interviewer: Like how?

Julio: When we were younger, it used to be like not so tight as we are now. [It was] not like if something goes wrong, like one of us shed a tear, the other one will cry.

Expressions of compassion were commonly heard among these 16 boys. Johnny, a 14-year-old Chinese American, tells his interviewer about his friend comforting him when he was sad: "I had this goldfish for a long time and it died. So I started crying and crying, I don't know why, but I went . . . [to my best friend] and I was crying and . . . you know, he comforted me, he talked to me." Although the severity of the loss that Julio and Johnny are experiencing might not be the same, the empathy and concern that their friends show them are. Crying along with a friend and comforting him are acts of feeling for and with a friend, defying the stereotype of adolescent boys as lonesome riders who prefer to keep their feelings to themselves.

Another way of being close among the boys in the first group related to a shared history, time, and family. Having known each other for a long time, spending almost all their free time together, and knowing their friends' families well was the fabric of these boys' intimacy. They spoke about eating dinner at each other's home, sleeping over, and calling their closest friends' mothers "Mom." Julio, who says he shares his "secrets" with his best friend, chooses to describe his closeness with his best friend in terms of time spent together at each other's home. He and his best friend have known each other since kindergarten:

Julio: We're best friends. I don't do the things I do with him, I don't do with everybody else. . . .

Interviewer: Like what?

Julio: Like he comes to my house. Hardly any of my other friends come to my house. I go to his house. Hardly any of my friends go there. [They] go to their [own] house instead of his house. Our relationship is tight, like, he's my brother.

Strikingly, going to each other's home was often described by the boys with great pride. Spending time in such a familiar environment seemed not only a consequence but also an enhancer of intimacy.

"Being like brothers" and "like family" were common expressions among these 16 boys when they were trying to convey the bond they felt with their best friends. For some boys, in fact, family status was a reward given to those who had been most loyal to them. Jonathan, an African American student, says this about his closest friends:

They are there for you. Even though your family can be there for you too, your family got to be there for you. Your friends, they don't have to be there, but they choose to be there and since they choose to be there for you, they make you want to accept them into your family . . . so you make your family bigger and bigger.

These boys expressed love and concern for each other by bringing their friends into the fold of their families.

An additional way the boys in the first group expressed feelings of intimacy for their close friends revolved around the concept of *protection*. Protecting each other was not only about "backing each other up" in fights (as we had originally assumed) but also about helping each other calm down, thus preventing a fight. Chris, a Puerto Rican student, repeatedly emphasizes how his best friend helps him stay out of trouble. For him, this is a crucial aspect of their friendship:

Interviewer: Why do you think your friendship with Mark is better than with other friends?

Chris: Well, with him when I'm in an argument with somebody that disrespected me and he just comes out and backs me up and says, "Yo, Chris, don't deal with that. Yo, let's just go on, you know," 'cause I could snap.

Another way the boys in the first group protected each other was by showing concern about harmful behaviors such as smoking, selling drugs, and cutting class. Jorge, a 14-year-old Dominican who is trying to help his best friend change, tells his interviewer that his best friend is like a little brother to him:

Interviewer: What do you not like about this friendship?

Jorge: That he smokes weed and that he sells drugs.

Interviewer: Is there something you would like to change about Benny?

Jorge: That! That's about it.

Interviewer: Yeah?

Jorge: Well, I'm trying to change him. He's, you know, trying to [stop] 'cause I told him. I be talking to him and he's trying to get off drugs and smoke.

A similar relationship is described by Jonathan. With his best friend, Jonathan is the "little brother," whereas his friend, who is almost the same age as Jonathan, acts as a protector. Jonathan says about his best friend: "He's honest, he never lets nobody try to harm me, and he's like a big brother that I never had. So, we've become closer than we ever have been." When asked what makes his friend like an "older brother," Jonathan answers: "He's taking care of me, he buys me what I need. Like if I need stuff for my birthday, or need something to go out, he'll buy me an outfit or some sneakers or whatever I'll need, he'll try his best to give it to me." In Jonathan's description, the nurturing quality of his friend's protection is readily apparent. Not only does his friend protect him against potential attackers, but he also takes on a parental role by providing for his friend.

All the boys in the first group were deeply engaged with their friends. Moreover, they expressed a commitment to their friendships that rested on the hope that the relationships would last into the future. The tone in which they spoke about their commitments was occasionally reminiscent of romantic relationships. Claudio thinks that he and his friend will be together for a long time: "We'll never be like split apart if anything happens." Gabriel emphasizes the strong bond between himself and his best friend: "Hardly nothing could break us up. Like we argue . . . same day, we get back together." Unlike the boys in the second group, who often defined good friendships by the absence of arguments, the boys in this first group told stories about arguing and "making up" with their best friends. James, the playwright, actually enjoys arguing and "making up" with his best friend and believes that it enhances the intimacy of their friendship.

Although there were multiple ways of being intimate with each other, all the boys in the first group seemed to have strong emotional ties to their best friends because they were able to share their personal thoughts and feelings with them, they considered them a part of their families, and they had known them for a long time. They were in relationships with other boys that consisted of much more than simply participating in the same activities.

Pattern 2: Sharing Jokes

Ten adolescent boys (24%) in the study seemed to have less intimate friendships than the boys in the first group. However, they considered their friendships to be close. Their definitions of *close* did not include confiding their personal thoughts and feelings to their friends or protecting one another, but rather sharing jokes, having fun, and playing games with each other. These boys were the boys who, in their emphasis on game playing, fit the stereotypical image of male friends (see Belle, 1989; Kilmartin, 1994). Yet, their friendships did not appear to be superficial.

Marcus, an outgoing Dominican, says that he and his best friend go to movies, play video games, "chill, smoke, drink, go to parties . . . Most of the times we hang." Marcus sees his friend every day, and he spends time with him and his cousin. They are close because "we have known each other for a long time and, you know, . . . [we] do what we want, he won't get mad, unless it's bad."

Friendships for the boys in the second group rarely involved arguments. Samuel, a seemingly popular African American, says about his friendships with other boys, "We never argue or fight, we just have a little argument here and there, but we never like really got into it, we never fought, we're just good friends." Unlike James, in the first group, who states that one way he enjoys his close friend is through the process of fighting and then "making up," boys such as Samuel claim not to have any arguments.

The emotional tone of these activity-oriented friendships was predominantly joyous and often involved teasing. Samuel says that he will argue with his close friends about "silly things" such as "who is a better fighter, Jackie Chan or Bruce Lee." Marcus says that he and his best friend will fight but only playfully, "like if I diss his mother, he just starts laughing, and if he disses my mother, I start laughing. We don't take it personally, you know, when the other person does something." He says about his best friend: "He's fun to hang out with . . . Like he does crazy stuff and makes me laugh." Samuel says that his friend is closer to him than his other friends because they spend so much time together "telling jokes and doing little pranks."

A few friendships in the second group of boys involved shared secrets, but these secrets mostly concerned romantic crushes and never included family or personal problems or concerns. Samuel says, "I trust [my best friend]. I tell him secrets, he don't tell no one." When asked whether he would share any serious concerns with him, Samuel says, "No." This categorical no was typical among these boys. When Justin was asked what types of things he shares with his friends, he says, "Nothing deep."

The boys in the second group gave no particular reason for not sharing their personal lives with their close friends. They implied or stated directly that they had no interest in sharing such information. Although we were initially tempted to interpret this kind of response as a sign that these boys were afraid to be vulnerable with their friends, we were convinced after listening repeatedly to their interviews that they simply had no desire to share their concerns with their friends. They were, however, willing to discuss girls with their friends, and that was clearly a vulnerable topic for many.

Unlike the boys in the third group, the boys in the second group (and first group) seemed quite satisfied with their male friendships. Marcus, Mitchell, and Justin say that they enjoy their friendships with other boys and that they do not want any other types of friendships. Part of the reason, perhaps, for their satisfaction may have been that they did not place primary importance on these relationships. Their hearts and minds seemed focused more on their families than on their friends. Samuel says: "I love my mother. I love her to death, yeah . . . She would do anything for me." The passion with which they expressed their feelings for their mothers, in particular, often contrasted with the relative lack of passion for their close friends. Their friendships were close, reliable, and enjoyable but did not offer the kind of support and affection their relationships with their parents did.

Pattern 3: Fearing Betrayal

When Kevin, a Puerto Rican 14-year-old, is asked to describe what his friendships are like with other boys, he tells his interviewer:

> Kevin: They're not really that great because I'm usually getting into fights with most of my friends. But I don't really have any friends that I trust that much. Most people I do trust [are in my] family. Most of my friends, I really consider them associates more than friends.
>
> Interviewer: Associates? What do you mean by associates?
>
> Kevin: Just people that I know, not people that I really rely on for everything.

Kevin vividly expresses a key theme that was evident among a group of 9 boys (21%) in the study who, when asked about their friendships with other boys, seemed consumed by their lack of trust and their fears of betrayal by their male peers. When asked about male friends, these boys typically stated that they had difficulties trusting any of their male peers and that, consequently, they did not have close or best male friends. Brothers and cousins, however, were occasionally exceptions to their general feelings of distrust.

Kevin says that he does have a male peer with whom he spends more time than his other peers. However, he does not trust this peer "that much." "I trust him maybe, I wouldn't trust him with my life. I trust nobody with my life, but I do trust him to hold, like my expensive things, or like to watch my back in a fight or something like that." Kevin makes it clear that trusting someone else with one's material items or one's "back" does not mean that one trusts the other completely. Scott says that he only trusts Dell to a "certain extent" "'cause I don't trust nobody really . . . I only trust my brothers. . . . I don't trust nobody because people are slick . . . I don't put nothin' past nothin. . . . Anything is possible to happen."

These "distrustful" boys spoke of having had close friends when they were younger but of losing these close friends as a result of their friends moving or going to a different school. Kevin says: "My best friend, I knew him since I was, he was like 4 and he lived on my block. And he moved away and that was the last good friend I had." Similar to previous qualitative research (see Way, 1996), the boys who voiced distrusting their peers often spoke of having had less difficulty trusting their peers when they were younger. Mark says: "When I was younger, my friends, they never dissed you, you know, [we] just had fun. Since I'm older, people dis you and they do different stuff." Michael says that his friendships were better when he was younger: "We were closer [when we were younger] because we used to do everything the same, but now we grew up . . . everybody's like separated." These boys expressed a yearning for the types of friendships they had when they were less "separated" and when loyalty was more assured.

Friendships with other boys often meant trouble. When Scott, a 15-year-old African American student, is asked what his friendships are like with other boys, he says:

Scott: It's alright . . . My friends are really my brothers [at home].

Interviewer: Do you have friends with boys who are not your brothers?

Scott: Not really . . . 'cause, I'm saying, I don't trust them.

Interviewer: Why not?

Scott: I don't feel comfortable around boys because when boys, when a lot of boys are together, they get into trouble. . . . And I don't like getting into trouble.

Scott explains how his friends are always starting fights or selling drugs and that he does not want to be a part of either of these activities. Kevin, in fact, says that he never got into trouble until he started making friends in the sixth grade. Once he began making friends and "hanging out in the streets," his grades went down. Now he is more selective of his friends. Michael says that he doesn't like the friends he grew up with because "they get me into trouble . . . Like right now, I'm on probation for selling, and they, you know, influenced me into selling and I got into trouble, so that's why I be stayin' home to stay away from trouble." He says, however, that he has one close friend who is not like other peers: "We do nothing wrong, as like, we won't have to take peer pressure. It's just us two, you know, trying to stay away from everything, like sellin' drugs and all that." Jermaine puts it poignantly when asked why he keeps to himself: "You're marked by the companies you keep . . . like if you be with someone who likes to argue, likes to fight or stab, or likes to murder or something they gonna think you do it too just because you be with them. And that's not always how it be."

Fears of, and actual stories about, betrayal are rampant in these nine boys' narratives of friendships. Scott provides an example of the kind of betrayal he fears: "All right like, I can be talking to a girl. [My best friend] could be talking to a girl. All of sudden . . . he could try to talk with my girl . . . and then boom! They start talking to each other. That would bother me." Although his best friend may not get Scott into trouble, he may steal his girlfriend, and consequently Scott limits the extent to which he trusts him.

When asked about his friendships with other boys, Michael says:

Michael: I'm not too tight with my friends.

Interviewer: What do you mean by that?

Michael: I don't trust, I don't trust 'em.

Interviewer: Why not?

Michael: 'Cause I don't trust nobody. I learned through the past that a lotta things happen. You can't trust nobody. . . . Like maybe one day, yeah, you leave your money there, and they don't touch it, but the next, maybe they will. . . . or another way . . . say I'm trying to get with this girl or something and my friend goes there and mess with that same girl, that's called disrespect . . . That's why I don't trust.

Their male peers stealing their girlfriends or material possessions was the fear that haunted the minds of these 9 boys.

In striking contrast with their discussions of their peers, the boys in the third group often spoke with passion about their relationships with their parents. Their lack of trust in their male peers did not seem to stem from a lack of trust in their parents. With the exception of 1 boy who explicitly stated that he did not trust anyone, including his family members, the remaining boys discussed trusting their mothers, occasionally their fathers, and one or two of their siblings. Mark, who moments earlier spoke about how he has difficulty trusting his peers, says that he has a very good relationship with his mother: "Suppose I have a problem with a girl or something, you know I could always talk to her about it, even like sex or whatever I wouldn't be afraid to talk to her about it. . . . She always listens to me." He says that his relationship with his father is also "pretty good" but that he wishes his father would show more affection toward him. He knows that his father loves him, however, and he trusts his father completely. Angel says that although he does not trust his friends to keep "his secrets," he does trust his mother. Jermaine says that he does not have close friends, only "associates." He describes his mother as his best friend, however, because he can "tell her everything" and "we do everything together." He also trusts his father, but his father is in prison, so he does not see him very often.

Parents not only were trusted and occasionally considered best friends but also, at times, were the reason the distrustful adolescents believed they had no close friends. Carlos says that he does not have many friends because "you can't trust like everybody" and because "my parents don't let me go out of the house as much. . . . I just wish that my parents would let me go out a little more." Carlos explains that his parents are worried about his safety when he "hangs out" with friends and that, therefore, they do not allow him to spend much time with friends outside school. The parents of many of the adolescent boys in the study feared for their children's safety and, consequently, discouraged them from spending time with friends after school. Some parents also appeared to emphasize to their children, perhaps as a consequence of their fears, that "family always comes first."

Although the boys who spoke of distrusting their peers did not have close friends, they often spoke of wanting such relationships with their male peers. When asked what he would like to change about his friends, Michael says: "Everything. I would like to have better friends . . . that I could trust as family." Scott says: "I would like one that I could trust. 'Cause then I could be able to talk to him about things or talk with him about things that I can't even talk to my family about." These boys typically stated that although they valued their relationships with their families, they still desired close male friendships. Carlos, who says that he does not have a close or best friend because he can't trust "nobody these days," would still like to have such a friend: "Yeah, as long as like, you know, I could talk to them about anything and if I tell them to keep a secret, to keep it, like I been telling you." Albert wants a best friend who "doesn't talk nothing behind my back, tell my personal problems to . . . not leaving me for another . . . You know, a friend that would be real tight to me, close, that I could tell him just anything." These boys spoke of not having but of wanting close and intimate male friendships, a pattern that was distinct from those heard among the boys in the first two groups. The boys in the first two groups suggested there was no difference between what they had and what they sought in their friendships.

DISCUSSION

Adolescent boys, who have so often been portrayed in the research literature as having friendships that are emotionally flat and that focus predominantly on activities rather than on sharing thoughts and feelings (see Kilmartin, 1994), were typically found in this study to either have or want friendships that involve sharing secrets, feelings, and problems. Over half of the boys spoke of having or wanting intimate same-sex friendships.[6] Less than a quarter of the boys described having *and* wanting the types of friendships that are typically presented in the research literature on adolescent male friendships. By listening to the stories told by boys in semistructured interviews, we were able to hear stories of boys' relationships that were different from those we have heard before.[7]

Furthermore, through the use of semistructured interviews, we heard the ways their experiences of intimacy, closeness, distrust, and loneliness were shaped. Intimacy among the boys in the first group involved much more than sharing thoughts and feelings with their best friends. It also involved physical and emotional protection, sharing each other's home space, knowing the other person over a long period of time, having arguments and "making up," and being "like family." Friendships among boys in the second group consisted of more than playing games. These friendships also involved laughter, shared jokes, and having fun. These boys reported having *close* male friendships, but the meaning of closeness for them was based on the extent to which they enjoyed their friends, rather than on the extent to which they could share their secrets or problems with them. The boys in the third group who spoke of distrusting their peers did not simply discuss their lack of trust; they also told stories of boys as troublemakers. Their distrust appeared to be related not only to their fears of betrayal but also to their concerns about being associated with the "wrong type of crowd." Friendships were potentially dangerous, and the boys were wary, consequently, of such ties. They also spoke of being hurt by their friends and of seeking more intimate male friendships. Their language seemed as vulnerable and emotional as the language used by the boys in the first group.

The adolescents' stories suggested that parents' restrictions on spending time with their friends, parents' messages about "family coming first," the quality of relationships between adolescents and parents, as well as experiences of betrayal by their peers may play an important part in explaining why particular patterns of relationships exist for some adolescents and not for others. The nature of our one-time interview approach, however, made it impossible to determine the factors that cause, for example, the high level of distrust among a certain segment of our sample. Such questions need to be examined in longitudinal, qualitative research studies. Understanding the types of familial, social, and institutional factors that lead to different types of friendship patterns is key toward understanding adolescent friendships (Brown, Way, & Duff, in press).

Longitudinal qualitative research is also needed to determine how friendship patterns shift over time. Indications in our study and in previous longitudinal studies (see Way, 1998) are that boys' feelings of distrust toward their peers grow stronger as boys grow older. The boys in the current study who had been held back in school and were, therefore, older than the other boys in the ninth grade were more likely to fall into the distrusting group than into any other group. Although this finding may be a consequence of being held back in school, it may also be a result of growing older and more cynical about the possibility of having close friendships with other boys. Longitudinal research is needed to determine whether, in fact, this pattern is consistently found among adolescent boys.

Before we conduct longitudinal research on the predictors of friendships or on the ways patterns of friendships change over time, we need a firm grounding in what we are trying to predict or follow over time. As this study suggests, what we thought were the typical friendship patterns of adolescent boys (based primarily on survey research) appears to inadequately represent the types of friendships that urban, ethnically diverse adolescent boys from low-income families are having or wanting. Such a finding has immediate implications for future studies of adolescent development. What other processes have been missed or overlooked because we have failed to listen to the stories told by our participants? By relying almost exclusively on survey, questionnaire, or observational research for descriptions of adolescent processes, developmental psychologists may be basing their theoretical predictions and explanations of such processes on insufficient grounding. Without the understanding gained from listening closely to experiences of adolescents, our knowledge of adolescent processes is seriously constrained and possibly inaccurate. Qualitative, interview-based research with ethnically and socioeconomically diverse populations will only strengthen our understanding of adolescent development and, consequently, human development.

NOTES

1. This study is part of a larger study of parent and peer relationships among urban, ethnic minority adolescents from low-income families. Ninety-percent of the students who attend the school in which the study took place are eligible for federal assistance through the free lunch program. The study was funded by a B/START grant from the National Institute of Mental Health, a New York University Research Challenge Grant, and a New York University School of Education Research Challenge Grant to the first author.

2. The large sample size required us to use professional transcribers. Some qualitative researchers prefer to transcribe their tapes themselves. That was not feasible in our project, however.

3. For further discussion of how gender, race, ethnicity, and social class may influence the analysis of qualitative data, see Way (1998).

4. The reason we indicate numbers or percentages of participants who suggested each theme and quote precisely the words of the adolescents is to give the reader an accurate representation of the interview data. Stating "the boys stated" rather than "50% of the boys stated" repeats an old problem in psychology: generalizing a particular finding to the entire sample when, in fact, the finding was only evident among some of the participants. Furthermore, stating "some boys said" is vague and leaves the reader unclear as to how we are interpreting *some*. Indicating the number or percentages of boys who stated each theme is our attempt at being clear and precise in our representation of the data.

5. The reason we occasionally indicate the ethnicity and age of the boys is to reveal the diversity and similarities of the adolescents within each of the three groups.

6. In addition to the boys already described in this chapter, three boys (who were a part of the seven boys in the study who did not fit into any of the three patterns) also expressed a desire for intimate male friendships.

7. Seven of the boys in the study did not fit into any of the groups described in this chapter. Three of these seven boys, however, seemed to form a pattern of their own. These three boys, all Chinese American, seemed particularly depressed and lonely. They spoke of having no close friends but of yearning for friends with whom they could share their secrets. They did not distrust other boys but found it difficult to make friends. They spoke of being repeatedly teased and harassed by other boys, and these experiences seemed to play a part in why they did not have close male friends.

REFERENCES

Belle, D. (1989). Gender differences in children's social networks and supports. In D. Belle (Ed.), *Children's social networks and supports.* New York: John Wiley.

Brown, L. M., & Gilligan, C. (1992). *Meeting at the crossroads: Women's psychology and girl's development.* Cambridge, MA: Harvard University Press.

Brown, L. M., Way, N., & Duff, J. L. (in press). The others in my I: Adolescent girls' friendships and peer relations. In N. Johnson, M. Roberts, & J. Worell (Eds.), *Beyond appearances.* Washington, DC: American Psychological Association.

Buhrmester, D., & Furman, W. (1987). The development of companionship and intimacy. *Child Development, 58,* 1101-1113.

Bukowski, W. M. (Discussant). (1997, April). *Examining children's friendship experiences: Conceptual and methodological innovations.* Symposium conducted at the Society for Research on Child Development, Washington DC.

Caldwell, M. A., & Peplau, L. A. (1982). Sex differences in same-sex friendships. *Sex Roles, 8,* 721-723.

Duff, J. L. (1996). *The best of friends: Exploring the moral domain of adolescent friendship.* Unpublished doctoral dissertation, Stanford University.

Eder, D. (1986). Serious and playful disputes: Variation in conflict talk among female adolescents. In A. D. Grimshaw (Ed.), *Conflict talk: Sociolinguistic investigations of arguments in conversations.* Cambridge, UK: Cambridge University Press.

Eder, D. (1991). The role of teasing in adolescent peer culture. In S. Cahill (Ed.), *Sociological studies of child development, 4,* 181-197.

Eder, D. (1993). "Go get ya a french!" Romantic and sexual teasing among adolescent girls. In D. Tannen (Ed.), *Gender and conversational interaction.* Oxford, UK: Oxford University Press.

Fine, M. (1991). *Framing dropouts: Notes on the politics of an urban high school.* Albany: State University of New York Press.

Gilligan, C. (1982). *In a different voice.* Cambridge, MA: Harvard University Press.

Hey, V. (1997). *The company she keeps: An ethnography of girls' friendships.* Cambridge, UK: Cambridge University Press.

Kilmartin, C. T. (1994). *The masculine self.* New York: Macmillan.

Merten, D. (1997). The meaning of meanness: Popularity, competition, and conflict among junior high school girls. *Sociology of Education, 70,* 175-191.

Miller, B. (1991). *Adolescents' relationships with their friends.* Unpublished doctoral dissertation, Harvard University.

Selman, R. (1980). *The growth of interpersonal understanding: Developmental and clinical analyses.* San Diego: Academic Press.

Thompson, S. (1995). What friends are for: On girls' misogyny and romantic fusion. In J. Irvine (Ed.), *Sexual cultures and the construction of adolescent identities.* Philadelphia: Temple University Press.

Way, N. (1996). Between experiences of betrayal and desire: Close friendships among urban adolescents. In B. Leadbeater & N. Way (Eds.), *Urban girls: Resisting stereotypes, creating identities.* New York: New York University Press.

Way, N. (1998). *Everyday courage: The lives and stories of urban teenagers.* New York: New York University Press.

Youniss, J., & Smollar, J. (1985). *Adolescent relations with mothers, fathers, and friends.* Chicago: University of Chicago Press.

CHAPTER 13

Capturing the Process of Family Therapy as Social Meaning Construction

Joy M. Tanji

Despite the growing popularity of family therapy and its origins in research, development of a methodologically rigorous research base has lagged, particularly with regard to systemic theory and its applications (Nichols & Schwartz, 1995; Sprenkle & Moon, 1996; Wynne, 1983). Early family therapy research emphasized a quantitative and experimental approach based on assumptions very different from those of systemic epistemology. Although important treatment outcome information may be contributed through the continued use of a positivist paradigm, exclusive use of a singular research paradigm poses challenges to practitioners seeking to understand better the reciprocal influence of family interactions and meanings. A more pluralistic approach to family therapy research may maximize opportunities to study systemic phenomena from frames more congruent with, and more adept at, capturing the social meaning construction process (Bednar, Burlingame, & Masters, 1988; Sprenkle & Moon, 1996). The inclusion of qualitative approaches may also enhance the overall rigor of family therapy research by providing an understanding of how the idiographic and probabilistic data are related.

Despite the call for increased use of qualitative research methodology in family therapy research (Hoshmand, 1989; Moon, Dillon, & Sprenkle, 1991; Sprenkle & Bischoff, 1995), little movement has been made toward increasing its use (Sprenkle & Moon, 1996). How might we as researchers and practitioners begin to move toward a more integrated understanding of the family therapy process? The following discussion outlines paradigmatic and methodological considerations that may be helpful in furthering our efforts. First, the study of systemic family process requires an epistemological shift toward an approach that acknowledges the therapeutic value of exploring the reciprocal influences of multiple perspectives. Second, the use of research paradigms that share postmodern assumptions with systemic approaches to therapy may enhance theoretical sensitivity but are likely to change the phenomena they are meant to capture. Third, given the assumption of reciprocal influence, methodological rigor may be enhanced through the inclusion of multiple methods of verification that enhance participant-observer reflexivity and credibility of data.

CAPTURING THE NATURE OF THE PHENOMENON: IDENTIFYING ELEMENTS OF THE EPISTEMOLOGICAL SHIFT

In 1993-95, I embarked on a study of a therapist, reflecting team, and family engaged in Milan systemic family therapy. A major challenge facing our research team as a whole was how to begin understanding the reciprocal influence of family meanings and interaction patterns.

Milan systemic family therapy uses a *reflecting team* to assist therapists and family members in generating multiple plausible hypotheses that may suggest opportunities for future changes in family interaction patterns and meanings. The team optimally consists of three to five consultants who meet and brainstorm with the therapist several times during a therapeutic session. The function of the team is to help punctuate news of difference that may have been previously misinterpreted or disregarded as noise. Reintroduction of lost information, especially the hidden differences of perspective, often offers the family new opportunities for change (Boscolo, Cecchin, Hoffman, & Penn, 1987).

In the original model, the team met with a family for a single consultation. The reflecting team observed from behind a one-way screen. During the session, the therapist intermittently consulted with the reflecting team to examine their divergent hypotheses. The therapist then returned to the family, where he or she shared some of the team's impressions (Boscolo et al., 1987). In subsequent variations of the model, the process was expanded to include multiple consultations, often scheduled a month apart. Depending on the team, the family also was offered the opportunity to observe the therapist's consultation with the team, allowing them to decide which hypotheses to pursue (Andersen, 1991). The greater inclusiveness in current variations of the model provides families with increased opportunities for change that may have remained hidden from them in the original model.

An initial challenge in researching this phenomenon involved pushing past my socialization as a positivistic researcher to understand the assumptions that were uniquely different in this therapeutic culture. Milan systemic family therapy is embedded in postmodern assumptions that emphasize context and relationship, rather than objects and latent or unconscious intentions. Postmodernism also regards humans as fallible knowers. Whether an absolute truth exists is not the issue. The issue is that it is not directly knowable with certainty. Fallibility results in a plurality of ideas about the world that is then storied through a process of social construction (Anderson, Goolishian, & Winderman, 1986; Epston, White, & Murray, 1992; Gergen, 1988; Karl, Cynthia, Andrew, & Vanessa, 1992; Lax, 1992; Sabin, 1986).

It quickly became apparent that, in designing a study, I would have to consider a paradigm shift toward a postmodern epistemology. The shift involved validating the relevance of intersubjective constructions as a medium for change. It also required a search for an approach to inquiry that would enable systematic and rigorous study of an evolving, narrative system. This required learning multiple "languages" and exploring the standards of rigor in the qualitative paradigm.

Learning to Speak the Language

I began by learning the systemic language. Operationalizing systemic constructs like circularity and neutrality were challenging. The team studied them in theory and in application, first through role plays and then in collaboration with families. Systemic theory challenged us to reconsider our assumptions about causality, epistemology, and clinical rigor.

General family systems theory conceptualizes a *system* as a cognitive-affective-behavioral meaning system with functional and structural rules (Guttman, 1991). Rather than people, the group is composed of a set of relational meanings. Anderson and Goolishian (1992) described family problems in terms of *problem-organized systems:* a constellation of meanings surrounding the same context and defined as "a problem" by the family participants. They observed that these problems were embedded in a medium of language and hypothesized that perhaps these problems could be deconstructed through an iterative process of what was earlier termed by Robinson and Hawpe (1986) "narrative repair" or "reauthoring" (Epston et al., 1992).

Circularity and neutrality are systemic constructs introduced by the Milan associates to describe what may be involved in this process of reauthoring. *Circularity* refers to the reciprocal influence of multiple perspectives on a family meaning system. Although troubling, these systems may be amplified through repetition until noticed. *Circular questioning* is an interview strategy designed to facilitate and enhance curiosity about relational information or differences in perspective (Boscolo et al., 1987; Fleuridas, Nelson, & Rosenthal, 1986; Penn, 1982, 1985; Selvini, Boscolo, Cecchin, & Prata, 1980: Tomm, 1987a, 1987b, 1988).

Neutrality is a term also introduced by the Milan associates to describe the process of reflexivity encouraged in the family consultations (Boscolo et al., 1987; Cecchin, 1987, 1992; McNamee, 1992; Selvini et al., 1980). Cecchin (1992) later referred to this strategy as "irreverence," a process of challenging invariant assumptions about human experience. He argues that clinical rigor requires reflexivity, a questioning of certainty. Neutrality assumes that therapeutic effectiveness is enhanced by our openness to the opportunities introduced by uncertainty (Cecchin, Lane, & Ray, 1992).

Therapy as Social Construction

Simultaneous with this exploration of systemic language was my exploration of narrative theory. Milan systemic family therapy focuses on changes in meaning that are embedded in a narrative medium, in the multiple stories shared by family and reflecting team members. Use of narrative process as a medium for change is not a new idea, nor is it unique as a concept to systemic family therapy. In fact, myths and stories have been used historically as a means of understanding human experiences and natural phenomena (Robinson & Hawpe, 1986).

Narrative process in therapy also involves the telling of personal stories. What has brought the family to therapy? What do family members perceive needs to happen before things change? Out of the steady flow of events, people intentionally and unintentionally select particular elements and link them together on the basis of a causal or motivational strategy. They construct a coherent interpretation based on what seems relevant to their personal sense of meaning (Gergen & Kaye, 1992; Robinson & Hawpe, 1986).

Although the narrative process has been used throughout history, research of this process, particularly in family therapy, has been hindered by a lack of available training in methodologies that can capture the process as it emerges, its circularity, and the reciprocal influence of family and team stories. If we assume circularity, the focus shifts from trying to gather historical data to determine interventions toward understanding what seems to be effective in getting the system unstuck. It was like discovering a way to study a Möbius strip systematically.

By the time I began to design my study, I was immersed in this strange new world. Despite 4 years of theoretical and experiential exploration, I still did not think I understood the essence of Milan systemic family therapy. I could parrot some of the literature, but I did not feel confident that I understood what really happened in the process. Because of the shared postmodern assumptions of the qualitative approach and Milan systemic family therapy, the qualitative method seemed well suited to capture the essence of systemic practice. I began meeting regularly with a debriefer while beginning my exploration of the qualitative paradigm. This enabled me to wonder aloud about the possible strengths and limitations of the model for the task ahead.

Exploring the Fit of a Qualitative Approach

Although the qualitative method and Milan systemic family therapy have their own particular jargon, their shared fundamental assumptions made immersion into the therapeutic system through a qualitative approach fairly rapid. The *isomorphism*, or parallelism, between the therapeutic and research methods might enhance the *theoretical sensitivity* of the study (e.g., knowing what might be meaningful to ask). But some of the dialectical distance between the two domains may have been lost. The lack of difference made it more difficult to assess what might be happening in the therapy process that falls out of the study because it cannot be translated into the qualitative-Milan systemic meta-language. In addition, given the similarity between the two interview protocols, it is difficult to determine whether one process may be punctuating the other and thus amplifying the outcome of therapy. Thus, isomorphism has the advantage and disadvantage of shaping the research approach to the phenomenon, the therapeutic process to the family system, and the family's epistemology to the therapeutic and research epistemologies.

Selection of a peer debriefer knowledgeable about qualitative method but more strongly socialized in the positivist paradigm was crucial to maximizing the strengths and minimizing the limitations of this isomorphism. Throughout the process, this debriefer challenged me to articulate my methodology, revisit my hypotheses, and sit with puzzling observations.

SEEKING METHODOLOGICAL RIGOR

Given the assumption of reciprocal influence, inclusion of verification methods that enhance participant-observer (researcher) reflexivity and credibility of data can improve the methodological rigor of qualitative studies. Strategies for enhancing methodological rigor include (a) a clear understanding of qualitative epistemology, including covenantal and critical ethics, (b) debriefing, (c) enhancing entry and immersion skills, (d) triangulation of data, (e) peer examination, and (f) conducting member checks with participants from multiple stakeholder groups. Method without epistemology, however, will not improve rigor. Qualitative method requires more than just learning a procedure (Lincoln & Guba, 1985).

Importance of Understanding Qualitative Epistemology

Qualitative method is an approach rather than a procedure. It is designed to be used in the study of emergent meaning construction, suggesting that even in the most carefully designed studies, the method will be shaped by the phenomenon being studied. Without a strong understanding of the qualitative epistemology, it would be difficult to apply the model systematically. When problems arise in the field, epistemology guides the researcher and the debriefer in managing threats to the rigor of the study (Lincoln & Guba, 1985).

Debriefings

The peer debriefer's role involves facilitating the researcher in clarifying what may otherwise remain implicit. The debriefer asks probing questions and plays devil's advocate. He or she challenges interpretations and collaborates with the researcher in managing methodological rigor. The debriefer also facilitates the researcher in increasing his or her awareness of positions taken, of processes used in arriving at and testing hypotheses, and in exploring how his or her values and beliefs affect what is knowable. The debriefer discusses, makes recommendations, and collaboratively problem-solves threats to methodological rigor as the study unfolds. The debriefer provides a safe environment in which the researcher can process feelings that may be interfering with his or her ability to be fully present and open in the field. The depth of immersion required in qualitative work is exhausting, time-consuming, and lonely. The debriefer can often be a vehicle for maintaining "binocularity": managing subjectivity and reconnecting with self after long periods of immersion in the field (Lincoln & Guba, 1985).

Because using the qualitative method reflexively requires a deep understanding of the epistemology, it is extremely important to seek out someone who is either familiar with qualitative epistemology and method or highly invested in learning it. Although the issue of selection criteria has not been widely discussed, I tend to seek debriefers who are inquisitive, observant, and reflexive, who have very different theoretical preferences than I, and who enjoy the stimulation of being immersed in the dialectical process.

Entry and Immersion as a Participant-Observer

The ability to immerse into the world of participants and to listen deeply to their stories requires an ability to establish deep, meaningful relationships with others. To achieve and maintain successful entry, it is important to consider how you might habituate participants to your presence. It is likely that you will still have an effect on the system, but by minimizing that impact, credibility or authenticity of your data will be enhanced.

When I began implementing my study, I had been a member of the therapy team participating in the study for 4 years. My first challenge was habituating the team to my presence in a new role. My principle strategy was to situate myself before anyone else arrived so that I might eventually become a part of the clinic environment. I wore the same dove colors and made only limited eye contact. Although I could not eliminate my impact on their behavior, I did what I could to minimize my presence. Within 2 weeks, I could sit next to reflecting team members at a research team meeting only to meet them in the hall, later, concerned that I had missed the meeting.

Learning to operationalize qualitative method and to immerse into the Milan systemic family therapy process as a participant-observer outside the treatment team involved not only habituating the team to my presence in a new role but also learning multiple languages or meaning systems, including my own meta-language connecting multiple systems into a larger system. As a *participant-observer* rather than an observer, I assumed that what was knowable would be a product of my own personal filters (Clifford & Marcus, 1986). The very act of formulating a question implied a valuing of what is meaningful to ask (Wolcott, 1992).

Rigorous participant observation requires immersion into, and the flexibility to move into and out of, divergent phenomenological spaces (Lincoln & Guba, 1985). What may be most challenging in accomplishing this is suspending core beliefs and values: to hear the voice of another above the din of a singular subjective approach to knowing (Andersen, 1992; LeCompte, Preissle, & Tesch, 1984). In addition, as one attempts to understand alternative perspectives, it is virtually impossible to escape the influence of the construction of reality that one is attempting to capture (Lincoln & Guba, 1985). Rigorous participant observation requires continual monitoring of "binocularity": maintaining an experience of both immersion and distance.

Triangulation

Triangulation is a verification method that also enhances credibility of the findings and interpretations. Reconciling the frequently discrepant verbal, written, and observational self-reports can reveal complex patterns and hidden meanings. The two most common types of triangulation involve triangulation by different sources and triangulation by different methods. When data are triangulated by *source* (e.g., different stakeholder groups), data are collected from different participants or participant groups; when data are triangulated by *method,* data are collected by different modes (e.g., interview, written, observation; Lincoln & Guba, 1985).

Implicit in the discrepancies between sources and methods can be rules, roles, and functions that implicitly structure interactions in the family system. Although these findings may be helpful to families seeking help from other Milan teams, the recursive approach required to generate these findings is so extensive that it is not likely to benefit the family currently participating in the study (Rafuls & Moon, 1996).

Peer Examination

In the study of the Milan systemic family therapy experience, a *peer examiner* with a different theoretical orientation was recruited to examine and comment on themes and categories as they emerged from the interview, session break, postsession debriefing, and counseling session transcripts and journals. The peer examiner was asked to code the data from her own theoretical orientation. Her coding strategy was then used to challenge the researcher's hypotheses.

The peer examiner, like the debriefer, played a crucial role in the data analysis process. It was the peer examiner's coding that suggested the structural nature of the participants' interactions. The shift of roles and functions across the mirror later proved to be an important part of the meaning change in the system, suggesting that parallel process occurs across the mirror whether or not the family and reflecting team have contact (Tanji, 1995).

Member Checks

Participants in the study were consulted during the analysis process and were asked to review the written conclusions and to offer comments, clarifications, and suggestions. Member checks invite participants to provide feedback on the accuracy of the researcher's conceptualization of the process. Member checks may be most generative to participants when inclusive variants of the Milan systemic family model are used. In cases where the team discloses only select hypotheses to family members, member checking may not be as informative.

Relational Ethics

Credibility of the data and subsequent findings are strongly influenced by the researcher/participant-observer's ability to negotiate a respectful and meaningful relationship with family and team participants. To the degree that the researcher succeeds, he or she will be able to elicit the idiographic experiences of participants and to avoid the party line or culturally rehearsed responses that may mask the true perceptions of participants (Kirk & Miller, 1986; LeCompte et al., 1984).

In the interaction between systemic family therapy and the qualitative method, each shapes the other as the process of social construction in both domains ensues. Given the recursive nature of both processes, it seems important to consider the relevance of covenantal and critical ethical concerns. Can fully informed consent be found in a changing system? Despite the more egalitarian framework assumed by the qualitative paradigm, the relative power differential between researcher and participants is still apparent. It is the researcher's prerogative to determine and ask the questions and to focus selectively on specific story lines. Perhaps the selective focus on the interactions contributes to the difficulty in seeing the participants (Deyhle, Hess, & LeCompte, 1992).

CONCLUSION

Qualitative method offers exciting possibilities for studying systemic process with theoretical sensitivity. The challenge of using the model ethically and effectively is awareness of the complementarity between qualitative and systemic family therapy approaches. Even with high standards of methodological rigor built into a design, the research method is likely to have an effect or influence on participants. Immersion into participant narratives facilitates immediacy and sustained reflection similar to that of therapy (Rafuls & Moon, 1996; Rennie, 1994). If researchers are to maximize the advantages and minimize the disadvantages of using research models more adept at capturing systemic therapeutic change process, it may be helpful to design studies that explore the interface between these isomorphic domains.

It will also be crucial for more family therapists and researchers to familiarize themselves with the qualitative paradigm. The epistemological shift required in effectively using a qualitative method will likely be transferrable to treatment skills. Given the complexity and process orientation of the model, however, it may be advantageous to seek out apprenticeships with others and to research what is most effective in training qualitative researchers.

REFERENCES

Anderson, H., & Goolishian, H. (1992). The client is the expert: A not-knowing approach to therapy. In S. McNamee & K. J. Gergen (Eds.), *Therapy as social construction* (pp. 25-39). London: Sage.

Anderson, H., Goolishian, H., & Winderman, L. (1986). Problem-determined systems: Toward transformation in family therapy. *Journal of Strategic and Systemic Therapies, 5*(4), 1-11.

Andersen, T. (1991). *The reflecting team: Dialogues and dialogues about the dialogues.* New York: Norton.

Andersen, T. (1992). Reflections on reflecting with families. In S. McNamee & K. J. Gergen (Eds.), *Therapy as social construction* (pp. 54-68). London: Sage.

Bednar, R. L., Burlingame, G. M., & Masters, K. S. (1988). Systems of family treatment: Substance or semantics. *Annual Review of Psychology, 39,* 401-413.

Boscolo, L., Cecchin, G., Hoffman, L., & Penn, P. (1987). *Milan systemic family therapy.* New York: Basic Books.

Cecchin, G. (1987). Hypothesizing, circularity, and neutrality revisited: An introduction to curiosity. *Family Process, 26*(4), 405-414.

Cecchin, G. (1992). Constructing therapeutic possibilities. In S. McNamee & K. J. Gergen (Eds.), *Therapy as social construction* (pp. 86-95). London: Sage.

Cecchin, G., Lane, G., & Ray, W. A. (1992). *Irreverence: A strategy for therapists' survival.* London: H. Karnac.

Clifford, J., & Marcus, G. (1986). *Writing culture.* Berkeley: University of California Press.

Deyhle, D. L., Hess, G. A., & LeCompte, M. D. (1992). Approaching ethical issues for qualitative researchers in education. In M. D. LeCompte, W. L. Millroy, & J. Preissle (Eds.), *The handbook of qualitative research in education* (pp. 597-642). San Diego, CA: Academic Press.

Epston, D., White, M., & Murray, K. (1992). A proposal for a reauthoring therapy: Rose's revisioning of her life and a commentary. In S. McNamee & K. J. Gergen (Eds.), *Therapy as social construction* (pp. 96-115). London: Sage.

Fleuridas, C., Nelson, T. S., & Rosenthal, D. M. (1986). The evolution of circular questions: Training family therapists. *Journal of Marital and Family Therapy, 12*(2), 113-127.

Gergen, K. J. (1988). If persons are texts. In S. B. Messer, L. A. Sass, & R. L. Woolfolk (Eds.), *Hermeneutics and psychological theory.* New Brunswick, NJ: Rutgers University Press.

Gergen, K. J., & Kaye, J. (1992). Beyond narrative in the negotiation of therapeutic meaning. In S. McNamee & K. J. Gergen (Eds.), *Therapy as social construction* (pp. 166-185). London: Sage.

Guttman, H. A. (1991). Systems theory, cybernetics, and epistemology. In A. S. Gurman & D. P. Kniskern (Eds.), *Handbook of family therapy* (Vol. 2, pp. 41-62). New York: Brunner/Mazel.

Hoshmand, L. S. T. (1989). Alternate research paradigms: A review and teaching proposal. *Counseling Psychologist, 17,* 1-80.

Karl, Cynthia, Andrew, & Vanessa. (1992). Therapeutic distinctions in an ongoing therapy. In S. McNamee & K. J. Gergen (Eds.), *Therapy as social construction* (pp. 116-135). London: Sage.

Kirk, J., & Miller, M. L. (1986). *Reliability and validity in qualitative research.* Beverly Hills, CA: Sage.

Lax, W. D. (1992). Postmodern thinking in a clinical practice. In S. McNamee & K. J. Gergen (Eds.), *Therapy as social construction* (pp. 69-85). London: Sage.

LeCompte, M. D., Preissle, J., & Tesch, R. (1984). *Ethnography and qualitative design in educational research.* San Diego: Academic Press.

Lincoln, Y. S., & Guba, E. G. (1985). *Naturalistic inquiry.* Beverly Hills, CA: Sage.

McNamee, S. (1992). Reconstructing identity: The communal construction of crisis. In S. McNamee & K. J. Gergen (Eds.), *Therapy as social construction* (pp. 186-199). London: Sage.

Moon, S. M., Dillon, D. R., & Sprenkle, D. H. (1991). Family therapy and qualitative research. *Journal of Marital and Family Therapy, 16,* 357-373.

Nichols, M. P., & Schwartz, R. C. (1995). *Family therapy: Concepts and methods* (3rd ed.). Boston: Allyn & Bacon.

Penn, P. (1982). Circular questioning. *Family Process, 21,* 267-280.

Penn, P. (1985). Feed forward: Future questions, future maps. *Family Process, 24,* 299-311.

Rafuls, S. E., & Moon, S. M. (1996). Grounded theory methodology in family therapy research. In D. H. Sprenkle & S. M. Moon (Eds.), *Research methods in family therapy* (pp. 64-80). New York: Guilford.

Rennie, D. L. (1994). Storytelling in psychotherapy: The client's subjective experience. *Psychotherapy, 31*(2), 234-243.

Robinson, J. A., & Hawpe, L. (1986). Narrative thinking as a heuristic process. In T. R. Sabin (Ed.), *Narrative psychology: The storied nature of human conduct* (pp. 111-125). New York: Praeger Scientific.

Sabin, T. R. (1986). *Narrative psychology: The storied nature of human conduct.* New York: Praeger.

Selvini, M., Boscolo, L., Cecchin, G., & Prata, G. (1980). Hypothesizing—circularity—neutrality: Three guidelines for the conductor of the session. *Family Process, 19*(1), 3-12.

Sprenkle, D. H., & Bischoff, R. J. (1995). Research in family therapy: Trends, issues, and recommendations. In M. P. Nichols & R. C. Schwartz (Eds.), *Family therapy: Concepts and methods* (3rd ed.). Boston: Allyn & Bacon.

Sprenkle, D. H., & Moon, S. M. (1996). Toward pluralism in family therapy research. In D. H. Sprenkle & S. M. Moon (Eds.), *Research methods in family therapy* (pp. 3-19). New York: Guilford.

Tanji, J. M. (1995). *Milan systemic family therapy as a training model: A grounded theory study.* Unpublished doctoral dissertation, University of Nebraska at Lincoln.

Tomm, K. (1987a). Interventive interviewing: Part I. Strategizing as a fourth guideline for the therapist. *Family Process, 26*(2), 3-13.

Tomm, K. (1987b). Interventive interviewing: Part II. Reflexive questioning as a means to enable self-healing. *Family Process, 26*(4), 167-183.

Tomm, K. (1988). Interventive interviewing: Part III. Intending to ask lineal, circular, strategic, or reflexive questions? *Family Process, 27*(1), 1-15.

Wolcott, H. F. (1992). Posturing in qualitative research. In M. D. LeCompte, W. L. Millroy, & J. Preissle (Eds.), *Handbook of qualitative research in education* (pp. 3-52). San Diego, CA: Academic Press.

Wynne, L. C. (1983). Family research and family therapy: A reunion? *Journal of Marital and Family Therapy, 9*, 113-117.

CHAPTER 14

Using a Qualitative Method to Study Clinical Supervision
What Is Effective Clinical Supervision?

Virginia O'Brien
Mary Kopala

Most experts agree that clinical supervision is an activity that occurs between a junior and a senior member of a helping profession and that the purpose is to enhance the therapeutic and professional skill of the junior member or supervisee while promoting the well-being of the actual clients with whom the supervisee is working. During the past 15 years, this definition has been fine-tuned, and some authors have extended this definition to include group supervision. But this chapter is not a discourse on clinical supervision, and so a thorough discussion of what constitutes clinical supervision is not necessary (if you are interested in the finer details, see Bernard & Goodyear, 1992). Suffice it to say that the role of the clinical supervisor is important in that at least two vulnerable people—the supervisee and the client—are the responsibility of the supervisor. Consequently, it is a role that should not be taken lightly. Unfortunately, many clinical supervisors are ineffective in their mission and often leave supervisees feeling injured and ineffective (Kopala & Keitel, 1991).

Kopala conceived of this study in response to a recognition that some clinical supervisors are helpful and supportive and encourage growth and development, whereas others evoke feelings of anger, distress, and inadequacy. It seemed that if counselors go through a developmental process from novice counselor to master counselor as is suggested by the literature (e.g., Worthington, 1987), then perhaps supervisors, too, must go through a developmental process from novice supervisor to master supervisor. That may explain why some supervisors are more effective than others.

Given the importance of the role of supervisor in the training of future counselors and the likelihood that new counselors will assume the role of supervisor sometime in their careers, how individuals develop in their role of supervisor seemed an important research question. Hess (1986) briefly addressed this issue and identified a 3-stage model that begins with a new Ph.D. making a transition from supervisee to supervisor. According to Hess, this process continues as one enjoys feelings of more confidence, competence, and enthusiasm in the role of supervisor in the second stage. In the third stage, a mutual respect between supervisor and supervisee increases, and the focus is on the supervisory relationship. But Hess said little about the development of supervisor effectiveness.

Both of us—independent of each other—have struggled with our own and our colleagues' ineffective supervisory experiences. We often asked ourselves, Am I responsible? when supervisory relationships seemed not to work well. In an attempt to gain understanding, each of us asked ourselves, What part did I play in the dynamics between us? Answers to these questions came with a greater understanding of the supervisory process, self-exploration, and the conviction that when a supervisory relationship was rocky, it was not entirely the fault of the supervisee. In fact, at times it just might be the supervisor's fault. These thoughts and experiences led the second author to explore further the relationship of clinical supervisor and supervisee.

It did not take long to discover that not only could the relationship between supervisor and supervisee be troublesome, but to study the relationship could also be difficult and troublesome. After all, how does one fit this dynamic relationship into a between-groups design? For nearly a year, countless hours were spent figuring out a way to study this relationship by using the tools acquired in graduate research methods courses. Attempts to use groups of supervisors and groups of supervisees were unsuccessful. No matter what was done, the question simply did not fit the research methodology. During this time, Kopala was still a graduate student attempting to design a dissertation study.

The issue was resolved one day when a different research methodology was discovered. A journal article suggested that $N = 1$ designs might be useful for answering questions in counseling. This idea was eagerly embraced as a feasible way to conduct the study. With the support of both her advisor and her dissertation committee, Kopala began a study of the supervisory relationship by using a single case design. On completion of the study, it was clear that the method was only moderately successful, and the investigator was not completely satisfied.

Kopala's interest continued in the area of supervision, and questions about the supervisory relationship continued to plague her. This happened at a time of great change and growth for her. Part of her responsibilities as a new assistant professor were to teach a class in supervision to doctoral students. At this same time, Dr. Leo Goldman, a new colleague, encouraged her to learn about qualitative research methods, and so she completed a course on qualitative methods offered in the graduate Department of Social Work at the university where she worked. To complete the methods course, she had to develop a research project. It occurred to her at this time that a qualitative approach could be the best way to study her questions about supervision. At last, it was all coming together—a way to study the area in which she was interested and, she hoped, to answer the question she had been asking all along: Why are some supervisors more effective than others? This class project was the first qualitative study designed and conducted by the second author.

THE PROCESS OF QUALITATIVE
SUPERVISION RESEARCH

The study was intended to examine whether student supervisors moved through a developmental process. Did they undergo changes as a result of a course in supervision and the activity of supervising master's level students? How did they understand their new role as supervisor for master's level students in counseling? Although the project was conceived as part of a course, the study was begun after the course had been completed. At this point, the study was conducted solely by the second author and without further assistance or advice. Like many novice qualitative researchers in psychology, there were few resources and individuals who could help.

Ten doctoral students enrolled in Kopala's supervision class and met weekly. All of these students were new to the area of clinical supervision, and each was assigned to supervise a master's level student enrolled in a field placement class. In addition to the supervision provided by the doctoral students, the master's students were also receiving supervision from professional counselors at their field placement sites.

The supervision class was conducted as a seminar, and students shared their fears, frustrations, angers, and successes each week as they related their experiences of supervising another individual. Much intimacy had developed among the class members and between the students and the professor. At the time, it seemed natural and appropriate to ask these students to reflect on their experiences as novice counselors. Kopala explained the project to the class and asked individuals to consider whether they would be willing to participate in the study. Those individuals who agreed to participate gave formal informed consent, and then in-depth qualitative individual interviews of nine of the students were begun during the last 4 weeks of the semester. One student declined to participate.

The Student Supervisors' Interviews

A semistructured interview schedule, with each interview lasting between 1 and 2 hours, was used. Interview questions were designed to enable respondents to describe various aspects of their experiences as supervisors. Students were asked to describe their experiences as supervisors, to evaluate the quality of their relationship with their supervisees, and to discuss the didactic information presented in class. As a follow-up to these open-ended questions, students were asked to reflect on and describe their feelings and behaviors during the actual supervision sessions. The final questions centered on how the students changed as a result of being a supervisor.

During the interviews, students often reflected on their own experiences as *supervisees*. It seemed quite natural for them to draw on these experiences because they were immersed in a long process of being supervised and were more familiar with the role of supervisee than supervisor. Often their own experiences were so current and formative that they had a significant impact on how the students acted toward their supervisees.

Because the interviews were intended to glean all relevant information on the topic of supervision, any new information that emerged during the interviews was explored, and respondents were encouraged to elaborate on each new topic area. (Questions about new topics were then added to the interview schedule and were asked during subsequent interviews.) Several respondents welcomed time to discuss what they thought were relevant areas of supervision. Perhaps the dialogue was able to continue because the students thought that, especially in this setting, they were somewhat like colleagues with their professor. Their hectic graduate school schedules were interrupted, and they were able to pause and share their more heartfelt experiences on a topic so central to their profession. Not only were they listened to with respect, but the graduate students' responses were considered noteworthy; the students felt as if they were making a valuable contribution to the profession.

This experience created an atmosphere of mutual trust and collaboration between the students and their professor and lessened the anxiety on the part of some students who had felt some pressure to present the right answers to the questions. The qualitative research design highlighted the reality that not all the definitive answers to research questions are in and that the process of exploring the questions can be a mutual learning experience.

Unfortunately for this new researcher trained primarily in quantitative methods, reflection about ethical concerns came from the perspective of a quantitative researcher. The researcher was open and up-front about the purpose of the project; no one was deceived. Informed consent was obtained, and students agreed to audiotape the conversations, but clearly the students were in a dual relationship with the researcher, who also happened to be their professor for a course in supervision. Yes, they were assured that they could withdraw or not participate at all and that they would not be penalized (participation or lack thereof did not affect their grades in any way), but did they really feel comfortable participating in this study? Did they feel coerced?

O'Brien, the first author of this chapter, was a member in that class. In preparation for this chapter, she wrote the following about this experience:

> This interview method seemed to work well since it was one in which the interviewer had considerable experience. Given that her own relationship with

the individual students was positive, the students generally felt free to give an in-depth response to her questions. However, since it was the first experience being a supervisor for many of the students, the interviews from the perspective of the students often caused some anxiety. The source of the anxiety seemed to center on the possibility that their weakness as supervisors might readily be exposed.

As the researcher and a new faculty member, Kopala knew little of the anxiety she evoked as the teacher of the class. She was more convinced that the anxiety detected was a result of this new role known as supervisor. Her own experiences as a new supervisor and faculty member fairly fresh from graduate school seemed to correspond with the feelings these novice supervisors reported.

I had developed rapport with the class members, and it seemed at the time the study was conducted that, in some ways, it was almost a participant observation study. True, I didn't study their behavior in the classroom, but the class experiences allowed the interviews to be conducted—or so I thought.

Analysis of the Student Supervisors' Data

All interviews were audiotaped. The tape recorder and microphone sat openly on the table between the interviewer and the respondent. All respondents were asked to give written and oral permission for the interview and taping to take place. The interviews were transcribed by Kopala. Each transcript was assigned a number to protect the confidentiality of the students. The task of transcribing the interviews was both painstaking and time-consuming. Given the length of the interviews and the fact that the participants were immersed in both theoretical knowledge and the practical experience of supervision, the amount of information obtained from each interview was extensive.

Following the completion of the transcriptions, the process of identifying the major concepts and ideas contained in the interviews was begun. Despite the relatively few interviews nine sessions of $1\frac{1}{2}$ hours each—mounds of data resulted. In an effort to be "close" to the data, Kopala waded into the data and felt overwhelmed and uncertain, with Strauss and Corbin (1990) always within easy reach. This part of the project required large blocks of uninterrupted time—time spent solely on the identification of themes and relationships. Each transcription was read and reread several times to identify major concepts and ideas. As themes emerged, charts were constructed that contained interview identification codes. The transcript pages and exact lines that corresponded to the identifying concepts were indicated.

In an effort to manage the extensive data, tentative categories were identified. The text was then reread to find all supporting evidence for the existence of that particular category. Characteristics of each category were examined to determine whether they were mutually exclusive of each other.

Themes From the Student Supervisors' Transcripts

Five categories emerged from the transcripts that described the experience of the novice supervisors: (a) the role of the supervisor, (b) the impact of the supervisory process, (c) supervision techniques, (d) the supervisor-supervisee relationship, and (e) supervisor judgments, attitudes, and opinions of supervisees.

The students often described feelings of confusion and self-doubt about their abilities as supervisors. This seemed to be developmentally appropriate because all the doctoral students were supervising for the first time, with the exception of one student who had participated in peer supervision during a previous semester. During the supervision sessions, the students reported that they did not focus solely on client diagnosis or focus solely on specific techniques of counseling. Rather, the tendency was to provide didactic information about the client problem that was presented or to answer specific questions the supervisee raised about the client or the client's issues.

The doctoral students seemed to be very cognizant of the attained skills presented by their supervisees, and consequently they tended to provide supervision in response to their assessment of their superviseess skill levels. They worked hard to meet the needs of their supervisees and tended to be more didactic if they thought a supervisee needed to learn skills. If the doctoral students were confident about their supervisees' competence, they were less directive in the supervision sessions.

Throughout the interviews, a great concern was expressed for the actual clients' welfare. The supervisors felt extremely responsible for protecting the clients from the novice counselors, realizing that the counselor-client relationship is one in which the counselor has a significant influence in the life of the client, who may be very vulnerable. This intense consciousness on the part of the doctoral students may also have been influenced by their own experience of being new in their role as supervisor and wanting to avoid any semblance of being incompetent, even indirectly.

Finally, the supervisors were sensitive to their supervisees as individuals and worked hard to establish rapport. They were cautious about being critical of their supervisees' work so as not to destroy their self-esteem. Perhaps they wanted to avoid some of the negative experiences they themselves had faced or were facing in their own advanced practicum sites. The students reported that they enjoyed the supervision experience, worked hard to prepare for supervision, and considered it an important professional activity.

EXPANSION OF THE STUDY TO PROFESSIONAL SUPERVISORS

After the interviews with the graduate students were completed and the transcripts transcribed, it became evident that some emerging themes pertained specifically to novice supervisors. The question emerged, How would more experienced field supervisors respond to similar questions on the topic of supervision? It was clear that if a theory of supervisor development was to be developed, this was the next logical step. Following the qualitative research paradigm, the study was expanded to include experienced supervisors. Although an expansive amount of data had already been collected, the need to expand the study to well-established supervisors seemed urgent to obtain a broader representation of the developmental stages of a supervisor (if, in fact, such stages existed at all). It was also obvious to Kopala that the project could no longer be undertaken by a solo researcher. The time required to conduct interviews, transcribe tapes, and then analyze the data was prohibitive. It had also become quite apparent that, at this time, finding an outlet for publication of the research may be impossible. As an assistant professor trying to juggle class preparations and teaching with service obligations and scholarly pursuit, it became difficult to spend time on the project despite the fact that the project was one of particular interest.

At this time, one graduate student from the original study (O'Brien, the first author of this chapter) was beginning a research project necessary to complete a specific doctoral degree requirement. Kopala invited O'Brien to join this qualitative research project. Quantitative research projects were the more acceptable norm on campus. Quantitative research was known to be the research that enabled one to become a scientist/practitioner, a professional that the majority of students were striving to become. Qualitative research did not make that cut despite the fact that authors (see Goldman, 1986) were calling for more of it, especially in the field of psychology. Students who "number crunched" were sought after by their colleagues and professors; those who engaged in qualitative research were fortunate if their projects were found acceptable. Despite this attitude, O'Brien found this invitation to be a welcome alternative. Here was an opportunity to explain issues directly related to counseling without reducing phenomena to measurable variables. Instead, the richness of the relationship between supervisors and supervisees could be studied in context with attention to the meaning of participants.

After collaborating with the lead researcher, the student who had a firsthand feel for the project because she had been one of the nine students interviewed joined the research team. This required that the student switch roles; instead of responding to questions, she began to develop interview questions based on those used in the original study. Switching roles was challenging, yet the collaboration between the two researchers worked well. A very positive mentoring relationship developed, and with dialogue based on mutual respect, the questions for the professional supervisors flowed rather naturally from those asked of the student supervisors.

The student was shown the beginnings of the data analysis from her class's interviews. For her, it was somewhat like looking at the beginnings of an architect's drawing and wondering what type of structure might emerge. Her own feelings were ones of excitement that something new and relevant to the field was being formed, mixed with the graduate student's ever-present anxiety that Hess's (1986) theory would not be supported.

From all the responses of the novice supervisors, four areas of questioning for the "expert" supervisors seemed to emerge: (a) expectations of supervision, (b) feelings about supervision, (c) behavior during the supervision sessions, and (d) thoughts and opinions on supervision. Questions were designed to identify how supervisors dealt with an issue currently, how they did so in the past, and how they thought they may approach it in the future. It was decided that each section would close with the open-ended question, Is there anything else you would like to tell me about this area of supervision?

As O'Brien became more aware of the possibilities for personal growth in her own role of supervisor, she often felt inadequate when meeting face-to-face with individuals whom she had not previously met and who had been supervisors for years. Considerable energy was spent managing her anxiety and being present with the supervisors so that spontaneous follow-up questions could be asked where appropriate. Often the questions on supervision echoed in her mind as she asked them while at the same time somewhat distracting herself with an outline of her own answer that she might offer if asked to engage in a dialogue on specific points. In her mind, the ideal graduate student was able to converse on every topic; therefore, it was difficult to remain open to the process and be with the person being interviewed, rather than search one's own memory bank for an appropriate response.

The Supervisors' Interviews

It was practice at this university that students completed supervisor evaluations at the end of each fieldwork course. O'Brien reviewed these reports, and supervisors were selected as potential participants in the study. Those chosen had been evaluated positively and were considered approachable by the graduate students who had completed the reports. Six supervisors agreed to be interviewed, signed informed consent papers, and agreed to be audiotaped. The supervisors who were interviewed worked in hospitals, schools, colleges, and community counseling centers. O'Brien conducted each interview at the supervisors' work site, and each lasted $1\frac{1}{2}$ to 2 hours.

Analysis of the Professional Supervisors' Data

The same procedure for analyzing the data that was used for the first part of the study was followed for the taped transcripts of the supervisors. Each transcript was assigned a number to protect confidentiality, and once they were transcribed, the process of identifying the major concepts and ideas contained in the interviews was begun. Initially, O'Brien took responsibility for analyzing the interviews, following the directions of Kopala.

Once again, the enormous amount of time it took to read and identify themes from the transcripts was surprising. The process often felt overwhelming, and I began to doubt that valuable data could emerge in any recognizable pattern.

And so the two researchers set up several meetings so that the analysis continued as a joint process. Through the joint effort of both researchers and after reading the transcripts several times, identifiable patterns did emerge.

Key quotations that best illustrated the responses of the supervisors were gleaned from the transcripts and organized under the pertinent headings. These quotations gave support to document the organization of the material in appropriate categories.

Themes From the Supervisors' Transcripts

The major themes from these interviews were (a) supervisors' understanding of the role of supervision, (b) knowledge of supervision techniques and theory, (c) impact of the supervisory process on the supervisor, (d) supervisors' judgments, attitudes, and opinions of supervisees, and (e) supervisor-supervisee relationship. Responses were often found on some point along a continuum that ranged, for example, from colleague to expert on one's perception of the role, from confused to clear on one's understanding of the role, from no sense to a strong sense regarding responsibility, and from no influence to a great deal of influence regarding past supervisors.

Understandings of the role of supervision varied. They contained reflections on an educative role that included a mandate to teach individuals to become psychotherapists, as well as more of a mentoring role that called for supervisors to model with their supervisees the care they were giving their own patients. Within each conceptualization, a clear theme was for a person who had considerable experience in the field to share that with someone who was more of a neophyte. The importance of both the person who was being supervised and the process of supervision was emphasized.

Knowledge of supervision theory was found to be limited. Only one supervisor who was interviewed had any formal course work in supervision. The other supervisors, though they all professed that supervision is an essential ingredient in becoming a counselor, had no formal training for the role in which they spent a significant portion of their professional time. Instead of using a theoretically based model of supervision, they seemed to apply their knowledge of counseling to supervision. One supervisor described her growth in the role as "pulling herself up by her own bootstraps."

The impact of the supervisory process on the supervisors included the realization that they got a certain satisfaction watching therapists grow. In some cases, a rich mutual learning experience occurred between supervisor and supervisee, wherein each person learned more about psychotherapy. In another instance, a supervisor reported being more of a "big brother" who shared his years of experience with younger counselors. One supervisor used her experience as a supervisor as a measure of how far she herself had developed as a counselor from the days when she was in supervision.

Supervisors expressed several judgments, attitudes, and opinions of their supervisees and the supervisor-supervisee relationship. One supervisor referred to the experience as "potty training" a new profession. Another reported that she trained her supervisees so that she could leave the counseling center early in the evenings for "the place is running itself." Others expressed the need to create a relationship that included mutual respect and openness and a place where students could bring their most challenging cases for collaborative consultation.

The need for the supervisee-supervisor relationship to be open was expressed by several participants. One supervisor expressed it in terms of a "two-way street" where communication needed to come from both participants. Another believed that supervisees needed enough freedom to be able to state that they were lost, without fear that they would be negatively judged. Situations that created a fear of judgment were found to prevent supervisees from returning to future sessions. Finally, one supervisor addressed issues of supervisees' countertransference in the sessions with their clients and the parallel process that often occurred in the supervisory sessions. Her reflections centered on how and when to process issues between herself and her supervisee without becoming the supervisee's therapist. Other supervisors reported struggling in their efforts to balance their need to be directive and their helping the supervisees become more autonomous.

When the results of both studies were examined together, only partial support for Hess's (1986) model was found. In addition, the rich data that resulted from the use of a qualitative method provided a better understanding of the supervisory process and insight into why some supervisors may be perceived as more effective than others. The use of in-depth interviews to study this group allowed us to understand better the perspectives of these novice and experienced supervisors. We also recognized, however, that these two studies represented only the beginning of an awareness of how the clinical supervisor develops.

DISCUSSION

The use of a qualitative method seemed to be a good fit as we researched the process that clinical supervisors undergo as they share their expertise with novice counselors. Now, many years later, as we have reflected on our study with a more sophisticated understanding of qualitative methods than we had when we first conducted the study, we have identified some issues on which we wish to comment.

One thing became immediately clear: We did not have the problem that many authors describe, that of gaining access to the group to be studied. Frequently, researchers are viewed with suspicion by gatekeepers as they attempt to gain entry to a setting, or once in the setting, the participants may be wary about revealing information to the researchers. Because one author was the professor of a class, participants were readily accessible and willing to participate.

This raises the ethical dilemma discussed earlier: Were the participants coerced? Faculty frequently invite students to participate in studies, of course, but this practice does not make it an ethical practice. The use of a semistructured interview schedule minimized issues regarding informed consent. At least some control regarding the topics and feelings that emerged was retained by the interviewer. This allowed for a more fully informed consent. At least students had a pretty good understanding of what participation entailed. In hindsight, at least one benefit may justify having had student participants: Many of the students reported that the interview gave them an opportunity to debrief the course, an opportunity they otherwise would not have had.

Further, it became apparent that the initial investigator's interpretation of the data was partly erroneous when she interpreted anxiety as a response to the new role of supervisor. Because her coauthor understood that some participants feared they would be discovered to be inadequate supervisors, this error was identified. However, not every study team has this insight. Perhaps here is the beginning of an argument for choosing research team members partly on the basis of their social location. Or perhaps the answer is one that Rennie (1996) put forth when he suggested that authors recognize clearly it is their interpretation of the data they present.

Finally, this study represents the evolution common to the use of qualitative methods. Interview schedules were changed in response to the interviews, and a second group of respondents was added to the original group. The "study" could continue; future studies may be conducted with other individuals in training by researchers who are not also the respondents' professor, or a group of experienced supervisors who have had training in clinical supervision could also be interviewed. Only one of our experienced supervisors had formal training.

REFERENCES

Bernard, J. M., & Goodyear, R. K. (1992). *Fundamentals of clinical supervision.* Boston: Allyn & Bacon.

Goldman, L. (1986). Research and evaluation. In M. D. Lewis, R. L. Hayes, & J. A. Lewis (Eds.), *An introduction to the counseling profession* (pp. 278-300). Itasca, IL: F. E. Peacock.

Hess, A. K. (1986). Growth in supervision: Stages of supervisee and supervisor development. *Clinical Supervisor, 4,* 51-57.

Kopala, M., & Keitel, M. A. (1991, Fall). Supervisees' perceptions of supervisor behaviors: A qualitative investigation. *New York State Journal for Counseling and Development,* 25-38.

Rennie, D. L. (1996). Fifteen years of doing qualitative research on psychotherapy. *British Journal of Guidance and Counseling, 24,* 317-327.

Strauss, A., & Corbin, J. (1990). *Basics of qualitative research.* Newbury Park, CA:
    Sage.
Worthington, E. L., Jr. (1987). Changes in supervision as counselors and supervisors
    can experience: A review. *Professional Psychology: Research and Practice, 18,*
    189-208.

CHAPTER 15

Relationship-Based Change

A Feminist Qualitative
Research Case

Michelle Maher

Feminist scholarship brings a concern for how domination and liberation function. By definition, it is driven by a political agenda to create social change, empower women, and end oppression. Of course, feminist discussions are full of debate about exactly what this might look like and how to go about it. Feminist researchers, theorists, and activists often recognize contradiction, tension, and paradox as an expected and welcome form of the complexity of their work (Maher, 1996). Feminists value relationship as a primary issue, especially because power (and thus possibilities for exploitation) functions within relationships. Feminist qualitative researchers focus on the complex issues of relationship and power within multiple social contexts, such as their subjects' lived experience and culture, as well as the research process itself.

In feminist qualitative research, the relationship between subjects and researchers is especially important. Because feminists seek to be self-reflective in their own research, they acknowledge that all researchers undoubtedly bring their own perspectives, politics, consciousness, and passion to the research process. Feminists also seek to supply the social context in which research claims are made in order to provide a broader scope of meaning. The relationship between researchers and participants (hereafter referred to as the research relationship) is an important part of the research process. Relationships by definition are continuously cocreated. The mutuality and negotiation of the relationship between subjects and researchers affect the data. The research relationship provides the context in which data are gathered. Although such relationships can be difficult to capture in writing, I argue that doing so creates

---

AUTHOR'S NOTE: All participants' names contained herein are names they chose to represent themselves.

more credible reporting of research because it deepens descriptions of the context in which the research took place.

In this chapter, I describe qualities of the research relationships created in a study I conducted on lesbians' experience of supportiveness in their therapy. First, I present a review of feminist concerns in qualitative research to provide the reader with the theoretical context of this study. Next, I overview my study and the participants' reports of their experiences in it. I interpret how our experiences in relationship may have bearing on the research.

FEMINIST QUALITATIVE RESEARCH

Feminist research is research for women "to correct both the invisibility and distortion of female experience in ways relevant to ending women's unequal social position" (Lather, 1991, p. 71). Feminist researchers seek methods that more accurately and comprehensively represent women's experience. For some, this work places the social construction of gender and other intersections of difference (race, class) at the center of analysis. Others consider that the qualities of the method make research feminist. None of these perspectives necessarily excludes the others. In all examples of such feminist inquiry, however, is considerable attention to issues of domination.

Some feminist researchers struggle with traditional science that has a history of exploiting women's labor and mystifying their experience (Allen & Baber, 1992) and seek other means of accurately representing the breadth of women's lives. Feminist theorizing has grown exponentially in the past few decades as an alternative to the worldview of patriarchal institutions, such as the discourse of academe, science, mass media, education, health care, and the justice system. Positivists interested in generalizability and institutional definitions tend to dismiss the everyday experience and perspectives of women as idiosyncratic, false consciousness and merely commonsensical. Many feminist researchers strive to legitimate everyday experience with qualitative methods (Smith, 1987). For example, in *The Everyday World as Problematic,* Dorothy Smith (1987) argues that the everyday experience of women in settings such as homes and low-status pink-collar jobs is "silenced through writing and print when the intellectual work that claims universality actually centers on and among men" (p. 9). The qualitative approach instead credits participants with the power and ability to narrate their own experience. This encourages their agency—their sense of personhood and ability to affect their own lives. In contrast, methods with predetermined questions and scope solicit information passively. Feminist researchers strive to understand the subject, not as an object from which to gather information, but as an active participant in the research process.

Because theory is said to emerge from analyses of subjects' voices in inductive research approaches (Blumer, 1969; Bogdan & Biklen, 1992; Glaser & Strauss, 1967), some feminist researchers see ethnographic/qualitative methods as appropriate means for feminist inquiry (Duelli-Klien, 1981; Mies, 1981; Rabinowitz & Sechzer, 1993). The qualities of feminist research include

(a) presenting the social context in which subjects are embedded, (b) having subjects help interpret data and develop theory, (c) acknowledging and accounting for how the researcher's location (e.g., literate, lesbian, white, educated, middle-class, female), voice, and perspectives enter the research, and (d) being careful in how research is presented to academe.

Some feminists, however, have critiqued such research. Trinh Minh-ha (1989) is concerned with how informants are represented and argues that the research process always creates an "us" and "them" and appropriates the experiences of subjects. *Appropriation,* a term found in critical theory, is used to denote the unethical usage of other peoples' cultures, including their stories. In other words, researchers take subjects' stories and may share them without permission or with an audience to whom subjects have tenuous links so that the subjects do not fully understand what their permission grants. For example, in speaking about ethnographic methods, Minh-ha says that it "is mainly a conversation of 'us' with 'us' about 'them' . . . in which 'them' is silenced. 'Them' always stands on the other side of the hill, naked and speechless . . . 'them' is only admitted among 'us,' the discussing subjects, when accompanied or introduced by an 'us'" (p. 67). For Minh-ha, the structure of ethnographic research and its academic audience objectifies, silences, and dominates subjects. Acker, Barry, and Esseveld (1991) also ask whether narrative research processes always inherently objectify subjects because their stories are the object of the researcher's gaze.

Other feminists take issue with researchers' authorial voice. They claim that authors reproduce patriarchal and Eurocentric relations by not making their social and political location explicit in the text (Fine, 1992; Haraway, 1988). Michelle Fine's (1992) notion of "ventriloquy" and Donna Haraway's (1988) "the God trick" critique the positivist notions of objectivity and "letting the data speak for themselves" when, in fact, the author's control, perspective, form of reporting, and analysis pervade the research. In *ventriloquy* in social research, the "author tells Truth, has no gender, race, class, or stance, treat[s] subjects as objects, . . . den[ies] all politics in a very political work of social research, . . . seeks asylum behind texts in which they deny their authorial subjectivities" (Fine, 1992, pp. 212-214). The "God trick . . . [is] that mode of seeing that pretends to offer a vision that is from everywhere and nowhere, equally and fully" (Haraway, 1988, p. 584). Fine, Haraway, and other scholars ask whether researchers truly "give voice" by opening a space for the informants' voices to be heard. One way to remove the hegemonic traces of patriarchy in qualitative research involves exposing the speaking subjects at all times and identifying their personal and political positions. As Patti Lather (1991) notes, "All researchers construct their object of inquiry out of the materials their culture provides, and values play a central role in this linguistically, ideologically, and historically embedded project that we call science" (p. 105).

Feminism in its contemporary form investigates the uses of power out of a concern for liberatory social change. Because such change must happen within institutional as well as individual relations, feminism also focuses on the processes and development of relationships. All the feminist issues mentioned above concern power within the research relationship, as well as power of institutions.

I am not arguing here that feminist methods move beyond the foundational critiques that Minh-ha (1989), Fine (1992), and Haraway (1988) allude to: those of objectifying the subjects, appropriating their stories, and presenting such research to an audience that has tenuous links to the participants. Although research continues to function within patriarchal relations, so does silence. We are unable, at this historical time, to create a purely liberatory, feminist/radical humanist methodology. The effort to do so, however, may be more linked to positivism than to the process of change. Marjorie DeVault (1991) argues that the struggle to move beyond hegemonic relations in research may be diverting time and energy away from tasks and work that provide possibilities for social change. For Alcoff (1991-92), the goal lies, not in silence, but in responsible speaking. She offers four guidelines for responsible speaking: First, look closely at the reasons for speaking. Second, make explicit how we account for the bearing of our location and context on what we are saying. Third, be accountable and responsible for what we say. Fourth, evaluate the potential and actual effects of speaking on the "discursive and material context" (p. 27). Responsible speaking must account for the contextual relationship developed with the people about whom one is speaking. This includes noticing the process of relationship development between researcher and participants. An ethical and mutual relationship helps prevent objectifying subjects, misrepresenting them, and appropriating their stories.

THE STUDY

The purpose of my research project was to understand lesbians' supportive and unsupportive experiences of therapy and to generate a theoretical model of those experiences. What follows is a description of the participants, method, and findings to give the reader a brief context of the study.

Nine women participated in my research project. In terms of socioeconomic class, one participant identified as homeless, two as working poor, two as working class, three as middle class, and one as upper middle class. In terms of other identities, one identified as Native American; one as Chicana and Caucasian; another as African American, Native American, and French American; six as primarily Caucasian; one as transgendered; and two as surviving a highly right-wing Christian heritage. Their ages at the time of the interview ranged from 18 to 60. All participants lived in or near a small city in the Northwest and were interviewed during the fall and winter of 1995. Seven of the nine were in significant relationships. Four participants were in long-term relationships ranging from 5 to 15+ years. In terms of religious experience, one identified as Jewish, four had Christian upbringings (one Catholic, one Southern Baptist, one Christian, and one Baptist/Lutheran/Catholic).

As a feminist researcher, I investigated the different perspectives these culturally and class-diverse lesbians had about their therapy experiences. Themes emerged from participants' perspectives about their experience. Participants reviewed, commented on, and approved their transcripts, codes I suggested representing their ideas, the main emergent themes, and the final manuscripts. I interpreted the themes from the codes. I was careful to notice and reflect on my coding, theme development, and theory building to analyze my assumptions and maintain open-mindedness about what "representing their experience" may come to mean. I kept an extensive journal, as well as included "analytic memos" concerning every interview to assist maintaining this inter-subjectivity. Having participants review and approve manuscripts helped double-check this process.

What follows is a very brief description of the study. It focuses on lesbian experience and generally excludes analysis of class and culture even though all these issues overlap. Participants' experiences fit into two main categories: unsupportive and supportive experiences in therapy. Unsupportive experiences fell into three subcategories: Participants perceived therapists as (a) marginalizing lesbian experience, (b) suppressing it, or (c) pathologizing it.

Marginalizing lesbian experience as a theme encapsulates the experiences of participants in which they or their lesbianism or both were discounted and reduced. This functioned at times subtly as well as overtly. For example, three participants spent extensive amounts of time in their therapy educating their therapists about lesbian issues even though lesbianism was not a reason they were seeking treatment. Thus, their real treatment issue was marginalized because the therapist was more interested in hearing about lesbianism. One subject thought she was blamed for her son's attention deficit/hyperactive disorder and treated disrespectfully and coldly since coming out. Sophie's experience is more overt:

> [T]hey assumed that I didn't want to be a lesbian. Well, a couple of them outright said, "Are you sure that you are gay?" And I would say, "Well, yeah, I am." And I had one therapist who said, "How do you know today if you haven't been with a man for 10 years?" She implied that I was copping out of dealing with men because of my abuse issues. I think my sadness and anguish at the time was being perceived because I was a lesbian.

Another theme was the suppression of lesbian experience. This occurred when therapists, from the participants' point of view, actively created environments where the client never felt safe enough to come out or where the therapist ignored or refused to talk about the client's lesbianism or denied that the client was gay. One participant's partner was never recognized as a coparent to her son in family therapy even when they were both present. Jesse shares that her counselor "strongly discouraged me from ever saying the words 'I am a homosexual . . .' He encouraged me to be in denial of who I was."

Five participants' stories contained examples of how their therapists focused on the cause or cure or both of lesbian identity, creating a theme about pathologizing lesbian experience. As Christina says, "[My therapist] . . . was just so focused on the lesbian issue that we never got to my problem. She just kept jumping to conclusions. She kept looking for something to blame it on." Others were told it was because they had a single mom or an abuse history. Not only did Christina and others not get to the issue for which they sought help, but "curing" their sexuality was seen as a valid treatment goal without their consent. Angelina was told she was "oppressed by Satan."

Instances of supportiveness of lesbian identity were strikingly similar to one another. All the subjects talked about being (or wanting to have been) accepted, supported, and not judged. This happened when, if they were interested in discussing the lesbian issue, the therapist listened, was supportive, and never assumed any problem with it. For many, the lesbian issue was simply a "non-issue"; the therapist was seen as accepting the participants' lesbian identity, and because it was not a treatment issue, it never came up. Participants also discussed qualities like demonstrating authenticity, providing a reality check for them, and asking open-ended questions. Here, therapists did not tell participants what to do or give advice about any issue, but instead encouraged clients to trust themselves. More specific themes did not develop here because the supportive experiences were so similar.

PARTICIPANTS' EXPERIENCE OF RELATIONSHIP

Lather (1991) explains that "through dialogue and reflexivity, design, data and theory emerge, with data being recognized as generated from people in a relationship" (p. 72). Because data emerge out of a relationship, how can researchers capture that relationship to better communicate the data's context? What follows is my effort at noticing different ways participants came to and experienced this research project and how the research relationship seemed to affect the stories I received. I did not receive foundational criticism from participants concerning the structure, direction, or interviewing strategies I used in the project. I wonder if my approach inhibited such commentary or if my sensitivity to these issues merely points to my front-end preparation and attachment to the project, whereas subjects' roles required less. Further development of such issues is needed; however, given space limitations, I primarily focus on participants' feedback. The following voices of participants come out of postinterview discussions that asked "What was it like, being part of this research?" "Why did you decide to be involved with this research?" and "What did you get out of it?" Participants' experiences and reasons varied, yet all chose to be involved because the therapy experience of unsupportiveness or supportiveness was important for them to share with others. A few participants thought their experience in the research was "fine" but did not elaborate. Some had difficulty putting it into words. Jesse articulates her experience and frustration about not having the words:

Fine, mildly frustrating when I couldn't think of how to answer something. Well, I just wanted to say something that made sense. That's the struggle of some of the things that we are talking about . . . at the time they are only a feeling, that words and vocabulary had not been put to it before. So, it was an emotional experience that I've been trying to put into words.

Jesse describes a tension that came up within our relationship: her frustration at trying to articulate experiences that functioned for her on a feeling level. Jesse described several experiences with different therapists. One told her to deny it, to not say the word *homosexual;* another overtly pathologized it, naming it sinful; and another accepted it to the extent, she said, that her sexuality became "not an issue." These intimate stories of betrayal and triumph were shared with me in trust by Jesse. In her narrative, I hear many kinds of stories. One is a story she told me because I am a researcher whose purpose she understood to make a difference for other people. I also hear in her story the process as it unfolded between us. Finally, I hear the story that she needed and wanted to tell for herself. She later said that it was good for her to put it all together, that she gained a different perspective as she put it into words. It is crucial that this telling happened in a mutual relationship. The genuineness and connection in the relationship provided the climate for her story to unfold. The challenge for feminist research is highlighted by the many aspects of Jesse's story: How do we capture the many pieces of experience, some of which are never put into words?

Sophie also discussed the power of putting her experience into words:

This [interview process] was good for me. I knew I had a feeling of why I didn't like [therapists who did not respect my decision making], why I hadn't got what I needed but I hadn't put it into words. So now when I meet someone, whether it is a teacher or a therapist or anyone who has authority to me, if I feel something from them that is textbook, that's how I am going to say it, and I get a textbook or clinical response from them, I get nervous. They aren't really responding to me. It is important to put it into words, to really say it and say what wasn't OK and what was so wonderful about my good experiences.

Sophie said that putting her experience into narrative form brought clarity; the interview process between us helped her make connections between her experiences and clarify her sense of being "met" versus just getting a "textbook response." She knew when her previous therapeutic relationships were genuine and mutual and when they were not. A response can only be "textbook" within a nonmutual relationship. Mutuality in relationship recognizes both the participant and the researcher as a part of the story the participant is sharing; it is not that it is co-authored, but co-constructed.

Angelina was sensitive, too, to interactions that did not respond "in kind" to her. She needed to develop and test rapport to discuss her experience. Like others, she described being nervous, guarded, and unsure what to expect during our first meeting:

Well, at first I needed to make sure that you were gay-friendly. You didn't have to be a lesbian, but I needed to know that you were accepting and I had to test that out. After that, I was just on a roll. I have had so much happen. What happened was life-threatening, and I needed to make sure that you were OK. It gives me some faith that there is acceptance.

She shared that she was ready to leave the interview if I was not accepting and reciprocal in our interactions. Here Angelina recognized the tenuous links between her openness to the moment-by-moment negotiations that can be a part of research relationships. As the Personal Narrative Group (1989) recognizes, research relationships are ones of "co-construction where context is considered from the standpoint of the subject of the personal narrative, as well as from the standpoint of the interpreter's analysis." In claiming her power to leave the interview if a mutual relationship (vs. Sophie's "textbook" one) was not created, Angelina reinforced the idea that we mutually came together to create the climate and develop the foundation on which she told me her story. For her, the telling would not meet her needs if I responded judgmentally or as a blank receptacle. We both had to "be open," as she said, to have mutuality.

Angelina was keenly in touch with what she wanted in the relationship, and she knew that. I, the researcher, came to the relationship with more institutional power. She came with a clear intention for me to present her story along with others in hope of making change in therapy for other lesbians. At the conclusion of our discussions, she said, "It felt good to talk about. I haven't ever talked about it in this way before, putting all of these particular experiences together." She gained something in telling her story.

I was especially struck by all participants' willingness to share their stories and by the fact that, for many, it was something they looked forward to, like Kelly:

Well, I'll tell you that I have actually been looking forward to [the interview] because I don't get to talk about it a lot. I'm out to my parents and all that, but it's not like I can just talk about the way it feels or how it affects other people that I deal with on a daily basis being the way I am. What I am and who I am. So it feels good to just talk about that. That's pretty much it. It just feels good to talk about it.

Participants reminded me how powerful the experience of telling one's story or truth is—for simply the purpose of telling. This quality is what makes it worthwhile and important. The meaningfulness of participants' stories, which resonated differently with each one of them, brought richness and passion to the data and theory building. Angelina continues:

These things shouldn't have happened. So I'm doing this to get that idea out there. I went through hell. I was so isolated, I was locked up with psychiatrists who would tell my parents what I said. I was told my eating disorder was because I wanted to look "female" for men. There wasn't a safety zone at all with therapists. There was all of this political propaganda on the walls of the counseling agency. And I want to be heard, I want what happened to me out there. I'd like to help prevent it for others.

Angelina chose to share her story to contribute to political and social change through and with me because I have the possibility to voice these issues in the field. Lincoln, too, used her positive experience and growth with the intention of helping others:

[My therapist] helped me figure out, to trust my own judgment, to trust my own emotionality. And that was really it. It made all the difference, and he hung in there with me. So in my first experience, I felt so judged, but this experience was different. So I want other people, other therapists, to hear this. The bad experiences I had [with therapists] just held me back from making my own decisions . . . So I want to give back this way and help others with my experience. That's why I'm [involved in this research project].

Lincoln shared these personal experiences with me out of a belief in her own experience, and she seemed to do so with a principle of feminist research in mind: to represent women's experiences as a way to change women's oppression.

In the process of this research, I recognized the unfolding of a parallel process. I felt a deep concern about the issues of supportiveness and unsupportiveness in therapy. I had read professionals' accounts of homophobia, heterosexism, and supportiveness in therapy but read no clients' voices in any of this work. I was also concerned that it did not capture the breadth or depth of the issue. Consequently, I was prepared to put together many women's experiences. In this study, Angelina, Lincoln, Sophie, and Jesse shared that they sought to tell their stories for themselves and also to help effect change in the field.

Although all participants mentioned that they were participating to help therapists understand the consequences of supportiveness and unsupportiveness of their clients, Jesse in particular hoped to further the liberation of lesbian and gay people seeking support in therapy:

Well, we pay for therapy when we get it, on some level, assuming that we have a therapist with integrity who is there because they want to be, they have a positive intent, and we are receiving something of great value from them, and part of what we then get to do, to make the process complete, is give back. We can't give back to the therapist necessarily, but that is not the point of giving back. The point of giving back is that I have benefited from somebody else's experience, I've got something that I might not have ever gotten, and I got that because somebody else gave that to them somewhere along the line. And so it becomes a chain not a circle. And so there was a link that was linked to them that got linked to me and it gets dead-ended. . . . It would just give it back to them. It goes on if I give it back to somebody else. . . . It may mean becoming a therapist or participating in a research project or any number of things.

Jesse is mindful of the need for ongoing community development and sharing in relationship. Her perspective links into the idea of the researcher as someone whose purpose is to give back to the community by conducting research for empowerment and social action. Of course, that is the ultimate purpose of feminist research.

CONCLUSION

My purpose in conducting this research parallels many of the purposes subjects had for participating. Our intentions link together via our research relationship, and we continue the chain of giving back. We were interested in social change for women and came to the project with intentions of actively contributing to that change. Participants were clearly interested in the research itself, were engaged in claiming what constituted supportive and unsupportive experiences, and made those issues known. We cocreated space to connect and generate knowledge with each other (rather than into a tape recorder). We engaged in a process that affirmed our agency. In Jesse's words, this is how we "kept the chain going."

Subjects were also interested in sharing their meaningful experiences as people connecting to other people. Qualities of the relationships had a bearing on both the research process and the data gathered. These various aspects of our research relationships provide more context for the study and make research more credible because research without context is suspect, at best.

Feminist researchers value relationship. They use a heightened sense of ethics to be responsible speakers. By this, I mean that feminist research seeks to tell the whole story, from the subjectivity and personal location of the researcher to contextualizing the social group of the subject. Feminists notice power differences because they are often in the form of domination. Thus, they search for possible use of power in an attempt to avoid objectifying subjects, misrepresenting them, and appropriating their stories. They attempt to put the research relationship on an equal plane, engaging subjects in the interpretation of data and development of theory. The research relationship is transformed from more standard forms of research in sometimes dramatic ways. As this chapter argues, it enables better and different access to data because the research relationship affects the data that are gathered.

Feminist qualitative research offers an alternative to how the U.S. dominant culture and the culture in some research circles today value relationship. Laura Brown (1994) explains:

North American dominant cultures treat emotional intimacy and the tasks of relationship development and maintenance in a profoundly ambivalent, often dismissive and destructive manner . . . One of the important contributions of a feminist deconstruction of value has been a valuing and privileging of the capacity to relate well and intimately to others, and the construction of the capacity as a source of strength, a style of competence, a type of agency, and a desirable and necessary outcome of adult development. (p. 92)

Often recognition of relationship invites claims of contamination and unreliability, yet relationships are essential to the human condition. This chapter is intended to initiate and continue discussions concerning how to account for such relationships to represent them more accurately and rigorously.

As an invitation for dialogue about this chapter, I close with Michelle Fine's (1992) words: "If feminist researchers do not take critical, activist, and open stances on our own work, then we collude in reproducing social silences through the social sciences" (p. 206).

REFERENCES

Acker, J., Barry, K., & Esseveld, J. (1991). Objectivity and truth: Problems in doing feminist research. In M. M. Fonow & J. A. Cook (Eds.), *Beyond methodology: Feminist scholarship as lived research*. Bloomington: Indiana University Press.

Alcoff, L. (1991-92, Winter). The problem of speaking for others. *Cultural Critique,* 5-32.

Allen, K., & Baber, K. (1992). Ethical and epistemological tensions in applying a postmodern perspective to feminist research. *Psychology of Women Quarterly, 16,* 1-15.

Blumer, H. (1969). *Symbolism interactionism: Perspective and method*. Upper Saddle River, NJ: Prentice Hall.

Bogdan, R., & Biklen, S. (1992). *Qualitative research for education: An introduction to theory and methods* (2nd ed.). Boston: Allyn & Bacon.

Brown, L. (1994). *Subversive dialogues: Theory in feminist therapy*. New York: Basic Books.

Devault, M. (1991). *What counts as feminist ethnography?* Unpublished manuscript, Syracuse University, Syracuse, NY.

Duelli-Klien, R. (1981). How to do what we want to do: Thoughts about feminist methodology. In G. Bowles & R. Duelli-Klien (Eds.), *Theories of women's studies* (pp. 25-46). Berkeley: University of California.

Fine, M. (1992). *Disruptive voices: The possibilities of feminist research*. Ann Arbor: University of Michigan Press.

Glaser, B. G., & Strauss, A. L. (1967). *The discovery of grounded theory: Strategies for qualitative research*. New York: Aldine.

Haraway, D. (1988). Situated knowledges: The science question in feminism and the privilege of partial perspective. *Feminist Studies, 14,* 575-599.

Lather, P. (1991). *Getting smart: Feminist research and pedagogy with/in the postmodern*. New York: Routledge.

Maher, M. (1996, August). *Embracing the oxymoron: The contradictory territory of "empowering" research*. Paper presented at the annual meeting of the American Psychological Association, Toronto, Canada.

Mies, M. (1981). Toward a methodology for feminist research. In G. Bowles & R. Duelli-Klien (Eds.), *Theories of women's studies II* (pp. 46-64). Berkeley: University of California.

Minh-ha, T. T. (1989). *Woman, native, other: Writing postcoloniality and feminism*. Bloomington: Indiana University Press.

Personal Narrative Group. (1989). *Interpreting women's lives: Feminist theory and personal narratives*. Bloomington: Indiana University Press.

Rabinowitz, V. C., & Sechzer, J. A. (1993). Feminist perspectives on research methods. In F. Denmark & M. Paludi (Eds.), *Psychology of women: A handbook of issues and theories*. Westport, CT: Greenwood.

Smith, D. (1987). *The everyday world as problematic: A feminist sociology*. Boston: Northeastern University Press.

CHAPTER 16

The Use Of Focus Groups Within a Participatory Action Research Environment

John O'Neill
Barbara B. Small
John Strachan

Qualitative methods were used to study issues surrounding employment for persons with HIV/AIDS (PWAs). As is seen in this chapter, the focus group methodology enabled researchers to address emerging issues in HIV/AIDS that have not been previously studied. To begin, the overall context of the research is described, including a discussion of how the focus group method fits into a participatory action research (PAR) framework. Readers will see how focus groups can contribute to the development of a research agenda within a changing environment. The mechanics of running the focus groups are briefly

AUTHORS' NOTE: This project is field-initiated research funded by the U.S. Department of Education, National Institute for Disability and Rehabilitation Research (H1336606101). When this chapter was written (Fall, 1997), the project was already ongoing and had begun more than 2 years previously with the writing of a grant proposal. The grant was awarded a little more than a year ago and will continue for another 2 years.

described, as well as how preliminary findings from focus groups have been used to enhance program design.

BACKGROUND AND CONTEXT OF
THE RESEARCH PROJECT

Four-Way Partnership

The project is a collaboration among individuals from four organizations that have an emerging partnership focusing on employment and quality of life issues for PWAs. The organizations are (a) the Counselor Education Programs at Hunter College of the City University of New York; (b) Mobilizing Talents and Skills (MTS), a nonprofit community-based organization providing employment services to people with HIV/AIDS; (c) the Department of Rehabilitation Medicine at Mount Sinai Medical Center; and (d) the Center for Essential Management Services, Inc. (CEMS), a nonprofit research organization. This organizational partnership reflects a history of working together on this and other projects. Each organization is making unique contributions to the research. A faculty member from the Counselor Education Program serves as project director, and results from this research will be integrated into the counselor education curriculum. MTS staff provide both access to the HIV/AIDS community and the technical expertise to use the research results to improve employment programs for people with HIV/AIDS. The Department of Rehabilitation Medicine is providing the survey technology and access to participants. CEMS staff are serving as the project's evaluators and providing technical support for both qualitative and quantitative analyses.

The research was initiated with a series of focus groups conducted with PWAs to gain a qualitative understanding of work, community participation, and quality of life. Findings derived from those focus groups will be further validated through quality of life and health status surveys on 200 persons with HIV/AIDS. Qualitative and quantitative data will also be collected on two logical control groups—persons with spinal cord injuries and persons with liver transplants—as well as a nondisabled group. These control groups will help in our understanding the dual impact of having a life-threatening disability, like HIV/AIDS, that also has a high degree of stigma associated with it.

Participatory Action Research

The organizational principals of *participatory action research* (PAR) that underlie this collaborative effort requires consumers of research to participate actively throughout the process, beginning with the initial design through data collection, analysis, interpretation, and use of findings (Whyte, Greenwood, &

Lazes, 1991). *Consumers* within this project refers to the counselors, supervisors, and administrators at MTS, as well as the clients they serve. The action component in PAR means that research is directed at solving practical problems and that results have direct implications for action and change. The professional researcher in the PAR model does not function as the expert directing all aspects of the research, but instead acts more as a consultant/facilitator mobilizing and maintaining the team's efforts and bringing in experts when necessary. This way of conducting research is in sharp contrast with the conventional or *expert model,* in which members of the community being studied are simply passive subjects who, at their greatest level of participation, authorize the research, provide data, and receive results. Also, in the expert model, the research often has no explicit action implications and is only conducted to satisfy the theoretical curiosity of the professional researcher.

PAR has several advantages. Consumers of research have a greater commitment to the process because they find the design, data collection, analysis, and findings credible. Professional researchers functioning as consultants/ facilitators are less likely to make serious blunders that almost always compromise their credibility with consumers. Finally, the PAR model creates a learning process in which insiders (consumers) and outsiders (professional researchers) benefit from each other's experiences while they continuously adjust and reinvent the research (Walker, 1993). This mutual learning, iterative process leads to more valid theoretical explanations.

Within this project, the PAR model has been implemented in at least two ways. Project staff purposefully recruited and hired two research assistants who are members of the community that will ultimately benefit from the research— PWAs. These research assistants have been able to represent effectively the insider's perspective in terms of women with HIV, gay men, and MTS clients because one research assistant is a former MTS client. The two research assistants are employees of MTS and, aside from their research responsibilities, have become integral members of the MTS program, helping with intake and screening and attending staff meetings related to in-service training, case conferences, and quality control. This has provided them with important information regarding the organizational culture at MTS, which is the site where the action implications of the research will be tested. A second expression of PAR is that all decisions regarding focus groups have involved selected staff from MTS (executive director, employment services manager, assessment counselor, and research assistants), along with the project director and project evaluator. This group of individuals has met approximately twice per month for 2 hours each meeting to consider the myriad issues surrounding focus groups, such as the number of focus groups, characteristics of participants, questions to be asked, recruitment, payment of participants, facilitation of focus groups, informed consent, confidentiality, transcription of focus group audiotapes, what food to serve, and analysis of focus group data.

Recent Changes in HIV/AIDS Realities

In the months since the field initiated research project was conceived, dramatic changes in the HIV/AIDS community have consequently affected the activities of the project and the qualitative process. The project's ability to adjust to these major changes demonstrates the effectiveness of the PAR model and the focus group methodology to respond flexibly to external changes to ensure that the research remains relevant.

Beginning in January 1996, significant numbers of men and women with HIV/AIDS had access to new classifications of drugs. The success of triple combination therapies (two nucleoside analog drugs plus a protease inhibitor) has changed the face of HIV/AIDS across the country. For the first time in the 16 years of the HIV epidemic, the number of AIDS cases diagnosed in the United States dropped in 1996. The number of AIDS deaths dropped 23% from 1995 to 1996 (Stolberg, 1997).

At last, the thought of staving off the ravages of HIV disease has moved from fantasy to fact. Access to the new drug therapies, in conjunction with primary medical care and a constellation of social services, has allowed countless PWAs to improve their health dramatically and to envision a future that is not automatically equated with disease and death. In New York, unlike most states, every PWA has access to the drugs through private insurance, Medicaid, or the AIDS Drug Assistance Program (ADAP). Luckily for New Yorkers, benefits of the therapies are available to all socioeconomic levels.

Although the new therapies do not benefit every PWA, the majority of persons taking the new drugs have seen improvement in their health. Cautiously, as PWAs now contemplate having a future, they also think of having a job. HIV/AIDS has disabled tens of thousands of hardworking individuals who are considering or may soon be able to consider returning to work on a permanent basis.

Prior to January 1996, when PWAs thought about entering or reentering employment, they thought about holding jobs on a short-term or time-limited basis because AIDS was perceived as a terminal illness. Now, 2 years later, may PWAs and their treatment providers view HIV/AIDS as a chronic condition similar to diabetes—a serious condition that must be carefully treated but can be controlled. This change in context makes employment much more crucial in planning for a life with a real future. Financial independence and self-sufficiency have become desirable and necessary goals as the supports offered to PWAs change with the changing perception of the disease.

Accompanying the optimism generated by the encouraging treatment results is a real sense of confusion and anxiety. Individuals who have spent the past several years preparing to die are now faced with the prospect of learning to live with this disease. This requires a total change in mental attitude. Career and financial planning, personal and business relationships, and identity and esteem issues must all be reconsidered for the long term.

The HIV community has a suspicion that disability benefits will be discontinued for those whose health improves. Cases of private disability carriers that have reevaluated claims and disallowed benefits have already been seen. Corresponding with this expectation is the fear that the effects of the new combination therapies may be temporary or time limited. Cessation of disability benefits is extremely serious if the beneficial effects of the therapies are only temporary. This fear must be considered as services are provided, but unfortunately only time can address its reality.

These changes in HIV/AIDS realities affected the planning of focus groups and content of the focus group questions. The emphasis of the research became more clearly defined as employment-specific, rather than as including related activities such as volunteer work. For instance, more information was solicited about benefits and health insurance because PWAs are now considering long-term entry into the labor market. Learning what benefits and insurance concerns were affecting employment decisions became more crucial in planning additional MTS services.

PLACE OF FOCUS GROUPS WITHIN THIS PROJECT

Use of Focus Groups in Grant Proposal Preparation

When preparing the grant proposal, it was discovered that scant published research related to HIV/AIDS and employment. Without such research information, it was difficult to conceptualize a substantive research agenda that was likely to be funded. To compensate for this weakness, project staff decided to collect some preliminary qualitative data by running a series of focus groups. They hoped the results from these focus groups would provide several hypotheses from which a research agenda could be developed.

Focus groups were held to elicit information from PWAs regarding the impact of their condition on their lives. In essence, these groups marked the beginning of the proposed research study as the results of the groups led to the formulation of the research questions and hypotheses.

Each focus group consisted of individuals who are or were recipients of services from MTS. Each group contained women and men of various ethnic groups (African American, European American, Asian American, Latino/ Latina) who had contracted the virus through intravenous drug use, heterosexual behavior, or homosexual behavior. The first focus group used an openended, brainstorming format to identify the most salient issues for PWAs who are involved or want to be involved in the labor market. Two additional groups were held in which similar participants responded to a series of questions that had been established as a result of the brainstorming. Many areas covered were related to issues concerning work, including reacting to the initial diagnosis by stopping work, deciding to disclose one's HIV/AIDS status or not, dealing with benefits as barriers to employment, seeking out support groups, determining the contribution of employment to wellness, dealing with employer discrimination, having general education about HIV/AIDS, and learning methods of accommodation on the job. Broader social issues, such as the impact of public policy through benefits and services designed for PWAs, the health care system, changing the focus to living rather than dying with HIV, and the economy of the HIV/AIDS industry were also discussed.

The recorder took detailed notes during the focus groups, in addition to the groups being tape-recorded. Recorder notes were supplemented and enhanced by listening to the tapes. The enhanced recorder notes were then reviewed independently by three researchers, who had been present at all focus groups, to identify the major themes. The researchers came to a consensus regarding the major themes and how these themes varied, depending on the characteristics of the focus group participants. Results of these analyses were used to plan additional focus groups for a more in-depth look at HIV/AIDS and employment, and this planning process established the research agenda for the grant application.

These focus groups provided several working hypotheses that pointed to the need to conduct further focus groups in a more in-depth exploration. A description of these hypotheses reveals the underlying logic behind the need for additional focus groups. It seemed that PWAs went through a developmental process related to the desire to work. When first diagnosed, PWAs tended to withdraw from the world of work and to focus on death, illness, health, and social/financial supports. After spending a prolonged period of time at home not working, boredom set in, and a desire to resume employment ensued. On returning to work, however, the need was to deal with a somewhat altered capacity and changed social demands relative to the work experience prior to the diagnosis of HIV/AIDS. These observations indicate the need to conduct focus groups with people at three points in time: (a) shortly after diagnosis, (b) when first considering returning to work, and (c) after returning to work.

Another issue of importance to focus group participants was disclosing one's IIIV/AIDS status to an employer. Many PWAs thought the job development conducted by MTS on their behalf was very helpful because it relieved them of the disclosure burden. Although MTS protects the confidentiality of all individuals it serves, it has a mission to educate employers who become open to hiring PWAs. As a result of this observation, it became apparent that we needed to explore the impact of MTS services on the problems surrounding disclosure by conducting focus groups of employees with HIV/AIDS who have and have not used MTS for job placement. The research team also observed that when selecting people who have not used MTS for job placement, it would be important to ensure that they had not used any other job placement service that "paved the way" directly or indirectly with employers.

The team also found reasons for conducting separate focus groups for gay persons, people who contracted HIV from intravenous drug use, and people who acquired it from heterosexual behavior. Several focus group participants indicated that the issues are different for these three groups. For example, gay men observed that they were somewhat more reluctant than individuals from the other two groups to disclose their HIV status because they had gone through one major life-status disclosure regarding their homosexuality that had not always resulted in positive outcomes. Extending this observation to heterosexuals with HIV/AIDS, the researchers hypothesized that this group may, for the first time, be grappling with a major identity change that puts them at risk for devaluation and that they are ignorant of the potential consequences. In contrast, people who acquired HIV through intravenous drug use observed that they were often receiving treatment for their addiction in therapeutic environments that value honesty and openness. It was hypothesized that this ethic tends to make these individuals more likely to disclose their HIV status.

Finally, it appeared that focus groups should be conducted to take a closer look at the issue of managing stress. It was apparent that several internal and external stressors affect the subjective well-being of PWAs. Participants reported experiencing much stress in managing interpersonal relationships with friends, mates, coworkers, and family. The issue to disclose came into play again, and once having disclosed, the need arose to manage other people's reactions. Another reported stressor was a tendency to overextend oneself when returning to work after a long hiatus. This overexertion sometimes led to a compromised health status or a relapse into substance abuse. Most important, all focus group participants thought that reduced levels of stress contributed to improved health and longevity.

Findings from these initial focus groups resulted in a proposal to conduct at least six additional focus groups. Three focus groups would be conducted with people at different points in time since receiving their diagnosis: (a) after being diagnosed with HIV/AIDS, (b) just after entering MTS, and (c) after completing MTS services and working for 3 months. An additional three focus groups would be held with those who contracted HIV/AIDS in different ways: (a) through homosexual behavior, (b) through heterosexual behavior, and (c) through intravenous drug use.

Changes in Focus Group Methodology

After the grant was awarded, participatory planning meetings were held to determine how focus groups should be structured. Our original plan to conduct six focus groups based on how one contracted HIV (heterosexual behavior, homosexual behavior, and intravenous drug use) and on the point in time since receiving the HIV/AIDS diagnosis (just after hearing the diagnosis, just after entering MTS, and after completing MTS services) was partially altered. The consumer research assistants were quite persuasive in convincing the planning team not to form groups based on how participants contracted HIV. Within the HIV/AIDS community, it has not mattered how one became infected. What has mattered is that people with HIV/AIDS come together in solidarity to effect sociopolitical change. In the light of this perspective, it would be counter-productive and impolitic to screen focus group members on the basis of how they became infected. The consumer research associates did point out, however, that two distinct cultures exist within the HIV/AIDS community—a gay/lesbian culture and a culture of individuals in recovery from substance abuse—and that people may identify with one or both groups. Homogeneous groups were *not* created to reflect these two groups. Instead, participants were recruited to ensure that each focus group had representatives from these two groups. Therefore, focus groups were heterogeneous for sexual orientation and being in recovery. This is a clear example of how the PAR methodology directly and substantively changed and improved the focus group methodology. Without the input of the consumer research assistants, professional researchers would have conducted focus groups that would not have seemed credible to participants.

The planning team decided that it would still be useful to understand the developmental process around employment after HIV/AIDS diagnosis. There-fore, the basic focus group structure was maintained such that participants were homogeneous for their place along the developmental continuum of participa-tion in the labor market after HIV/AIDS. At this time, project staff have conducted four focus groups. One group consisted of people who had received MTS services and were currently employed. The second group was receiving MTS services to obtain employment. The third group consisted of people not associated with MTS who had not been employed or participating in an employment program within the past year. The fourth group was composed of individuals who were considering employment and had signed up to receive more information regarding MTS services.

A fifth group is in the planning process. This group will consist of unem-ployed people who are receiving private insurance benefits. The reason for conducting this focus group is that MTS staff would like to extend employment services to this population. Many of these people are taking protease inhibitors and may be losing their private insurance benefits because of improved health status. Loss of benefits will make employment a paramount concern.

Mechanics of Running Focus Groups

Recruitment for the first two focus groups was not difficult because all participants were either current or former clients of MTS. More effort was required to recruit for the third and forth focus groups because participants had no connection with MTS. Each focus group had between 7 and 13 people in attendance.

Considerable effort was required to ensure that women with HIV/AIDS were present at all focus groups. Following the principles of PAR helped in this effort. A woman with HIV who had a history of community organizing was hired as a research assistant. Her knowledge of community programs serving women with HIV/AIDS was very constructive when recruiting women. She had also been an MTS client, which allowed former and current MTS clients, particularly women, to identify with her easily and feel comfortable attending focus groups

To maintain confidentiality, all focus group participants were given numbers and were asked to identify themselves by their numbers prior to making statements during the focus group and to refer to other group members by number. This procedure for protecting the participants' identities was required by New York State's strict confidentiality laws regarding HIV/AIDS.

Each focus group had a moderator, a note taker, and a timer. The moderator gave an introduction to the project, reviewed the main points regarding informed consent, and described the focus group process. To ensure that all points were covered by the moderator in a standard manner, a focus group script was developed (Vaughn, Shay-Schumm, & Sinagub, 1996).

Even though all focus groups were tape-recorded, to the degree possible note takers wrote down each participant's comments. These notes served two purposes: (a) They provided back-up data if the audiotaping did not work or if the tapes were destroyed or lost, and (b) they were used to provide immediate feedback to staff in lieu of transcribed audiotapes, which can take a considerable amount of time to produce. The immediate use of the notes was to identify additional issues (e.g., spirituality, family) to be included in subsequent focus groups.

Between 9 and 13 questions were asked at each of the different focus groups. Each question was structured to be either a *how* or a *what* question. General questions usually had specific probes that were asked only if the general question did not elicit the desired information (see Table 16.1 for a sampling of the general questions and their related probes). Because general questions were asked first and many questions were interrelated, we often found that later questions had been partially answered.

Contribution of Focus Group Findings to
Program Design and Implementation

MTS integrated the two research assistants into the full range of MTS meetings and responsibilities. The MTS policy is to employ PWAs whenever possible and to maintain a staff roster that is approximately 50% PWAs, but fluctuations with staff turnover always occur. MTS firmly believes that services must be driven by the needs of clients and that staff members must represent the community served. Thus, employment of the research assistants was in line with MTS policy and practice.

The research assistants have had direct impact on MTS services because they shared the concerns of PWAs they were hearing in focus groups and individual interviews. Their comments were particularly relevant in the biweekly client

TABLE 16.1 Examples of Focus Group Questions and Probes

How has spirituality played a part in you dealing with HIV?

If spirituality has *not* played a role in dealing with HIV or the decision to work, what
   has helped you sustain your sense of hope?

How did you decide to return to work?

What caused you to make the initial decision to return to work?

What were your initial visions, hopes, or expectations about returning to work?

How have these initial visions, hopes, or expectations "panned out" or been realized?

How has employment affected your lifestyle or quality of life?

What has happened to your health status since returning to work?

How have you coped with stress on the job?

What issues have gone unresolved as a result of returning to work?

What factors interfered with your return to work?

How were benefits a barrier to returning to work?

How did friends and family affect your return to work either positively or negatively?

How did the availability of health care present a barrier to returning to work?

services meeting and the monthly quality conferences. The research perspective
added another dimension to discussion about direct services and client needs.

Two concrete examples of changes that MTS made as a result of the research
assistants' comments are the enhanced training in the Business Service Center
(BSC) and the planning of case management services for mothers with
HIV/AIDS. Feedback about the BSC training from the research staff indicated
that more one-on-one training by management would benefit the trainees. Over
a period of 5 months, BSC management, in cooperation with our training staff,
was able to identify and implement a series of individualized training techniques that appear to have improved trainees' acquisition of skills and to
improve self-esteem.

The problems of mothers with HIV/AIDS who want to work were repeatedly
highlighted by one research assistant. In response, MTS is seeking additional
funding for case management services for this population. The anecdotal
summary of interview responses has enabled MTS to make a convincing case
for the services and to address a previously unmet need.

In conclusion, the qualitative research approach of using focus groups has
contributed greatly to this research effort. When scant published research was
available in the area of employment and HIV/AIDS, focus groups were used to
begin developing hypotheses and setting a fundable research agenda. The
combination of focus group and PAR methodologies allowed researchers
enough flexibility to respond effectively to a changing research environment.

And the action implications of the research have begun to be implemented because consumers of the research have been involved throughout.

REFERENCES

Stolberg, S. G. (1997, October 14). AIDS drugs elude the grasp of many thousands of poor. *New York Times.* Available: WWW.NYTIMES.COM

Vaughn, S., Shay-Schumm, J., & Sinagub, J. (1996). *Focus group interviews in education and psychology.* Thousand Oaks, CA: Sage.

Walker, M. L. (1993). Guest editorial: Participatory action research. *Rehabilitation Counseling Bulletin, 37,* 2-5.

Whyte, W. F., Greenwood, D. J., & Lazes, P. (1991). Participatory action research: Through practice to science in social research. In W. F. Whyte (Ed.), *Participatory action research* (pp. 19-55). Newbury Park, CA: Sage.

CHAPTER 17

Qualitative Research in Program Evaluation

Leo Goldman

Evaluation is clearly an applied area of psychology. Its purpose is primarily to find out—to put it simplistically—whether something works. If it does, the client has justification to continue the program or activity; if not, the question why it didn't work up to the expected standards remains. Obviously, someone thought it had possible merit, or it wouldn't have been started. So, in a way, it resembles an experiment; the major difference between the two processes is the main goal: In an experiment, it is to test a theory, hypotheses deduced from the theory, and possibly a method or technique and to generalize to other situations. In an evaluation, as conceptualized here, the goal is much more limited: whether a given program or intervention in a school, agency, or company accomplishes what is wanted.

If the results of an experiment fail to support the hypotheses, the experimenter is likely to question the hypotheses and even the theory and often also the suitability of the research method and instruments. The evaluator, like most qualitative researchers, is more likely to question *why* the program, activity, intervention, or an entire organization did not meet the level of effectiveness desired. Was it something about the person(s) involved? Was it the way the intervention was done? Was it something about the time or place? Was it the attitudes of the employees, participants, or trainees: Were they, for instance, not adequately oriented to the procedure so that they would participate willingly? Some of these questions are rarely raised in experimental studies and even, indeed, in survey studies.

The kinds of evaluation we are concerned with here may be classified in the following three categories:

1. *External/Formal:* A school, college, company, or agency (called hereafter the client) contracts with an outside person or organization to conduct an evaluation

of its total operation or, more often, of specified programs, departments, or activities. The evaluation may be required as part of a grant, or it may be initiated by the client because of dissatisfaction or concern with the status quo—poor achievement by students, poor performance by workers, low morale, or any number of other considerations.

2. *Internal/Formal:* The client's staff itself plans and conducts the evaluation. This often is done when the organization cannot afford the cost of an external evaluation, when confidentiality is a concern, when the client believes that an outsider would not understand the organization and its problems well enough, or when the client believes that the evaluation would be of most value if insiders did the planning and the entire study on their own or possibly with some assistance from a consultant.

3. *Internal or External/Informal:* This might be considered a "quick-and-dirty" evaluation, usually done without a written plan and possibly without a written report. "Let's talk to a few people" and "Make up a questionnaire and give it to everybody" are examples. Even such an evaluation may be of some value; at least people are acknowledging that something should be evaluated.

Although the methods discussed in this chapter are applicable to applied psychological activities in industrial, agency, and other settings, the illustrations are drawn from my experiences in evaluating counseling programs in educational settings.

EXISTING PROGRAM VERSUS
A PLANNED INTERVENTION

The work of an evaluator is quite different in two types of situations: one where the task is to study an ongoing program or organization, the other where a new program or activity is being introduced. In the former, one encounters a finished product and must learn quite a bit about it before even preparing a plan for the evaluation itself. With a new program, the evaluator may possibly be present during the planning meetings and thus can suggest ways in which the project could be conducted that would provide more and better data for the evaluation. If the evaluator comes into the picture only after the program has been started— or even worse, after it has run for some time—it may be too late at that time ever to retrieve formative data that cannot be collected after the fact.

The other valuable opportunity in a new program is to collect data before it begins—whether through interviews, questionnaires, or other methods—with which the later formative or summative data can be compared. This would be, in effect, a self-comparison or even test-retest design that permits more certain assessment of the effects of the intervention. In addition, the evaluator may in some instances suggest that a control or comparison group be included and that the experimental and comparison groups be selected from the outset in such a way as to make them maximally comparable.

COMPARING QUANTITATIVE AND
QUALITATIVE APPROACHES IN EVALUATION

Some evaluators prefer to use only quantitative methods, some only qualitative methods, and others a combination of the two. The issues here are illustrated in two recent evaluation studies. In the first, an attempt to evaluate the national School-to-Work (STW) program in the 1990s included both types of evaluation. The quantitative type consisted of frequent reports by schools of such students' career-related involvements as counseling and internships and such data as grades and absence rates. The qualitative type consisted of visits to a sample of schools that included interviews and observations. The opportunity to observe both types of research led me to have more confidence in the qualitative approaches. Although the quantitative data may seem to be more "objective," more is hidden than revealed. For example, 100 students in each of two high schools may have been reported as participating in a program of visits to work sites. But in one school, those may have consisted entirely of a quick walk through a plant; in the other, careful preparation of the students so that they would approach the visit itself with purpose and later review in school what they saw and heard. Similarly, an internship could consist mostly of observation week after week, or it could include a planned sequence of hands-on activities. At least the interviewer or observer can ask questions of the participants and even in some cases observe a field trip or visit an internship site.

THE ISSUE OF SUBJECTIVITY

It is often assumed that numbers per se are more objective than the reports of observers and interviewers. Some also argue that the reader of a qualitative evaluation report has no way to judge the competence of the qualitative evaluator and the validity of the conclusions reached. In fact, it is much more common in qualitative than in quantitative reports to find information about the credentials and point of view of the evaluator and to find details about how the data were collected. It is also generally assumed that numbers resulting from tabulation of multiple-choice questionnaires are more objective and therefore more credible than an observer's or interviewer's descriptions and interpretations. In fact, we usually know little about the respondents to a questionnaire—how each of them perceived each of the questions or items and what they intended to convey by their response to each, and in fact what their attitude was to the task and to what extent they were being candid in their responses.

What it comes down to is that both approaches rely very heavily on the competence and perceptiveness of the person(s) doing the study. But this is rarely stated or acknowledged in quantitative research reports. Numbers do not speak for themselves; the competence and perceptiveness, beliefs, and attitudes of the quantitative researcher come into play in selecting or designing instruments, in the way they are administered, and in the way the results are interpreted and reported.

ONE CRUCIAL CONCLUSION IS WORTH . . .

An evaluation study in a counseling center illustrates the contention that sometimes one major recommendation can be of greater value than several small points. The evaluators were asked to examine the counseling department of a college, with the general charge to see whether it was functioning as well as it might. The counseling staff were all doctoral-level psychologists, and all saw students who requested help on a one-to-one basis and by appointment. In addition, students on academic probation were required to see their assigned counselors on a regular basis (some would argue that "required counseling" is an oxymoron, but that was not an issue to be dealt with in the evaluation). All the counselors saw the probation students in individual interviews, and all reported that quite often these students failed to appear for scheduled interviews. Asked what they did with the hour, most indicated that they might read or chat with a colleague but that it was not feasible, while waiting to see whether the student would appear, to undertake any productive activity. Each week, quite a few hours were wasted this way.

The solution offered: Schedule probationary students in small groups. This could have several advantages. First, if, say, five or six were scheduled for a given hour, chances are that at least two or three would show up and the time could be used productively. Second, most students would probably get more out of a group than a one-to-one session: They could get ideas from each other and might recognize themselves and their behavior when listening to other students in the group and thus gain more self-awareness than in one-to-one interviews. They might also feel less on the spot; after all, one-to-one is not truly an equal relationship when one is a student (especially one having academic problems) and the other is a (usually older) college staff member. Having several students together helps even the odds.

When this suggestion was made in a conference with the dean of student services before the written report was prepared, it became clear that most counselors had had no real preparation for group work and were oriented almost entirely to individual counseling. This led the evaluators further to recommend training for all counselors in the use of groups and continuing follow-up meetings to exchange experiences and increase skills. This one recommendation was probably of greater significance than all the others combined.

PARTICIPATION OF INVOLVED PEOPLE

From action research, community psychology, and other conceptual frameworks (see, e.g., Danish & Conter, chap. 12 in Goldman, 1978) has come a point of view that evaluation studies will be the most productive if as many as possible of the parties involved in the situation participate actively in planning and conducting the evaluation, interpreting the results, and formulating conclusions and recommendations. A school, for example, has many groups with major concerns regarding how well it functions—students, parents, the PTA, neighborhood residents, taxpayers, community organizations of various kinds, staff of the next schools the graduates enter or employers of the school's graduates, school administrators, supervisors, teachers, counselors, psychologists, nurses, and others. If a problem arises, it is likely that several of these groups are dissatisfied with the status quo and have ideas for change.

The community approach would start by bringing together as many as possible of the parties mentioned to give them real involvement in the process; the goal would be to have all represented in discussions of the situation and to be kept informed and be asked for feedback during the course of the evaluation study. A smaller group drawn from the large one might serve as an executive group that would meet much more frequently and be actively involved in policy making and in overseeing the study process. This approach would increase the number of ideas feeding into the evaluation and would give all groups a sense of ownership of the study and therefore a greater readiness to accept its results.

Too often, advisory committees are for show-and-tell and are given no real role in the process. Some are selected because they can contribute funds or services or will add credibility to the conclusions and recommendations emerging from the study. The basic rationale for the participatory approach is that the evaluation will be better done because the evaluators understand the situation from various points of view. To accomplish that, the participants must be genuinely informed and involved and their opinions heard and taken into account.

QUALITATIVE METHODS AS
ACTION RESEARCH IN EVALUATION

The basic position here is that evaluation is action research (Nuttall & Ivey, chap. 3 in Goldman, 1978). Its purpose is to ascertain whether changes would enable the client organization to do its job better. When the charge from the client indicates concern about, or dissatisfaction with, the organization's functioning, then the evaluator's task is troubleshooting—using research methods to isolate any problems and to recommend ways to fix them. This is not quite as simple as the troubleshooting done by an auto mechanic; people in the client organization have to be actively involved in the process even as they are observed and interviewed. They are, indeed, often asked what they see as the problem or need and what ideas they may have for remedying the specific problem or just for improving the work of the organization in general. But before we can do any evaluating, we must establish what is to be evaluated and how.

Negotiating the Evaluation Agreement

The negotiation of an agreement that A is to conduct an evaluation of B can range from a telephone call to a public announcement inviting written proposals to conduct an evaluation. However the process begins, the evaluator must first establish clearly and openly what is wanted and what is to be done (which may not be exactly the same). Certainly, it should be quite clear whether the client wants quantitative data and whether this is what the evaluator thinks will provide the necessary information or is willing to do in any case.

In some situations, the client knows what is wrong and even what should be done and really wants an outside recommendation to that effect. In one case, for example, an important student service in a college was known to have deteriorated over a period of years. The cause was known to the administrator in charge (though not communicated to the evaluator until later on): The head of the office drank on the job to the extent that he was hardly functioning much of the day. The solution would seem obvious: Remove him from that job and, in fact, from the college staff. But this is so difficult to accomplish in most educational institutions that it is rarely tried. The administrator no doubt hoped that an external evaluation would strengthen his hand and possibly lead to acceptance by the staff member of rehabilitation or early retirement.

In all cases, the evaluator must know enough about the organization and what the client expects from an evaluation. This is not always easy to do: In one evaluation, after a draft of the report, which was quite critical of the management of the program, had been submitted to the client for feedback on errors or omissions, an angry reaction and demands from the client for changes in the report led to the realization that what the client had expected was a strong positive assessment that could be used in seeking further funding for the project. Perhaps this problem could have been avoided if the prospective evaluator, when negotiating the study, had made a greater effort to ascertain what the client really wanted.

The scope of work should be agreed on and a budget established before any work begins. This helps prevent later arguments and complaints, but this cannot always be done; sometimes the evaluators discover partway through that data not included in the initial plan are needed to answer the questions. This may call for further discussion and negotiation with the client. If the amount of additional work is relatively minor, the evaluators usually absorb any additional costs.

LEARNING FROM EARLY EVALUATION ACTIVITIES

Unless the evaluator knows the organization well—as would be the case in an internal evaluation—some of the early study is somewhat exploratory and leads to a sharpening of the focus for the remainder of the work. In one evaluation, for example, where the main technique was the interview, the first five or six interviews with people who had different relationships in and with the organization produced conflicting perceptions on the effectiveness with which the experimental program had been started. Those within the school saw no problems. Others, however—funding foundations and advisory board members—thought that arrangements at the outset had been inadequate to ensure funding for the multiyear project. Others among them complained that the project had not focused on what they understood it was going to. This was kind of a reverse triangulation; getting a variety of viewpoints produced different perceptions rather than their confirming each other. From the evaluator's point of view, however, this helped direct the remaining interviews—checking out each person's view of the issues on which disagreement occurred.

This process is very much in keeping with a basic premise of much qualitative research: that one begins with pretty much a clean slate rather than well-defined theory and hypotheses. Then, by using an inductive process, tentative hypotheses are formulated and tested by collecting further data.

Another early activity is to get some sense of the human and other resources available in the client organization. One staff member may be especially well-informed and aware of many aspects of the organization; that person could be very helpful by sharing insights into people and activities and perhaps some of the secrets (Deep Throat!). Also, the evaluator should have a tour of the premises and be introduced to as many staff members as possible. Assuming that several visits will be needed, it is important that staff (and students, if it is a school) see this person as a welcome, nonthreatening visitor whose purpose for being there is to help improve the program.

METHODS AND TECHNIQUES IN
QUALITATIVE ASSESSMENT

What follows is not a thorough presentation of each of these methods but instead is intended to show how they are used in evaluation studies.

The Interview

The interview as used in evaluation studies has been cited above several times and obviously is highly valued. Compared with the questionnaire, for example, it has several advantages. One is that the interviewer has the opportunity to observe the nonverbal behavior of the respondent. Another is that one can adapt the questions to each person's level of comprehension and articulateness. If the interviewer doubts that the respondent has understood a question or has given a full response, the interviewer can ask follow-up questions. Detailed discussion of the interview as a qualitative research tool may be found in many sources (see, e.g., Patton, 1987).

Concern about objectivity of the interviewer is certainly a pertinent issue, as it is with observation and other qualitative methods. The interviewer's professional credentials and reputation need to be established before the evaluation assignment is made. Beyond that, a second interviewer might speak with a few respondents as a cross-check. At the least, the evaluator should review and discuss the collected data on a continuing basis, perhaps with a supervisor or colleague, to help become aware of any bias, misjudgment, or unsupported conclusions.

Observation

Depending on the situation, a great deal can be learned by observing the client's site and the various facilities and people there (Balaban, chap. 5 in Goldman, 1978). The first walk-through can tell something about the organization from such observations as how much time one's escort takes, whether doors are opened and rooms entered, and whether the evaluator is introduced to people who are encountered. One can also get some sense of the relationship between one's escort and the people encountered.

In one school, impressions were mixed. Physically, the building was in much need of repair; some classrooms and the auditorium, in fact, were totally unusable. Some counselors and other support staff did not have their own offices and met with students either in a large room where others were present (even in the cafeteria!) or scrounged for a vacant room where privacy could be assured. Despite these conditions, almost all the staff spoke quite openly with the evaluators, many welcoming the opportunity to tell with enthusiasm about the projects they were engaged in, and all meetings and classes were open for the evaluators. A real sense of caring and commitment was obvious despite the physical conditions.

Observations such as those can reveal quite a lot. The way a student approaches a staff member or is treated when entering a room can tell much about the atmosphere in the school. Seeing students "hanging out" in nearby streets who are supposed to be in school provides questions to ask of responsible school staff. In one school where the visitors were impressed by the conduct of meetings, one exception was found—this, in fact, a team that was supposed to work together. One member of the team didn't show up at all, a second spent the entire time on the telephone, and the remaining members each spoke with the evaluators only, without any interaction with each other. It was clear that they all went their separate ways and rarely met as a team.

These and other observations provide a wealth of questions to pursue in further evaluation activities. It is also instructive to see how the client reacts when given tentative oral reports of some of these observations—whether with surprise, denial, resigned acceptance, or an invitation to the evaluator to suggest possible changes.

Records

In some evaluation projects, records are available that can contribute to the overall study. In one instance, a social worker's records were available for part of the evaluation of a family counseling program. Because the records were confidential, the social worker provided the data from each case folder orally to a research assistant. The resulting numbers were of some value: number of meetings with each family, number of referrals for each, number of telephone calls, and facts about services and materials received by the family from other agencies. Means and standard deviations were calculated for these and other data, and they provided useful information about the amount of work done. But with our qualitative emphasis, we placed greater emphasis on the social worker's interpretations, judgments, and conclusions regarding how much was accomplished with each family, which was, after all, the object of the program and the most important criterion of its effectiveness. Subjective? Yes, but from a professional person with excellent credentials who impressed the evaluators as being able, reasonable, unbiased, and honest.

Records can be of particular value when they provide a baseline against which to compare the results of a new program. Grades in school, dropout rates, absence records, numbers of counseling clients seen, positive rehabilitation outcomes, jobs obtained by career counseling clients—these are some kinds of situations where past records may be helpful in longitudinal comparisons.

REPORTING RESULTS OF THE EVALUATION STUDY

Evaluators should have a clear and specific understanding with the client, before beginning to collect data, about what kinds of reports will be required and to whom. Occasionally, a brief oral report is all that is required, but in almost all cases a written report is wanted. This can be brief, consisting essentially of conclusions and recommendations, or it can comprise many pages that give full detail of methods used, people seen, and data collected. Usually, the report is to be delivered to a senior person in the client organization. If that person wishes, the dissemination plan may also include oral or written presentations to other staff members, members of a board of directors, or an advisory group.

TWO COMPLETE EVALUATION STUDIES

Up to this point, we have focused on separate components and aspects of evaluation, with illustrations taken from parts of several studies. Now the following two evaluation projects are summarized to show how the pieces were collected, assembled, and finally integrated into a report.

A Brief Evaluation Study

In this instance, the evaluators were asked to review the graduate program in counseling at a small liberal arts college and to make any recommendations they saw fit. Implicit in the charge was the question of the viability of the program. The evaluators spent 2 days on campus and spoke with all faculty involved in the graduate program, a few students enrolled in the program, chairs of other departments, and several administrators.

Diverse views of the program were given, but one major fact was that it was one of only two master's programs at this college; the other was for graduates who wished to prepare to teach. A second important fact was that no faculty were teaching full time in the program. Instead, all the teaching was done by faculty from several academic departments and counselors from the student personnel department of the college, each typically teaching one course in the program. In fact, few courses were offered, and there was little systematic coverage of areas such as career development and group counseling—topics usually required of all students in a master's program in counseling. Instead, the heavy emphasis was on internships, which many students entered with very little course work.

A natural question was why this program was offered there at all; a university was within perhaps an hour's drive. But several faculty spouses and other residents of the area, many with young children, had prevailed on the college president to establish the program for their convenience. Several faculty members, especially counseling center staff, welcomed an opportunity to teach in the program, although none of them identified with counselor education as a discipline, published in professional journals, or participated actively in professional associations; some did not even maintain memberships.

The evaluators concluded that the college could go in one of two directions: either close down the program or meet the usual expectations of a master's program in the field as defined by professional associations. Although a great deal of student time devoted to well-supervised professional experience is in itself a positive feature, each student's range of experiences was limited by the kind of setting of the particular internship site. This hit-or-miss situation could not substitute for courses in basic areas, at least some of which are taught by faculty with primary identification as counselor educators.

One option suggested was to develop a cooperative arrangement with the university; at least certain courses could be taken at the university, and others perhaps taught at the college by faculty from the university.

All the options were spelled out in a conference with the college president and later in a written report. When the evaluators left, the president was considering all the options.

A More Extensive Evaluation Project

The setting was an inner-city high school with many problems, including high rates of absence and dropout, teen pregnancy, drug use, and poor achievement. The evaluators were asked to review all the guidance and counseling activities of the school and to make recommendations.

The school had a very large program of counseling, home visits, and specially funded projects and also housed the offices of several community agencies—some 15 separate programs. The principal and administrative staff obviously valued these support services and were exceptionally successful in obtaining additional funds from within the school system and from outside organizations.

One program provided a classroom-size room for each grade, freshman to senior. In each, at least one counselor or other staff member was always present, and students were encouraged to see the room as a kind of home base where they could go when they felt the need for immediate help. The organization and activities of the four rooms varied greatly. The most highly organized and proactive one conducted many counseling groups of various kinds and for varying numbers of students, depending on the topic and the purpose. Staff even arranged for students to be assigned to clusters that were scheduled to have their classes together as far as possible—almost a mini-school arrangement. The staff had regular meetings, with agendas announced in advance. By contrast, the other three grade rooms did little or no proactive work and ran almost no scheduled groups. Staff meetings varied from none to a daily 15-minute agenda-less touching of bases.

Two community organizations had established offices in the school building, each occupying a classroom. They were well staffed by social workers, but it appeared that their target clientele and their goals were similar to those of various guidance personnel in the school. In addition, a nearby hospital had installed a clinic in the school, open to all students and dealing largely with pregnant students.

The evaluators were able to attend a meeting of a home visitors program whose staff monitored absence records and visited homes to try to help parents become more involved in their children's school activities. In the process, they tried to help parents deal with problems in their lives that made it difficult for them to function adequately as responsible parents. The meeting functioned at a high professional level and included good staff development activities. It was held in a large open space, however, surrounded by several offices. During the meeting, parents and others who had appointments in those offices had to walk around the meeting to reach those offices.

A project sponsored by a citywide community organization occupied an attractive office with a small library of occupational information materials. The staff had been trained to do a specific task of conducting group and individual sessions designed to promote career development. Observation of a group in progress indicated that they did that job effectively and with obvious enthusiasm. Interviews with the staff, however, suggested that they were serving as technicians rather than as professional counselors—trained to perform a limited set of functions and unaware of career development theory and practice more broadly. Further, they had little or no contact with the many guidance personnel in the school and worked essentially in isolation. Again, a mix of pluses and minuses.

Several other special programs were aimed at bilingual students, actual or potential chemical abusers, low-achieving students, and others. The staffing of these and some other programs mentioned previously often consisted of teachers who were assigned to that activity for 1 period a day; many of them had only minimum graduate study in guidance and counseling. Within some programs there was good supervision, in others not, but there was no system for communication and coordination among these 15 or so separate programs—18 if one counts each of the four "homerooms" separately.

In reviewing the findings based on several visits to the school, the evaluators were impressed by the large number of people assigned to various support and special activities; the school clearly was committed to meeting many of the students' needs. The negative aspects of these activities included the fact that several programs were trying to reach and serve the same relatively small number of students; group guidance and counseling methods were used very little; several programs were reactive rather than proactive and reached few students; much of the guidance and counseling work was performed by teachers for whom this was a minor function; many programs and activities had little or no contact with each other; and space was inadequate, especially for individual and small-group activities.

Recommendations followed directly from that summary. One overarching conclusion was that, although the school had very extensive offerings in these important service areas, they had grown by accretion as funds and staff became available for specific purposes, rather than as parts of an overall plan. The first recommendation, therefore, was that an appropriate group should develop such an overall plan that would serve as a framework for all proposed additions and changes to try to ensure that duplication of effort was kept to a minimum and that all major areas were being given at least some coverage.

The second recommendation was that staff time assigned to all these programs be restructured so that the work would be done by people with total, or at least substantial, commitment to their guidance and counseling work and that all should be fully qualified as professional counselors. This would admittedly be difficult to do because many teachers saw the 1-period assignment as a plum, reducing their teaching load and giving them the opportunity to work with students individually instead of in a class.

The third recommendation was that an extensive program of in-service education on proactive programming be set up with an emphasis on a variety of scheduled group activities. Where groups were used, they served many more students, covered many topics and needs shared by students, and gave students a chance to share feelings and problems and give each other support in their school and school-related lives.

Fourth, because work in the area of career development and career counseling seemed to be dispersed, uncoordinated, and quite inadequate to meet the needs of this population, the evaluators suggested that a comprehensive program be developed, including in-service education for counselors, as well as classroom teachers, who could at least help their students see the career implications in their subjects.

Fifth, space needed to be rearranged so that rooms of varying sizes suitable for different kinds of groups would be available for counseling as well as staff meetings. Also needed were small rooms suitable for one-to-one conferences with privacy. In view of the overall lack of space in the building, these spaces could be shared by many people and offices on a scheduled basis. This would further underscore the need for advance planning and coordination.

Finally, a need for better communication among all these services and programs was indicated. Occasional meetings of all support staff would at least bring them into the same room on a regular basis. Those occasions and regular newsletters could keep everybody informed of new developments and encourage people to exchange ideas and information.

On completion of the study, the evaluators first met with the principal and a few key administrators to give the highlights of the recommendations and to seek feedback. Later, the evaluation team met with a smaller group selected by the principal and head of student personnel services to discuss the findings in greater detail. The final detailed report was prepared after these meetings and took account of some of those reactions.

CONCLUSION

Perhaps the one point to be emphasized is that, over and over in the evaluation studies mentioned, qualitative methods such as observations and interviews offered facts and insights that would not have emerged from quantified data from tests, questionnaires, and other sources.

REFERENCES

Goldman, L. (Ed.). (1978). *Research methods for counselors: Practical approaches in field settings.* New York: John Wiley.

Patton, M. Q. (1987). *How to use qualitative methods in evaluation.* Newbury Park, CA: Sage.

Afterword

Mary Kopala
Lisa A. Suzuki

The chapters in this text address the current state of the use of qualitative methods in the field of psychology. In the first section of this book, the authors discussed foundational topics relevant to the use of qualitative methods. In the second section, the authors discussed their struggles and triumphs as they sought to gain understanding of the meaning of participants' experiences through application of qualitative methods.

The complexities of the qualitative process are clearly illustrated through the challenges the authors identified. For example, in an attempt to be an ethical qualitative researcher, one cannot rely on traditional solutions. Informed consent is no longer a one-shot deal, but rather an ongoing process. In addition, new technologies enable researchers to access new sources of data, and with this comes new ethical questions that must be resolved. Qualitative researchers reported their struggles to enter the scientific community characterized by a quantitative culture.

Evident is a need to develop further a community of qualitative researchers whose members support and encourage each other in the usage of these methods and to continue the dialogue regarding these dilemmas. As training in qualitative methods increases in psychology programs, the potential network of qualitative researchers will also increase. It is our hope that the unique strengths of qualitative methodologies have become clear as a result of reading this volume and that other researchers will become a part of this movement.

The historical roots of psychology are more closely affiliated with qualitative observational methodologies in the understanding of human development. Over time, an emphasis on making psychology a hard science led us in the direction of quantifying variables and using statistical probabilities. Those of us who received our training a decade or more ago are likely to have been trained solely in quantitative methods. Thus, we use this framework to formulate questions and to design studies. We are comfortable at thinking about research from an experimental perspective or using sophisticated statistical analyses.

The authors of this text have posed numerous objections to the quantitative paradigm. These concerns seem to lead us back to our qualitative roots. Yet the qualitative-quantitative debate continues. To some, the foundation and philosophical premises underlying each methodology appear incompatible. For others, however, the movement toward a bimethodological identity appears imminent.

It is not likely that we will abandon our quantitative understanding in favor of qualitative methods; however, we can learn to understand and appreciate the contributions of both the qualitative and the quantitative approach to understanding psychological phenomena more clearly.

Index

About the Editors

Mary Kopala, Ph.D., is Associate Professor at Hunter College, City University of New York, in the Department of Educational Foundations and Counseling, where she teaches research methods. Many of her presentations at national and regional conferences have focused on the use of qualitative methods. She is actively involved in research, both quantitative and qualitative. She has also written numerous book chapters and articles.

Lisa A. Suzuki, Ph.D., is Assistant Professor in the Department of Applied Psychology at New York University. She is a coeditor of *Handbook of Multicultural Counseling* (with Ponterotto, Casas, & Alexander) and of *Handbook of Multicultural Assessment.* She has given presentations about qualitative methods at national conferences and is actively engaged in projects using qualitative methods.

About the Contributors

Kenneth Chavinson Asher, M.Arch., received his master's degree from the University of Oregon. He is a writer who has collaborated on several qualitative research projects, including a study (and its pilot study) presented in this volume.

Nancy Salkin Asher, Ph.D., is a counseling psychologist who lives and works in Portland, Oregon. Her research interests include body image, social support, and performance enhancement. She has worked for the past 7 years in a wide variety of clinical settings with a focus on adult women.

Cori Cieurzo, M.A., is a doctoral student in counseling psychology in the Graduate School of Education at Fordham University. She received her master's degree in general psychology at Wake Forest University, her master's thesis focusing on the link between external health locus of control and children's optimism and fears in a healthy and chronically ill sample. She has counseled college students and children and has presented at national professional conferences on the following topics: eating disorders and body image in adolescents, children's conceptions of illness and trauma, and neuropsychological functioning in children with brain tumors.

Constance T. Fischer, Ph.D., ABPP, is Professor of Psychology at Duquesne University, where she has participated in the department's development of empirical phenomenological research methods for more than 20 years. She is editing *Qualitative Research Methods for Psychology* and is a Consulting Editor for *Methods: A Journal for Human Science, The Humanistic Psychologist,* and *Journal of Humanistic Psychology.* She coedited Volume II of *Duquesne Studies in Phenomenological Psychology* and is author of *Individualizing Psychological Assessment.*

Leo Goldman, Ph.D., ABBP, Counseling Psychology, twice-retired Professor of counseling and counseling psychology (from the City University of New York [CUNY] and later from Fordham University), now teaches program evaluation in the Graduate Counseling Program at New York University as an Adjunct Professor in the Department of Applied Psychology. He also continues a 20-year relationship as Senior Research Associate at the Center for Advanced Study in Education of the CUNY Graduate Center. He has held national office in both counseling and psychological organizations and has been Editor of the journal of the organization now called the American Counseling Association. He is the author of *Using Tests in Counseling* and *Research Methods for Counselors.*

Ingrid Grieger, Ed.D., has been Director of the Counseling Center at Iona College since 1989 and the Coordinator of the Women's Studies Program from 1994 through 1996. She is also an Adjunct Associate Professor in the Department of Psychology at Iona College and in the Graduate School of Education at Fordham University. In the past, she has worked in college and university counseling centers, in community mental health clinics, and in private clinical practice. A frequent presenter at professional conferences, she is a published writer in the area of women's issues in psychotherapy and multicultural concerns.

Lisa Tsoi Hoshmand, Ph.D., is Professor and the Director of the Division of Counseling and Psychology at Lesley College. She is the Editor and principal author of *Creativity and Moral Vision in Psychology: Narratives on Identity and Commitment in a Postmodern Age.* Her other published works include *Orientation to Inquiry in a Reflective Professional Psychology* and *Research as Praxis: Lessons From Programmatic Research in Therapeutic Psychology.* She has been the Associate Editor of the *Journal of Theoretical and Philosophical Psychology* and has served on several editorial boards, including *Contemporary Psychology, Journal of Constructivist Psychology, Journal of Community Psychology, Journal of Counseling Psychology,* and *The Counseling Psychologist.*

Merle A. Keitel, Ph.D., is Associate Professor in the Graduate School of Education at Fordham University and has served as Coordinator of the Master's and Professional Diploma Programs in Counseling and Personnel Services, as well as the APA-accredited Doctoral Program in Counseling Psychology since 1994. She has published and presented at national professional conferences primarily in the areas of health psychology, stress and coping, and grief and loss.

Patricia O'Brien Libutti, Ph.D., earned a master's degree in library science in addition to her doctorate in educational psychology. She has worked with the National Library of Education as Chair of the Working Group on Web Design for the National Education Network and is associated with The Libraries for the Future as a Research Fellow. She is editing a book entitled *Librarians as Learners, Librarians as Teachers: The Diffusion of Internet Expertise in*

Academic Libraries. Using qualitative research methods, she has studied how individuals develop Internet expertise.

Michelle Maher, M.S., received master's degrees from Syracuse University in cultural foundations and from the University of Oregon in counseling psychology. A doctoral candidate in cultural foundations of education at Syracuse University, she focuses her research interests in feminist and multicultural studies, children and trauma, and qualitative research methods. She is a Child and Family Therapist at the Child Center in Springfield, Oregon. She has published and presented extensively on using qualitative methods and addressing multicultural issues from a feminist perspective.

Elizabeth Merrick, Ph.D., is a qualitative researcher, educator, and psychologist. Her qualitative study of childbearing among lower socioeconomic, black American adolescents led to an interest in research methods and epistemology. In addition to seeing clients and teaching, she is a Postdoctoral Fellow at New York University's Department of Applied Psychology, where she is involved in a qualitative study with middle school students in a lower-income, urban community.

Virginia O'Brien, Ph.D., received her doctorate in counseling psychology from Fordham University in 1996. A licensed psychologist, she works in private practice and for Kenwood Psychological Services in New York City and is a consultant at the Notre Dame School in Manhattan. In addition, she is an Adjunct Assistant Professor at Hunter College, City University of New York. She has presented at national conferences on her research interest of mathematics self-efficacy in adolescents.

John O'Neill, Ph.D., is Professor and Coordinator of the Counselor Education Programs at Hunter College, City University of New York. He is actively involved in research in community integration and quality of life for people with traumatic brain injury. He has received numerous grants focused on rehabilitation counseling and is conducting collaborative qualitative research in the area of HIV/AIDS.

Kerstin Pahl, is a doctoral student in the Human Development Program in the Department of Applied Psychology at New York University. Her research interests focus on adolescent development and adolescents' relationships and the experiences of adolescent immigrants to the United States.

Joseph G. Ponterotto, Ph.D., is Professor in the Counseling and Counseling Psychology Programs at Fordham University, where he teaches regularly the qualitative research course and the multicultural counseling course. He is a Fellow of the American Psychological Association (Divisions 17 and 45) and of the American Association of Applied and Preventive Psychology. In 1994, he was co-winner of the APA Division 17 Early Career Scientist/Practitioner Award. His research specialty is in multicultural counseling, a field in which he is coauthor or coeditor of several books and author of numerous journal articles. His current book project is the second edition of *Handbook of Racial/Ethnic Minority Counseling Research* (with J. M. Casas), which has a heavy qualitative research component.

Maria Prendes-Lintel, Ph.D., is Coordinator of Psychological Assessment and Multicultural Services at the Lincoln (Nebraska) Medical Education Foundation Behavioral Health Center. She specializes in post-traumatic stress disorders and lectures on the bio-psychosocial model and multidisciplinary collaborative treatment. Her research with the refugee population addresses mental health intervention and the vicarious traumatization of service providers.

David L. Rennie, Ph.D., is Professor in the Department of Psychology at York University, Toronto. After a period of quasi-experimental research on counselor training, in recent years he has applied the grounded theory method to the study of the client's reported experience of psychotherapy. This transition has stimulated an interest in the philosophy of human science. Among his recent publications are *Psychotherapy Process Research: Paradigmatic and Narrative Approaches* (edited with S. Toukmanian) and *Person-Centred Counselling: An Experiential Approach.*

Daniel Sciarra, Ph.D., is Assistant Professor at Hofstra University, Hempstead, New York, in counselor education. The author of a forthcoming book on multicultural counseling, he has research interests in racial identity development and multicultural family counseling. He has made numerous presentations at national conferences and published extensively in the area of multicultural issues in counseling, specifically with Latino families.

Barbara B. Small, B.A., is Executive Director of Multitasking Systems of New York/Mobilizing Talents and Skills (MTS), a nonprofit organization servicing the employment and training needs of men and women with HIV/AIDS. She is also President of Small and Associates, Inc., a consulting firm specialized in developing vocational programs for persons with barriers to employment. She received her B.A. in psychology from Duke University.

Sally D. Stabb, Ph.D., is Associate Professor in the Counseling Psychology Program in the Department of Psychology and Philosophy at Texas Woman's University. Her research interests are in the areas of couples' relationships (infidelity, attachment, therapy), women's issues (development, emotion, cross-culturalism), ethics, and needs assessment. She serves as an ad hoc reviewer for qualitative research manuscripts for *Psychology of Women Quarterly,* and within

APA Division 17 she is a member of the Qualitative Research Special Interest Group and a member of the Program Committee.

Amena Stallings, M.A., is a doctoral candidate in school psychology at Michigan State University. Her master's degree, also in school psychology, was earned at New York University. She has copresented with Lisa Suzuki at the National Convention of the American Psychological Association on the topic of Cuban refugees.

John Strachan, B.A., is a Research Associate with Multitasking Systems of New York/Mobilizing Talents and Skills (MTS), a nonprofit organization servicing the employment and training needs of men and women with HIV/AIDS. Research projects focus on quality of life and employment issues for persons with HIV/AIDS. He is enrolled in the Graduate Program in Rehabilitation Counseling at Hunter College, City University of New York.

Joy M. Tanji, Ph.D., is an adjunct faculty member in the Clinical Psychology Program of the American School of Professional Psychology/Hawaii Campus. She is a lithographer and Counseling Psychologist by training and is interested in humanistic, narrative, and systemic approaches to human change; qualitative approaches to inquiry; the application of social constructionist thinking in both academic and clinical settings, particularly with respect to diversity issues; Eastern philosophy; and fine arts.

Niobe Way, Ph.D., is Assistant Professor of Applied Psychology at New York University. Her main research interests are in the development of urban poor and working-class adolescents. She is the Coeditor of *Urban Girls: Resisting Stereotypes, Creating Identities.* She is also the author of *Everyday Courage: The Lives and Stories of Urban Teenagers.*

Lauren Wertlieb, M.S., is a doctoral student in counseling psychology in the School of Education at New York University. She received her master's degree in counseling at New York University and has done counseling with cancer patients and substance-abusing adolescents and their families. Her research interests include adolescent identity formation, trauma and resilience, and qualitative research methods.